The Leaf Key

Susan A. Mills

Trilogy Christian Publishers
A Wholly Owned Subsidiary of Trinity Broadcasting Network
2442 Michelle Drive
Tustin, CA 92780

Copyright © 2021 by Susan A. Mills

All Scripture quotations, unless otherwise noted, taken from THE HOLY BIBLE, NEW INTERNATIONAL VERSION®, NIV® Copyright © 1973, 1978, 1984, 2011 by Biblica, Inc.® Used by permission. All rights reserved worldwide.

Scripture quotations marked (KJV) taken from *The Holy Bible, King James Version.* Cambridge Edition: 1769.

All rights reserved, including the right to reproduce this book or portions thereof in any form whatsoever.

For information, address Trilogy Christian Publishing
Rights Department, 2442 Michelle Drive, Tustin, Ca 92780.
Trilogy Christian Publishing/ TBN and colophon are trademarks of Trinity Broadcasting Network.

For information about special discounts for bulk purchases, please contact Trilogy Christian Publishing.

Manufactured in the United States of America

Trilogy Disclaimer: The views and content expressed in this book are those of the author and may not necessarily reflect the views and doctrine of Trilogy Christian Publishing or the Trinity Broadcasting Network.

10 9 8 7 6 5 4 3 2 1

Library of Congress Cataloging-in-Publication Data is available.

ISBN 978-1-64773-714-6 (Print Book)
ISBN 978-1-64773-715-3 (ebook)

To King Jesus,
my Lord and Savior
and the King of my heart.

Contents

Foreword 7
Acknowledgments 9

Kara 11
Elspa's Cottage 33
Diversions on the Path 39
On to Averton 57
King Vespes 71
Lady Vallora 75
Dominic 79
A New Friend 83
The Windfolk 89
The Alliance 93
Mira 97
The Tunnel 103
The White Wolves 107
Preparations 111
Time to Leave 117
The Crossing 125
Arten 129
Silvenia 137
The Road to Rondival 147
Julia 151
Goldie 157
The Scroll 165
The Mysterious Picture 171
The Bird 177
A Secret Room 183

Back to Icelandia	197
A Joyful Reunion	203
The Proposal	211
The Silver Palace	219
Jonathan	229
Marta	233
Gaelyn	243
Secrets	249
Hidden	257
Journey to the Palace	265
Treachery	269
Confessions	277
Will	287
A Windfolk Spy	291
Arrival of the Empress	297
The Battle Begins	309
The Tree in the Meadow	321
Hope	327

Foreword

Susan Mills is a friend and a fantastic storyteller. *The Leaf Key* will captivate your imagination as Susan unravels the story of how Kara, a nursing student, seeks and finds direction and wisdom for life in the magical land of Paredonia. Her journey is met with many colorful characters, wise counsel, and mystical creatures. Once you open the pages to *The Leaf Key*, you will instantly see the world through Kara's eyes, as she discovers new desires, directions, and her destiny.

When Susan asked me if I would write the foreword to her first book, I felt incredibly honored because I believe that a writer's first literary piece is sacred. As an author myself, the opportunity to be one of the first to experience Susan's work was an opportunity I could not pass on.

Susan is an artist and visionary, whose words, imagination, and creativity will paint into your minds a whole new world, a Kingdom, that will challenge you to believe for more.

—Jonnathan Zin Truong, pastor, God Manifest, Houston, Texas
and author of *Buddhists, Mormons & Jesus*

Acknowledgments

First and foremost, I am grateful to God who provided me with the daily inspiration needed to create this book. I want to thank everyone who prayed for me, assisted me, and encouraged me on this journey—especially my husband, Ian, and my children, Shelby, Melanie, Joseph, and Peter. I love you dearly.

Thank you to Terri Savelle Foy, who is also an inspiration and my cheerleader of dreams! A special thank you to my mom, Evelyn Mealy, who is also the artist for the cover of this book. You and Dad's steady love, support, and encouragement spurred me on. I am so grateful that God made you my parents!

Thank you also to Kristy Mapp, who helped me fine-tune my illustrations inside this book and provided much-needed technical support. Thank you Jonnathan Zin Truong, my friend and pastor, for being one of the first people to read this book and for writing the foreword. Also, thank you to Ashley Welch, Christy Phillippe, and the entire editing and production team at Trilogy publishing and TBN for all your help and support in making this book a reality.

Kara

Kara Alder

Skidding to a quick stop on my bike, I pick up the orange-green-and-purple leaf lying on the path in front of me. I hold it in my hand and look at the vibrant coloring. It brings back memories of when I was a child skating on the frozen pond by Aunt Debbie's house in Northern New Hampshire. I found a frozen leaf in the ice once and took a picture of it. There was wonder in the world around me. Magic in the woods. Snapshots of memories frozen in the back of my mind. Riding my horse through the woods on a dusty path. Watching for dwarves and elves and unicorns as I went along. I enjoyed being alone and let my imagination run wild.

I didn't know I was being watched.

My path is set before me, and I walk on to my familiar bench by the pond, which is simply a fallen tree close to the water's edge. Turning the leaf over in my hand, I decide to keep it and put it in my pocket, even though I know it will quickly dry and crumble. The water is still, and the air is quiet, except for a few birdcalls in the distance. The blackbird's caw echoes and fades. I scrunch up my knees under my chin and sit with my back to the woods.

This has always been my spot to get away and think, but today my mind is foggy and jumbled. I need to focus on a plan. I need to figure out my next step. *Where do I go from here?*

I will be twenty-four in a few days, and I am supposed to know what to do with my life. I am in my third year of college, studying nursing, but I have no desire to be a nurse. "Follow your passion!" people have told me, but my passions seem to consist of things that don't make much money, except for the select few. As an introvert, I spend most of my time reading, writing, and drawing sketches, and I have no clue how to proceed with my life.

I feel trapped in my current job as a nursing assistant at Sleepy Oaks Hospital. It pays well, but it drains me. I do not like spending each day around the very sick and elderly. Instead of lifting them up, I feel like I am being pulled down into a place of darkness and despair. The clinical, chemical smell of the hospital permeates my very soul and makes me feel sick inside. Some of the nurses I work with are very kind, and I enjoy helping them, but I think they can see that my heart is not in this kind of work. I feel guilty and out of place, but I don't want to let down my parents, who have been paying for my training. I know they will be understanding and encourage me in a new direction, but I have no idea what direction to go.

And then there is Tom. My heart aches with sorrow every time I think of him, but we have ended it after three years together. I thought we would get married, but things between us had shifted. The attraction, romance, and even, I would say, love that we felt for each other couldn't hold us together. We had been slowly drifting apart for some time now. We loved each other for a time, but we didn't have the intimate qualities of true friendship to hold us together. I think we both realized this, but it was harder for me to face this and let him go.

He is walking away from me now; I can't be the person he wants me to be. We are too different to see eye to eye anymore. He loved the social scene, even thrived in it. I preferred a small group of friends, and I was most happy when it was just the two of us. I pretended he was happy that way too, but inside I knew different. He is moving on now. I have to let go.

Four months have gone by now, and I've only heard from him once. My heart is shattered, but apparently, he is doing okay. It seems everywhere I go now, we had gone together, and I can't keep the memories from popping up again, uninvited, in my head. A couple of times I thought I saw him in a crowd, but it wasn't him. He's living in Boston now, getting on with his life. Much as I resist this fact, I have to let it sink in and find the strength to press on without him.

My best friend Sonia is a great comfort to me during this time, but she can't fix the gaping hole in my heart. I go to work every day feeling like I am slowly bleeding out, my strength sapping away as I force a fake smile for the patients I am tending to. Most of them are elderly, and it is a relief to me when they are asleep and I don't feel like I have to make conversation. I quietly go about my duties, the dull pain continually throbbing in my chest. The time there seems to pass by very slowly, and I know I need a change.

Yes, a change of scenery will do me good. I need to escape. Take a vacation, escape from reality. Escape from the pain. I need a new beginning. What is that going to look like? I wonder. I close my eyes and let my mind wander. I think of places far away. Beaches, Europe, Australia. *You need money for that,* I chide myself. I want to dream again. My path ahead feels bleak and dark.

"What do I do now, God?" I say into the air.

The sun is setting. It is my favorite time of the day—I love seeing all the pink and orange colors in the changing sky. Breathing in the outdoor air, I pick up my phone and take a picture of the fading sky. As I glance at the picture on my phone, I hear a rustling in the trees behind me. Probably a squirrel, I think, turning to look at the woodland path behind me. Was it my imagination, or did I just see someone or something dart behind a large pine tree? I've never been afraid to be alone here. This is a well-traveled path, and there are usually people walking or passing by on their bikes.

"Hello?" I call out. No answer. My eyes scan the woods—nothing. I must be imagining things, I tell myself. It's time to head back, anyway; the sun is setting, and soon it will be dark. I slip my phone in my pocket and turn and head back the longer loop around the pond, avoiding the area where I thought I heard something in the woods. Better to be safe than sorry, right?

The wind has picked up now, and the trees sway and rustle around me as I bike down the leafy path. I pick up my pace and pedal faster. There are some kids ahead of me on the path, walking a small dog. I zip on past and am already thinking about taking a nice, hot bath when I get home. That will help me relax and, hopefully, get to sleep tonight.

As I pull up in our driveway, I see the lights are on in the kitchen. I'm sure my parents are in there, my mom probably straightening up and my dad staring at his computer or reading a book. My sister, Julia, must be out again somewhere, as her car is not here. I roll my bike into the garage and almost trip on Percy, our fluffy gray cat. He darts off into the bushes, and I call out to him, "Sorry, Perc!"

He slowly comes back out and saunters over, expecting to be petted. I oblige and crouch down to do so. "What's up, Percy? Where have you been?" I scratch under his chin, and he gives me a raspy meow and rubs against my leg.

Our home is set in a valley of sorts with woods and farmland surrounding us. We live in the small town of Nesterley, New Jersey, about thirty miles from the coast and twenty miles from Palleton, the closest city. I like our small community of country homes and farms. I especially like the fact that there are many horses around. I like to ride occasionally and have taken lessons from a lady down the street, but mostly, I just enjoy watching them.

I give Percy a final pat on the head and rise up to head inside. "Hi," I say as I push through the door into the kitchen.

My mom turns from the sink. "Oh, hi! How was your ride?"

"Just fine," I say. "The sunset was really pretty."

"Did you want anything else to eat before I put this food away?"

"No, I'm good. I think I'll head up for a bath soon."

"Okay," she says, giving me a quick hug. "That sounds good. Oh, and I took your clothes out of the dryer and put them up on your bed for you."

"Thanks, Mom. Love you!" I say as I head for the stairs. As I head up, the phone in my pocket vibrates, and I pull it out to see who's calling me. Seeing it's Sonia, I answer, "Hi, how are you?"

"Good, good," Sonia replies. "Just checking on you. How was work today?"

"Oh, you know, same old, same old," I answer.

"Want to come over and watch a movie or something? I've got popcorn," she adds enticingly.

"No, thanks. I'm beat. I think I'm just going to take a bath and then read until I fall asleep."

"That's no way to spend a Friday night!" she protests. "Come on, I'll pick you up and we can watch a fun movie. You can spend the night, and I'll treat you to doughnuts in the morning on the way home. What do you say?"

"It's hard to resist a good doughnut. Okay, I'll get ready."

"Be there in fifteen minutes," she says, hanging up.

I sigh as I get my overnight bag out of the closet, but my heart is warmed by the thoughtfulness of my friend. She always knows how to pull me out of my shell, and we've been good friends to each other since the fourth grade, when we were paired up as class helpers in Ms. Gutchen's class. We started eating lunch together every day along with our other friends, Margie and Barbara. I am very thankful to have a good friend.

Reaching in my pocket, I pull out the colorful autumn leaf and set it on my dresser. Then I begin to put away my clothes. I like my room to be neat and organized—the exact opposite from my sister, Julia, whose room usually looks like a tornado went through it. I have just finished stuffing some pajamas in my bag when, glancing out my window, I see Sonia pull up in the driveway.

"Be right out," I text and start to head downstairs again.

"Bye, Mom and Dad! I'm going to spend the night at Sonia's," I call out.

"Oh, okay. Have fun, then!" Mom replies, sticking her head out the kitchen doorway. "See you tomorrow."

Sonia smiles at me as I get into the front seat.

"Hi," I say. "Thanks for picking me up."

"No problem. I'm just glad you changed your mind and decided to come over."

"What are we watching? Do you have something picked out?"

"I was thinking a classic, maybe? Like *Jane Eyre* or *Wuthering Heights*…or maybe we should watch something funny. What do you think?"

"*Jane Eyre* sounds good. I haven't seen that one in a while."

"*Jane Eyre* it is, then." Sonia lives just about ten minutes away from me in a small apartment that she shares with her sister, Carol. "Carol's working late tonight," she says as she pulls out the popcorn. "I'm not sure what time she'll be home. Have you eaten already? We could order some pizza if you're hungry."

"No, thanks. Popcorn will be perfect. Do you have any ice tea or sparkling water? I'm trying to stay away from soda."

"Umm, let me look," she says. "All we have is some ginger ale. Will that work?"

"Perfect," I say, grinning as she hands me a can. "How was your day? Work going okay?"

"Yeah, it's fine. Except I've got to stop eating so many of the leftover cupcakes after work. I just hate to throw them away. I brought home two extra chocolate ones today. Want one?"

"Absolutely," I say. "I could use some chocolate therapy."

Smiling, Sonia puts them on two paper plates for us. She works at Carlotta's Cupcake Factory on Main Street in town. "They're asking me if I want to be an assistant manager now. What do you think?"

"Oh! Would that be a decent pay increase?"

"I think so. I don't have all the details yet, but I know I'd probably have to put in more hours. I'm seriously considering it, though. I really need to save for a better car."

"Well, you could try it out for a while and see how you like it. It's not like you have to stay there forever."

"Yeah, that's what I was thinking too. I have the weekend to think it over. Anyway, let's see what's going on in the world of *Jane Eyre*," she says, popping in the DVD.

We stay up late after the movie is over, just lying on the couches and talking. "I just love how everything works out for Jane in the end after all her suffering," I say.

"I know! I especially like how this version really portrays them living happily ever after in the end."

"Yes, I agree. This definitely is my favorite version," I say. "So what about you? Has that guy Mark from your work asked you out yet?"

"Not yet. I can't tell if he's just a big flirt or if he is really interested in me."

"From what you've told me, I'd say he sounds pretty interested. Maybe he's just a little shy?"

"Yeah, we'll see. At least I have somebody fun to work with." She smiles.

"Is he fun?"

"Oh yeah, he makes me laugh all the time. Sometimes it's hard to keep a straight face with the customers because he's in the back, making crazy faces or something."

"He sounds great. I definitely would want to be with someone who makes me laugh. Do you know anything more about him? Is he a college student?"

"Yeah, he's taking some classes at the community college. I'm not sure what he's pursuing, though. Speaking of college, have you decided what to do about your nursing classes?"

"No, I don't know yet. I have been thinking about it a lot. I don't want to bring it up with my parents until I figure out what direction I'm going with this. I just wish I knew what it is I should do."

"I hear you. That's why I've taken time off from school to just work until I figure things out. Maybe that's what you should do too."

"Maybe," I say. "I know I've got to make some kind of decision soon. I've got some major exams coming up, and I'm so not ready. Whenever I try to study, which hasn't been much lately, I find myself reading the same paragraph over and over. My mind just doesn't want to focus on anatomy and physiology."

"Kara," she says firmly, "just drop the nursing classes! Take a break. Your heart's not in it, and from what I can tell, it never has been, and you need to take some time for yourself to figure things out."

"I know, but I'm close to the end of the semester, and my parents will be so disappointed."

"Are you just living to please your parents? It's time to figure out what pleases you. What do *you* want to do with your life?"

I blink with the revelation. To hear someone else say what I've been thinking, out loud, gives me clarity. "Okay!" I say. "I'll go talk to my counselor tomorrow."

"Attagirl!" She smiles and gives me a hug. "It will all work out, you'll see."

"Thanks, Sonia. You're a good friend."

"Of course I am." She grins. "The very best!"

"And humble too," I add with a laugh.

We continue talking until the wee hours of the morning, until we finally drift off to sleep. At some point, I hear the front door open and close again as Carol returns home. Easing back into sleep, I drift into a dream.

My mind is active with colors and faces interweaving together. I see Tom; he is talking to some people in a crowded room. I'm trying to get his attention, but there are too many people blocking my way. He is in an animated conversation with a small group of about three people.

I push through the crowd and finally get close enough where he can't miss seeing me. I'm waving at him and saying his name, but my voice sounds quiet and muted. It seems the harder I try to speak louder, the softer my voice sounds.

Briefly he glances up at me. "Tom," I whisper. He seems to look right through me. I feel invisible. I stumble over to a door as I feel my heart rapidly racing. I just need to go outside for a moment and get some air. I push on a large wooden door, but it appears to be locked. "Drat!" I exclaim and head to the other side of the room to look for another exit. The room feels dark and stuffy. I've got to get out of here, I think.

I'm pushing past person after person. Everyone seems deep in conversation. I walk past a table filled with various food and drinks and stop to get a cup of punch. Hearing a snippet of conversation, I swallow the too-sweet concoction down slowly.

"When was the last time you saw her?" a young woman's voice says.

"I think last November," comes the reply. Her voice sounds vaguely familiar, but my back is to them, and I don't want them to think I'm eavesdropping, which I clearly am.

"I can't remember when the last time I saw her was," says the woman. "Probably high school senior year. We had the same history teacher, Mr. Perlman."

Mr. Perlman? I remember that name. He was my history teacher too. Could they be talking about me? Who are they? I turn to look but am jostled by another group of people and can't see their faces. I don't recognize anyone else. I look around again for an exit door; I need to get out of here and clear my head. Turning, I see a large framed picture at the end of the table. I feel drawn toward it.

I head over to it and stand there frozen. Stunned, I am staring at a photograph of me! I look at the photo as if staring at a stranger—brown hair, light-blue eyes, familiar smattering of freckles. It's definitely me. Why is my picture here? What is going on? I wonder.

I've got to go back over to Tom and ask him—he'll know what this is all about. I look around the crowded room, and he is nowhere in sight. "Excuse me," I say to a stranger, tapping him on the arm. "Can you tell me what is going on here?" The man I'm addressing doesn't even turn his head. What is this? I realize I must be dreaming. This isn't reality. I just need to pinch myself or something to make me wake up.

I pinch my arm, hard. Nothing happens. People mill around me, talking and drinking punch. Taking a deep breath, I remember I need to head toward the exit. Just find a doorway out of here, I think.

I see another large wood-framed doorway to my left. Heading toward it, I see a short man gesturing with his hand, like, "Come here!" He's standing right next to the door. As I get closer, I look into his eyes and realize he is gesturing to me. He can see me! He must know what is happening here, I think, and I make my way over to him.

His appearance seems a bit odd, which makes sense, considering this is probably all some sort of strange dream. Curiously, I look at him. He appears to be a short middle-aged man, slightly bald, with a scruff of a beard. He is wearing a brown suit jacket, no tie, a checkered flannel-type shirt, and brown shoes. As I get closer, he turns to reach for the door handle and opens the door. I look from him to the open doorway. It is dark, and I can't see where it leads to. He begins to walk through it and then turns his head back to look at me and says, "Come on!"

I don't know this man. Hesitantly, I put on the brakes with a feeling of uncertainty. Should I follow him? I need answers; I want to leave this room. My curiosity gets the better of me, and I follow. When I reach the doorway, I feel a gusty breeze and a sort of magnetic pull in the air. This must be an exit to the outside. I step through and find my feet on dry earth. It's a bit brighter now, and I can see a path before me with trees on both sides. The man is standing a few feet ahead of me on the path, waiting. Slowly, I walk up to him.

"Greetings!" he says. "My name is Dominic. I'm so glad you decided to come."

"Who are you? And where am I?" I ask in bewilderment. I'm convinced I must be dreaming now.

"The leaf was your invitation," he says. "Your key to this place."

"What leaf?" I ask, and then I remember the leaf on my dresser. "You mean the leaf I found on my bike ride the other day?"

"Yes," he says. "You picked it up and received the invitation to come here. And now that you've entered through the doorway, you are in the land of Paredonia and on the pathway to Silvenia. I will be your guide to get you safely to the inner gates. It's not safe to be out here alone on the paths these days."

I pinch my arm again, *hard*. Nothing happens. "I don't understand," I say. "What is Silva…?"

"Silvenia," he says again. "I've been waiting here for your arrival ever since you picked up the key."

"The leaf," I say again. "The leaf is a key?"

"Yes," he says, turning toward the path and beginning to walk. "Follow me. I'm sure you have many questions, but we must begin our journey now before the moons rise and it becomes more difficult to travel unnoticed."

"Why do we want to be unnoticed?"

He looks at me and begins to open his mouth to speak and then clamps it shut.

"Never mind all that now," he says. "Let me explain to you where we are going first."

"Okay," I say as I take in my surroundings. The trees are tall and vibrant, with many different-colored leaves. The leaves—there are many with similar coloring as the one I picked up on the path back home. There are also trees unlike any I have seen before, with willowy branches of dark blue and green and tall piney ones with large white cone-shaped flowers. There are birds also, small ones that flit around from tree to tree, and large ones with silvery wings that perch up high. What is this place? I am very curious but also feel a sense of alarm rising in me at my displacement.

"Come along now," he says, not seeming to sense my apprehension. We mustn't linger. Now, as I was saying, we are heading to the kingdom of Silvenia." I give him my full attention now, eager for him to clear up my ignorance of this place. "It's about a twelve-day journey from here by foot."

"Twelve days?" I respond. "I'm not sure I should be going to this place. What is it? And how will I find my way back? My family will be worried!"

"Your family will wait for you," he says with a smile. "There's a task you must complete before you go back."

"A task? What kind of task?"

"It will be given to you at the proper time. Until then, you will have to be content with me to guide you along the path."

"But I don't even know who you are! Why should I trust you?"

"It is your choice to trust me or not. You may not be acquainted with me, but since I have been assigned as your guide, I have become acquainted with you."

"What do you mean?" I say. "Who assigned you to be a guide for me?"

"I've been dispatched by Vale, high commander under King Vespes of Silvenia, in this land of Paredonia."

I stare at him, bewildered. "Where is Paredonia?"

"You're standing in it. All this land is Paredonia, and we're heading to the kingdom of Silvenia to receive your instructions."

"Instructions! What kind of—"

"You've been asking for direction, have you not?" he interrupts.

"What? How could you know?" I stutter. "I mean how do you know me?"

"It is my duty to become acquainted with the ones I am assigned to guide. And right now, you are my primary assignment of utmost importance."

"Of utmost importance to who?" I ask.

"Well, to the king, of course. He has his reasons, I'm sure. We mustn't keep him waiting." I notice he has picked up his pace a little more. I hurry to keep up with him.

"Is this king wise?" I ask. "Is he king over all this place?"

"There are many kings here. King Vespes is ruler over the kingdom of Silvenia. He is young and learning from the wisdom of the elders, his father's advisers. His father, King Rufus, has been ruling for over forty years in Silvenia, but since the accident, his son has had to step up in his place."

"What accident?" I ask, wrapping my arms around me as we walk. The wind has been steadily increasing.

"You must be cold," he notices. "We will find shelter in the town of Vicor. I know of a loyal subject to the king who lives there now. A former nursemaid to King Rufus's children. Her name is Elspa. We should reach her home before the moons have risen. You'll need warmer traveling clothes too. Elspa may have some you could use, or we can find some in town."

I nod, looking forward to shelter from the wind. "What happened to King Rufus?" I ask. "You said there was an accident?"

"Oh, yes, King Rufus went riding near the Copper Hills one afternoon and his horse was spooked by a serpent. He fell and hit his head on a rock. It did not kill him but has left him with frequent headaches and significant memory loss." He rubs his chin thoughtfully. "It is very sad. He was a wise and respected king, but now he remembers nothing of his royalty. His attendants care for him now, and Vespes, his son, has taken up his rule."

"What is King Vespes like?" I ask as I pull a leaf from an extended branch. He grabs my arm to stop me.

"You mustn't," he says firmly.

"Why? Are these all keys too?"

"No," he replies. "Only certain ones are. But you do not know the difference and may hinder another's path."

"This is all very strange to me. I think I must be dreaming." I say this loudly, as if this will awaken me somehow.

"Dreams come and go, but who's to say what is the dream and what is the reality?"

I am about to argue that I know very well what reality is for me when he suddenly grabs my arm and pulls me behind a tree next to the path.

"What is going on?"

"Shhh!" he whispers with a finger to his lips. "Let us see who approaches."

I hear the sound of horse hooves up ahead on the path and look up to see two men on horseback. They are dressed in brown and green, with hooded coats that are pointed on top with sharp edges. They both carry bow and arrow on their backs, and one of them has a long sword strapped to his side. They are riding along quietly together at a slow pace. Looking upon their faces, I cannot tell if they are friend or foe.

"Hunters," he whispers to me and seems to relax a bit.

"Is it safe?" I ask.

"I believe so," he says, stepping back on the path. I follow him cautiously, stepping behind his small frame.

"Greetings, gentlemen. What news from Vicor?"

The one with the sword approaches first. He has dark eyes and a short black beard and long dark hair.

"All is quiet in Vicor, not many about. Is that your destination?"

"It is," says Dominic. "We are visiting a friend there."

"And what sort of traveling clothes are these?" says the other rider, looking directly at me. He is ruddy and thick, with shaggy red hair and a long beard. I snap to, realizing he has directed the question to me. I look down at myself and realize I am still wearing the same navy sweatpants and long-sleeved pink and white T-shirt I had worn to bed at Sonia's house. Thankfully, I am not barefoot; I have my white sneakers on, which are now covered in brown dust from the path. I glance from him to Dominic and realize my clothes must look very odd in this new place. I'm trying to think of something intelligent to say, but nothing is coming to me at the moment.

"These are her riding clothes," says Dominic.

"Where is her horse? Have you been robbed?" says the red-haired one.

"Oh, no. This clothing was made for training purposes. She works with the pull-ponies at Redmonton." Dominic smiles back at me and nods, as if to say, "Smile and nod." So I nod and smile at the rustic pair.

"She doesn't say much, does she?" says the first one, grinning at me.

"What is your name, lass?"

"Kara," I reply. "And what is yours, good sir?" I say boldly, thinking this is a place where you would definitely say "good sir."

"I am Devon, and this is Brecco, milady. We are hunters in these woods."

"And what is it you are hunting?" I ask now with more confidence.

Devon pulls back on the reins as his horse stomps impatiently. "We hunt for many things, but currently we are seeking to find the great sterrador. I wonder, have you seen any sign of her along this path? Her feathers are bright gold and terrillion." (Which I find out later to be a brilliant metallic teal color.)

"No, we have not," says Dominic. "But we wish you well and hope you find your treasure! I beg your pardon, but we must be heading off now to get to our destination by nightfall."

"Of course. Safe journey to you both!" he asserts with a parting glance.

"Goodbye, sir. Goodbye, milady." Brecco nods, tipping his hood forward and nudging his horse along.

Once they are farther down the path behind us, I ask Dominic, "What is a sterrador? And why are they hunting it?"

"A sterrador is a large pheasant-like creature with tawny fur and gold-and-teal-colored wings. It has talons like an eagle. There is one called the great sterrador, which is very large. I've heard it's about the size of a small horse."

"Oh! Is it dangerous? Is there a chance we will come across it?" I ask.

"No, I don't think so. It knows how to stay well hidden, and the great sterrador has not been seen in these parts for probably about twenty years or so."

"Well, maybe it's dead, then, or has migrated to somewhere else."

"I don't know. Sterradors are known to live very long lives and, as I mentioned before, are very good at staying hidden from people."

"Have you ever seen one?" I ask curiously.

"Yes, once, when I was a child, up in the mountains of Shazir."

"Was it beautiful?" I ask, trying to picture it in my mind.

"Quite so, yes. It was about the size of a small ram. Its chest had golden fur, and its feathers glistened in the sun with an iridescent brilliance. It shot me a glance and then jumped off the cliff's edge, sailing down into the canyon below us. I tried to run up farther to watch it, but my father held me back."

"Was your father hunting them as well?"

"Oh, no, my father would never hunt a sterrador. He believes in the old tales about them."

"What sort of old tales?" I ask, swiping branches away from my face in the path. The woods are getting thicker now.

"Oh, there are many different stories. I suppose the best known one is that if you bring back to them one of their lost feathers, then they will be obliged to take you where you desire to go. Their feathers are rare and beautiful and sold for a high price in the markets."

"So why do those hunters seek to kill one, then?"

"I'm quite sure they are not hunting to kill. They probably want to capture the great one and bring it to a king for a large monetary reward."

"To King Vespes?"

"Possibly, though I'm quite sure he would not know what to do with it. It is more likely they would bring it to one of the kings in the southern region, to a kingdom like Castor or Rondival, where there are big rewards for rare treasures like that."

I ponder this as the path ahead begins to open up once again and I see what looks like small barnlike structures up ahead in the distance.

"Ah, we are approaching Vicor. The house of Elspa is not very far now."

It is getting darker now, and quieter. Even the birds have stopped their rushing about and twittering.

"Look, the first moon rises," he says, pointing. "We must hurry."

I quicken my pace a bit to keep up with him.

"There are two moons here?" I ask, rubbing my arms again to keep warm. "Are we not on Earth?"

"We are in Paredonia, a sister world of Earth, from another dimension in time. When you stepped through the doorway, you entered back into this dimension, which we call Paredonia."

"But there are two moons here," I reason. "My Earth has only one."

"In this place, there are two, but that is a historical lesson for another time. Look, I see Elspa's cottage just up ahead on the hill."

I look up and see a small home made of stone with a thatched roof and smoke rising from a chimney. There is a short wooden fence around the back of the house, where I see a few goats grazing. There is a light in the front window. I feel myself relax a bit, as the cottage looks warm and inviting.

"Come along now," he says, prodding me along. "Let's get you warm and safe inside."

"Why are we hurrying so much?" I ask. "I'd like to see the second moon."

"Oh, it won't rise for another hour or so, and it is better if we view it from the safety of the cottage."

I look at him with questioning, as many thoughts about this place continue to bombard my mind. But I am also growing tired and feeling cold, ready to be warm and rest my tired feet. Soon we are at the aged-looking wooden front door, and Dominic raps three times. A dog barks from inside as we wait on the stone doorstep.

"Who is it?" a woman's voice calls from inside.

"It's Dominic from the castle, on errand for King Vespes."

There's a slight pause and then a rustling sound. "I'm coming. Just a moment, then." The door opens, and we stand there before a short, robust, red-cheeked woman with a candle in her hand. She is wearing a long skirt with an apron and a knit sweater on top, and her gold-and-gray hair is pulled back in a loose knot at the back of her neck. Her black-and-white farm dog sniffs and circles us curiously.

"Come in, come in," she says cheerfully, "and welcome!"

I look around at her modest domain. We've come into the largest room, with two smaller rooms I can see off to the back. There is a fireplace with red embers glowing, and I head off in that direction, following Dominic. The dog walks along beside us, tail wagging.

"Yes, be warmed by the fire. I've got some stew still warm from dinner. Let me get you both some."

She heads off to a little kitchen area to the right that is filled with pots and pans of many sizes hanging from the walls.

"And who is this fine young lady you've brought with you today?" she asks as she spoons up the stew for us.

Dominic takes a seat on a bench by the fire, and I follow his lead. As I sit down, the dog decides I am safe and rests his head on my knee to be petted.

"That's Shepp," she says. "I see he's taken a liking to you already."

I smile and pat his furry head.

"This is Kara," says Dominic. "I am her guide to bring her to meet with King Vespes."

"The young king himself? What sort of meeting, if I may ask? And would you like some water, or some hot tea perhaps?"

"Tea, if you please," says Dominic.

I nod in agreement. "Yes, tea would be lovely, thank you," I add.

As she prepares the cups, Dominic continues, "It is a private matter known only to the king. We will be given more information once we arrive at the palace."

"Oh, I see." She nods. "How interesting. You are not from around here, then?" she asks, noticeably eyeing my sweatpants ensemble.

"No," I reply, "I am not," unsure how to explain this.

"You will be needing some traveling clothes, then. I'm sure I have some nice, warm garments that will fit you from my younger days at the castle. I'll be glad for you to put them to good use." She smiles warmly.

"Thank you very much," I say with a returning smile. The stew has warmed me up from the inside, and I feel cozy and quite peaceful.

"Dominic, I'll make a pallet for you by the fire, and, Kara, you can make use of the second bedroom tonight. How nice to have some company on this cool autumn night."

"Where is your son and daughter?" asks Dominic. "Have they gone out on their own now?"

"Sam is tending his own farm now, not far from here, and Cassie is newly married. She lives in Averton now, but they both visit me quite often. It's just me and Shepp now most nights, but you can see he's good company." She smiles.

"Yes, he's a very sweet dog," I reply, glancing toward the window. "Will we be able to see the second moon soon?" I ask.

"Aye, you should be able to now," says Elspa. "But why do you want to go out into the cold again? I'm sure you know the vayaklos will be out. The woods will be full of them with both moons bright in the clear sky tonight."

I glance over at Dominic and notice he's pulling something out of his jacket pocket. It's a pipe, I realize. He grabs a twig lit from the fire and lights it expertly. Pondering what a vayaklos might be, I ask them, "Is it safe to go outside, then?"

"Of course," says Elspa. "As long as you are smart enough to not engage them. It's quite safe here in my pasture. But why are you so eager to see the moons?" she asks, handing me a woolen wrap that she has just pulled out of a trunk.

"Oh, I just enjoy seeing the night sky before I go to bed at night," I say, glancing over at Dominic.

"It's a beautiful thing, to be sure." She smiles.

Dominic grunts in agreement and puffs out a billow of smoke from his pipe. I look at him entreatingly, and he slowly gets up and pulls his outer jacket back on.

"Come on, let's take a look, then," he says, gripping the pipe in his teeth.

I smile with anticipation and wrap the heavy cloak around me. Elspa turns and leads us down the little hall to a back door. "I'll join you in just a minute. Let me grab my other wrap."

Dominic opens the back door, and we step out into the back pasture. A curious goat approaches but doesn't get too close. We walk out farther into the field. The night sky is full of stars now, much more than I am used to seeing.

"Where is the second moon?" I ask, looking around with wondering eyes.

"There, coming up behind those trees. Do you see it?"

I look in the direction he is pointing and can just make out a small glowing light shining through the trees.

"Soon you will see it plain. It is much smaller than the first moon."

I look around to where the first moon is. As I turn and look, I hear what sounds like a high-pitched cricket song. It's musical and rhythmic, and the closer we get to the trees, the louder it gets.

"What is that sound?"

"Sounds like crickets mixed with vayaklos song to me."

"And what is a vayaklos?" I ask, pulling my cloak tighter around me.

"Like a firefly, but smaller and quicker. Their wings make that melodic sound."

"It's a lovely sound," I say, walking closer to the edge of the field by the woods.

"Be careful, they like to draw you deeper into the woods with their song. You hear their sound, then see a flitting light or two and want to follow. The rhythmic sound is like a siren song, soothing and lulling you to sleep. They like shiny objects, and their little caves are full of glittery buttons, earrings, and coins that they take from people while they are asleep."

Fascinated, I peer into the forest beyond, searching for the little lights. "I don't see anything."

"When both moons are high in the sky in the middle of the night, that is when they like to come out and are more likely to be seen. They live in the deep woods."

"What do they look like?" I ask.

"I've never seen one up close, but I've heard they look a lot like little people with wings and that their skin glows with a soft, luminous light."

"You mean like storybook tales of faeries?"

"Yes, I suppose so," he says, puffing out another plume of smoke from his pipe.

I close my eyes and listen to the high-pitched hum in the trees. I feel myself being drawn to it, and I can see how it is like a siren song. I hear footsteps approaching and open my eyes to see Elspa has joined us.

"Ah, it is a lovely night, to be sure," she says. Shepp runs out to the edge of the field and begins to bark. "Shepp! Come back here! Be quiet!" Obediently, the dog turns back and runs over to his master. "Good dog, Shepp. Leave it be."

The second moon has now risen above the top of the trees, and I gaze at it. It is smaller but glows brightly, with a pale bluish-green color. I stare at it, wondering why the night air feels so different now. There is an edge of fear as I gaze into the forest now that I didn't feel before. This small and oddly shaped moon, I find both strange and eerily beautiful. I resolve to question Dominic about it later. A cool gust of wind blows the woolen cape off my shoulder, and I pull it back quickly.

"Yes, it is getting colder now," says Elspa. "Are you ready to turn in for the night?"

"Yes, I am. Thank you," I say, turning back toward the cottage.

We all head back, and soon I'm in her cozy little guest room. There is a colorful quilt on the bed, a small dresser, and red-and-white-checkered curtains on the window. Elspa comes in behind me and closes the window's wooden shutters.

"You should be warm enough underneath those quilts," she says, turning toward a small closet. "In here you will find warm clothes for tomorrow. We can sort through them in the morning. Here's a gown for tonight." She pulls out a long flannel shirt and lays it on the bed. "There's water in the pitcher there. Is there anything else you'll be needing before morning?"

"Just...is there a place to...umm...relieve myself?"

"Oh, yes, the privy is just down the hall, through the back door. Do you have to be off early in the morning? I was thinking we could go to the town marketplace tomorrow to help you find some traveling boots."

I look down at my dust-covered sneakers. "Yes, I think that would be a good idea."

"Very well. Good night, then." She smiles and gently closes the door behind her.

I stand there for a moment, wondering what a *privy* is. "She must mean an outhouse. What century are we in?" Another important question for Dominic tomorrow.

The only light in my room is from a little candle sconce on the wall beside my bed. As I start to undress, I pat my pocket and realize I have no money with me to buy anything. "I guess Dominic will have to help me sort that out as well."

I climb into the soft, warm bed and feel sleep coming upon me quickly. I lie there thinking what a strange day this has been. I wonder what tomorrow will bring.

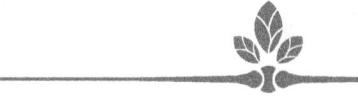

Elspa's Cottage

I awaken to what smells like bacon and slowly open my eyes. Disoriented for a moment, I remember I am not at Sonia's but in this strange, new world. I climb out of bed and open the wooden shutters to look out. Outside, the sun is shining on the green grass in the field, where goats are grazing. There is a little red barn just behind them.

I wonder what time it is and start to reach toward my clothes to retrieve my cell phone, which I realize I don't have with me now. Not that it makes much difference here. It must be sitting on Sonia's coffee table. Is she wondering where I am? Is my family looking for me? I remember back to my dream of being in that room with all those people gathered, conversing about someone being gone or missing. I remember the picture of myself on the table. "Is this really happening?" I must really be in another place, or dimension, as Dominic calls it. Either that or this is one of the longest, most detailed dreams within a dream I've ever had. I've always been a vivid dreamer. But this seems so real.

I close my eyes and pray, "God, I don't know what is happening, or why I am here in this dreamlike place. Please guide my steps and help me find my way. Bring me safely home in Your perfect timing. In Your name. Amen."

Looking in the closet, I find only long skirts and dresses. They are made of thick cotton and flannel, made for cold weather. I try on a long dark-blue skirt and beige top and then pull another cream-colored wool sweater on top of that, as it is quite chilly. I remember she said we could find some traveling boots in town, so I head out to the kitchen to find Elspa.

I find her in front of the fire, humming and frying up some eggs in a large iron pan. There is bacon already set on a plate, and some strawberries in a bowl.

"Oh, there you are! Would you like some hot tea?" she asks, handing me a steaming cup.

"Yes, thank you very much," I reply, taking a seat on the bench. "Thank you for all this."

"It's no trouble. I enjoy having company."

"Where is Dominic?"

"Oh, I asked him to bring in some firewood from the barn. He's already had his breakfast, so I put him to work." She smiles.

"I hope I didn't sleep in too long," I say.

"Of course not, dear. Here, have a plate and I'll join you."

I like Elspa. She is warm and friendly and seems somehow familiar to me. "So," I ask, "what was it like to work for the king? Did you live in a castle with them?"

"Yes, I did. King Rufus has a grand castle. In Silvenia it is called the Silver Palace, and it has three towers. I was the nursemaid for Prince Vespes, who is now the king, and his two sisters, the princesses Delvana and Trea. Princess Delvana is now married to the king of Volkenland, King Greffen. Princess Trea just celebrated her sixteenth birthday and still lives at the castle."

"How long did you live there?"

"For many years, until King Vespes had his eighteenth birthday. I could've stayed on longer, but I was ready to come back to my little farm in the country. I do miss them, though. For a time, they were like my own children, but I have my own son and daughter nearby now. They visit me quite often, especially since my dear husband passed away. From what I hear, things are much different in Silvenia now. King Vespes has been making lots of changes, some good, and some not so good."

"What kind of changes?"

"It saddens my heart to say it, but King Vespes is not the same kindhearted young prince that I used to know. Ever since his father's accident, his focus seems to be on acquiring more treasures for the kingdom and palace courts. He should be looking to the welfare of his people." She shakes her head. "And I do not approve of the rapid betrothal and marriage of Delvana to King Greffen. She was barely seventeen and still reeling from her father's accident. So many changes…" Elspa pauses for a moment, as if deep in thought, then clears her throat. "I shouldn't be saying so much about the young king. He is learning as he goes and has had to take on a lot of responsibility rather quickly."

"When did his mother die?" I ask as I bite into some toast.

"It was not long after she gave birth to Princess Trea. The baby was breech, and the queen lost a lot of blood. During the process, she was greatly weakened. She never fully recovered and passed away a few weeks after Trea was born. The entire kingdom mourned the loss of her."

"What was her name?"

"Queen Adele. She was lovely and had a quiet wisdom about her. The people greatly respected her. Princess Delvana resembles her in her beauty and manner. Trea is more spirited and lovely in her own way. She is more like her father. Anyway, I'm sure you will meet her at the castle when you visit."

"Yes, I hope so. I would like to meet her. Meeting with the king sounds a bit intimidating, though. I wish I knew what this meeting was all about."

I'm just finishing the last of the eggs on my plate when Dominic comes back in the house. "Ah, good morning, Ms. Kara. Are you ready to continue our journey today?"

"Not before she gets some good traveling boots!" Elspa interjects. "Would you like me to accompany you both to the market? I'm sure I'll be much more helpful than Dominic when it comes to women's clothing." She smiles.

Dominic raises an eyebrow. "Aye, but we can't spend all day there. We've got to be getting back on the road soon."

"I don't have any money with me," I blurt out.

"Don't worry about that," says Dominic, patting his pocket. "The king made sure we had money for the journey."

"Why does he want to meet with me?" I ask again. "Maybe he has me confused with someone else, do you think?"

"Oh, no, that specific key came to you for a reason. You were drawn to it, and it was drawn to you. There is no mistaking it."

"What kind of a leaf is it? How was it drawn to me?"

"It is a leaf from the mountains of Shazir, where Lady Vallora dwells. The trees in that forest are very old and very large. The starlings make their nests there. They are the messenger birds, and they answer only to Lady Vallora and her sister, Sabine. She is the keeper of the keys and lives in the sacred forest of Elmwood."

"Are we traveling there on our way to the castle?"

"No. That would be going in the opposite direction, and it's high up in the mountains. The forest itself is protected by the white wolves of that territory. No, to enter the sacred forest, you must be welcomed by Lady Vallora herself."

"Do the wolves answer to her as well?"

"In a way, yes, in that she communicates well with all animals."

I listen, fascinated by this tale. "So how did the leaf get to me?"

"When a leaf falls from one of the sacred elms, it is picked up by a starling and brought to Lady Vallora. If the leaf is a key, it is for a specific person and will have a name revealed on it by the Great One that can be seen by her. The Great One has given the windfolk the gift of seeing things we cannot. They were put here to help the people of this land. So if a name appears on it, she gives the leaf key back to the messenger bird to be brought to that specific person. A starling brought the leaf key to you and placed it in your path knowing you would be drawn to it."

"But how did they know how to find me? And how did they get to my Earth?"

"It's been said that when Lady Vallora presses the leaf to her heart, she can see the person it's meant for. This image is then somehow transmitted to the leaf and the bird knows whom to look for. Their vision is keen, and their memory is sharp. Carrying the leaf, they fly to a portal in the sky above the sea. It is a fracture in the atmosphere caused by a large meteor that fell from space a long time ago. This is the same meteor that hit your Earth's moon in 1652, causing an indentation on the surface. But it released tremors that opened up a fragmented portal into this dimension from your Earth.

"It is said there was a battle in skies between Mercurio—in your Earth he is called Lucifer—and the angels of God. He was trying to keep the new Bibles that had just been printed from spreading throughout the Earth to the people. But in this dimension, that same meteor split our moon in two pieces, causing the appearance of a second, smaller moon. When this happened, it caused changes in our dimension of Earth—a great earthquake followed by a massive tidal wave that swept over a great portion of land. People were swept through the portal in the sea to this place, which we now call Paredonia. There weren't many people who had Bibles at that time, but there were some. The Ancient One allowed this portal to open up in the sea, so instead of drowning, many were swept up here to this place, the uttermost part of the sea. There was a chest of Bibles that went with them and was later discovered by a fisherman close to the shore of the Great Sea a few years after the people arrived here.

"At first, the people were very excited to have these Bibles, and they read and studied them. Mercurio realized what had happened and influenced a wicked man, named Danere, to put a spell on the second moon. Mercurio is a trickster and masquerades as an angel of light, but he is the ruler over darkness and evil. He distracted the people with this spell. They lost interest in reading the truth from the Bible and started focusing on the magical happenings of the night. Trolls and other dark creatures appeared in the land. Some of the vayaklos that used to just give night-light like fireflies and make music with their wings became mischievous. More dangerous animals roamed the forests and attacked when the second moon was high in the sky, so people became afraid and let fear control them more and more. They forgot the truth in the Word about how God loves them and protects them. How he sent His own Son to save them. This world may seem beautiful and magical, but it is on the verge of being taken over completely by the evil one. Perhaps you are familiar with this scripture from His Word: 'For we do not wrestle against flesh and blood, but against principalities, against powers, against the rulers of the darkness of this age, against spiritual hosts of wickedness in the heavenly places'" (Eph. 6:12).

I nod, listening intently. "Yes, I remember hearing that before."

"So getting back to the starlings, when they get to the portal above the Great Sea, they follow the path of the winds to the place where the person they are looking for dwells. They fly over the area where the wind becomes still, searching for that person until they find them. Sometimes it can take weeks or even months to find their person, but they never give up."

"Don't the leaves dry up and crumble by then?"

"Not these, no. These are special leaves from the great elms that live by the brook in the sacred forest. Take your leaf out of your pocket and see. It is still colorful and vibrant."

"I don't have it with me," I say. "It's back on my dresser at home."

Looking at me with alarm, he says, "What? That's not possible!"

"Well, that's where I left it."

"The leaf key is what opens the door to this world. Didn't you have it with you when you came through the doorway?"

"No, I didn't. You told me to come, and I simply followed you."

"But how did you get to the door?"

"All I know is, I was at my friend Sonia's house and I fell asleep. In my dreaming, I was in this room with a lot of people and I was trying to find a way out. That's how I came to the door."

"Oh my, I must say, this is most unusual. I have never heard of a person entering this world without their key." Dominic frowns and rubs his bearded chin. "I am perplexed. We must consider what to do about this."

"What do you mean?" I ask.

"You will need your key to return home again."

"What?" I say, the alarm rising in my voice. "You don't mean I'm stuck here?"

"I cannot answer that, but we will meet with the king and his advisers. There will be an answer for you."

"Oh my gosh, oh my gosh!" I sit down on the floor by the fireplace, feeling suddenly light-headed and unsteady.

Elspa comes to my side and pats my shoulder gently. "Don't you worry, dear. Dominic is a good soul and an excellent guide. He will help you find your way." She looks up at Dominic as he paces the floor, stroking his beard thoughtfully.

He stops abruptly and looks up. "We mustn't linger, then. Let's go get Kara her traveling boots. To market!" he says, pushing open the front door.

Diversions on the Path

The market turns out to be a clearing place in the woods, filled with gypsy-like carts and caravans with many different wares. They find me some brown leather boots lined with soft wool that fit quite well. Elspa ends up buying some food for herself and for their travels. I, dressed in Elspa's clothes, blend well into my surroundings and am able to enjoy this outing among the other local villagers.

Soon we are back at Elspa's cottage, and Dominic is bundling up our sack of food in a little knapsack, which he slings over his shoulder. Elspa helps me to pack some more clothing of hers in another bag with straps to wear on my back.

"Here, take this extra wool blanket too," she says, stuffing the last item inside.

"I think we're ready, then," says Dominic. "Let's be away. And thank you, good woman Elspa. Your kindness will not be forgotten."

"Yes, thank you so much for everything," I say. "I hope I will see you again."

"You're more than welcome. Just stay close to Dominic and all will be well, my dear." She gives me a quick hug, and for a moment, I wish to stay and not hurry on. But I must get back home. I must find a way.

We head down the path again, and Shepp follows us a short way and then turns back at Elspa's call.

"Goodbye, Shepp!" I call fondly. He zips back to the cottage, and as I turn to look, I see Elspa standing in her doorway, waving.

My heart beats with a strum of sorrow, and I realize it's because she reminds me of my grandma Mary, who died a few years ago. She always treated me like I was her favorite person in the world, and I loved her a lot. She was warm and caring and could make me laugh.

At the end of her life, she lost her memory, so it felt like I lost her a couple of years before she actually passed away.

"Are you all right?" asks Dominic, noticing my somber mood.

"Yes, I'm fine. She just reminds me of someone I used to know."

"Ah, I see. And who would that be?"

"My grandma Mary," I reply. "She was my favorite relative when I was a child. She passed away a few years ago."

"I'm sure you miss her very much. What was she like?"

"She had a merry heart and liked to play games with me and my sister when we were little. We always had fun whenever we got to stay at her house, and she was an amazing cook too." I smile, remembering the dress-up game she played with Julia and me. Pretending to be gypsies and princesses, we would put on different sets of clothing and colorful scarves—she had tons of them—and then come out and say, "What do I look like?" And she would say, "Oh! You're a princess from a Turkish land!" or something like that. Then we would twirl around and laugh and just be silly. I suddenly realize I can't remember feeling that happy or lighthearted in a long time. I've forgotten.

"What are you thinking?"

"I was just remembering how it felt to be little and carefree. I'm not sure I'm ready to be a responsible adult yet," I say with an embarrassed smile.

He stops for a moment and looks me in the eyes. "Never lose that child in your heart. It's the very essence of who you are." He clears his throat and begins to walk again.

"Right, of course," I say. "It's just that, with becoming an adult, there are so many new responsibilities, bills, and demands. Everything's so serious."

"And then there're the valleys of heartbreak and loss."

I look at him. "You know about Tom?"

"Yes, I do."

"But how?"

"Before I was assigned as your guide in this place, I was given glimpses of significant moments in your life by the Ancient One. Not knowing what to do with these visions, I was sent by the windfolk to visit Gadir on the Blue Isle of Havendor. He is old and wise, a relative of theirs, I believe. He is the one who told me I must go to visit Commander Vale in Silvenia—that the king had an assignment for a young woman named Kara that was of great importance and that I was assigned to be your guide."

"And what did you see in those visions?"

"I saw many events in your life, some good and some not so good. Quiet days when you felt alone and small, sitting in the tree in your backyard. Fun times with your sister sledding on the farm hill. Being the new girl at school and finding new friends. Feeling misunderstood and betrayed by some of those same friends later on. I saw your first car accident on the freeway that you walked away from unharmed. Riding your horse at the ranch. I could go on."

"Wow, you've seen a lot of things in my life. Are you, like, my guardian angel or something?"

"No, I'm not an angel, that's for sure. This is my assignment, my 'job,' as you might call it. My gift is to help others along the path on the journey of life. Sometimes you have to completely change your surroundings to get a new vision or perspective on things, to get unstuck. I'm here to help you get unstuck and find your way."

"Am I dreaming all this? I'm glad you want to help me, but I'm concerned that I need to get back home. My family must be worried sick about me by now."

"You have great concern for others. That is an admirable quality. But you mustn't worry. If your burden of cares becomes too heavy, you won't be able to complete your assignment here."

"What assignment? What does this king want with me?"

"You will find out soon enough. Right now we must have patience and focus on our steps for today."

I sigh with uncertainty. "Okay, so where are we headed now?"

"We are headed to the Baton Bridge to cross over the river to the east. To the west lies the swamplands, so we must cross over the river before we can head back toward Silvenia."

"Okay. So can you tell me more about the—"

"Watch out!" he interrupts, jerking me back by the arm. I narrowly miss stepping into what looks like a large muddy puddle.

"What's wrong? It just a mud puddle!"

"Maybe, maybe not. We are getting close to the swamplands now and need to watch out for the sinkholes."

"Sinkholes? Do you mean like quicksand?"

"Sort of. It's a trap, set by Mercurio. Some of these innocent-looking 'mud puddles' are set that if you step in it, it opens up a trapdoor down a slippery tunnel to his underground catacombs and caves. There are many passages underground, and it can be very difficult to find your way back to the surface again."

"Are you serious? Why are we even walking on this path, then?"

"It's the only safe path I know of through these forests to Silvenia. Don't worry. I didn't let you fall in it, did I?"

"No, but why didn't you tell me about this danger sooner?"

"I don't want you to walk in fear. We must be brave and clear-headed on this journey."

I look at him with resignation. "Okay, so I just need to meet with this king, do some sort of task, and then he will somehow help me to get back home. I feel like Dorothy in the land of Oz! All right, let's get there, then!" I quicken my pace and then pause again for a second. "Is there anything else you might want to tell me about before we go on? Any other dangerous surprises that might be lurking ahead?"

"Let's take them as they come." He smiles. "Come on, stick with me and you'll be fine!"

We walk together, and now I am very alert to any muddy-looking areas on the path ahead. To the right, there are pools of water throughout the woodland floor. Long plumes of grayish-blue moss hang from the tree limbs, and there is a sour stench in the air. I hear a swishing sound, and to my left I see a brown snake slither off into the water. Up high in the trees, there are a few crane-type birds with silvery wings and long beaks. Their call is sharp and loud and echoes in our ears. We walk on in silence for a while, while the setting sun filters an orange light through the trees. I am focusing on watching my step, and then I remember to ask, "Tell me again—who is Mercurio?"

"Mercurio is an evil being that reigns in the underground world. He is always trying to capture unwary travelers and imprison them below. He has many agents working on his behalf aboveground as well."

"How can we be safe from him?"

"Just like in your Earth, by putting your trust in the Son of the Ancient One. He has made a way of escape and is much more powerful than Mercurio or any of his evil cohorts."

I look at Dominic, contemplating this. "So you're talking about God, right? And Jesus and salvation."

"Yes, I am. He is the very same God in your Earth and mine. We are in different dimensions, but He is Lord over all."

"Well, I gave my heart to Jesus as a young child, and I still believe in Him. So does that mean I am safe here too?"

"It means He will always be with you and never leave you or forsake you. It does not mean you won't have any troubles in life. In fact, there could be many tests of your faith and things to overcome, but the great Overcomer is with you, so do not be afraid."

"How did you become so wise?"

"By reading His book."

"You mean the Bible, right?"

"Yes, that is exactly what I mean."

"I haven't done much of that lately."

"I always carry it in my knapsack, and you're welcome to read it anytime."

"Thank you. I used to do that a lot when I first became a Christian. It just seems so confusing sometimes."

"Ask the Holy One to reveal its meaning to you. The Word is alive and powerful to help you in time of need. You should read it every day."

"Okay," I say, feeling a spark of hope ignite in my chest. I inwardly vow to renew my habit of reading the Word daily.

"We are in the swamplands now. The bridge is not far, maybe another two to three miles."

"And it crosses over the swamp?"

"No. We will be turning away from the swamp and crossing over the river Baton."

"And then where will we be spending the night?"

"I know of an inn. It's in the town of Averton, just a few miles from the bridge. We should get there by nightfall."

As we walk, I suddenly realize the birdcalls have died down and the rhythmic sound of the crickets is increasing. Dominic seems to quicken his pace, and I hurry to keep up with him. A gray squirrel darts across our path and runs into the swampy woods. I follow him with my eyes, and in the changing light through the trees, he looks like a gray cat—like my cat, I think. I blink my eyes and try to focus. My mind must be playing tricks on me.

"Keep your wits about you," says Dominic. "The vayaklos will begin to be out and about soon."

To my right, I hear it. *Meooww!*

"Oh my gosh, that sounds like my cat, Percy!"

"What do you see?"

"I think I saw a cat in the forest to our right. He was gray and looked like my own cat back home."

"There was a gray squirrel that just crossed our path. Maybe that's what you saw?"

"Yes, I know. I saw the squirrel. But then I saw a cat—and oh! There he goes!"

I see him run up a tall willowy tree deeper in the forest. He is calling out pitifully, *Meooww, meow!*

"I need to go check," I say, heading toward the tree.

"No! You mustn't," he says. "It's a trick to lure you deeper into the forest! It's not your cat, Kara."

I look at him, torn between panic and caution. "Is it the vayaklos?"

"It could be, or worse, it could be one of the agents of Mercurio leading you into a trap."

"But it's so real! Even if it's not my cat, maybe it's a cat from here who's lost or hurt and needs our help."

"I don't like it, but if you must go to it, let me lead the way."

"Okay," I say. I really just want to get closer to make sure it's not Percy; hearing him feels like a piece of home, and I have to get a closer look.

THE LEAF KEY

"Slowly now, watch your step." Dominic leads us gingerly through the woods around puddles and onto boulders sticking up in jagged patterns. Some of them are covered in slimy moss, and I feel my boot slide a bit as I get my balance.

"Are you okay?" he says, reaching his hand out to steady me.

"Yes," I say, grabbing ahold. "I'm fine."

Meowww, moans the cat again. I see it's gray tail twitching in the tall tree up ahead.

"It's up so high," I say. "I can only see its tail."

"I still think it's a trap. We shouldn't go any closer."

"Percy!" I call out. "Come here, Perc!"

Reoowwr, he calls back.

"Kara, the tree he is perched in is surrounded by thick, muddy water. Let's turn back."

"There's that one big boulder by it. I can step up on it and reach its lowest branch. The branches look thick enough to hold me so I can climb up closer and see where he is perched. I promise I'll be careful!"

Dominic frowns as I gently step toward the mossy rock by the tree. Suddenly, I hear a rhythmic flapping sound and look up. To my right, approaching swiftly is a large colorful birdlike animal flying directly at me.

"It's a sterrador!" cries Dominic. "It's hunting prey, the prey in that tree! Stay back, Kara!"

"No! I can't let it! Get back!" I wave my free hand at it and yell louder as I reach for the nearest branch. "Shoo! Get out of here!" I pull myself up higher and closer to the cat now. I can feel a breeze from the large wings swooping down close to my face. My adrenaline is pumping now, and I'm determined to save the cat. I see the creature's large talons descending close to the tree as I reach the spot. I put my hand up to grab it, and a gray squirrel jumps past me and shoots down the tree out of sight. I look up at the sterrador, and it gives a loud screech. It swoops right past me, and I feel the tip of its wing brush against my arm. A bright, teal-colored feather flutters down in front of me, and I reach out to grab it, but miss. It settles on the leaves of the branch just below me, farther out over the swampy water.

"Kara, are you all right?" Dominic calls up to me. "I'm right below you now. Just slowly make your way down to me."

"Yes, I'm fine. I'm coming down." As I reach for the branch beneath me, I steady myself for a moment and then lean out to grasp the elusive feather. I can see it clearly, its iridescent teal color vibrant and beautiful, and just out of my reach.

"You're almost down, Kara. Just a little farther…"

I straddle the branch with my legs and inch out a little farther over the water. *Don't look down*, I think. *Just grab the feather and climb back down. I can do this.* My hand is upon it now, and I hear a cracking sound. I freeze for a moment, and it stops.

"Kara, hurry!"

I shimmy back and climb down the trunk quickly, grasping the colorful plume in my hand. Dominic grasps my other hand and leads me.

"Stay close to me now. We're heading back to the path."

I follow him obediently, and soon we are back on the firm ground of the path. Catching our breath, we both sit down there for a moment. He looks at me. "What's that in your hand?"

"I got a feather. Maybe it can help me. You said they were valuable."

"Yes—extremely rare and valuable. But you almost got yourself killed in the process! Quite headstrong, indeed!"

"Sorry, Dominic. You were right, it wasn't my cat at all. It was the squirrel from the path, but it looked and sounded so real. How could that be?"

The thrumming of the crickets is increasingly louder now. Dominic shakes his head. "I do not know, but it's trickery indicates darker powers are at work. It could be the vayaklos, but the sun is just setting, and they are not fully awake yet. Speaking of that, we need to hurry now on to Averton to get there before dark. We don't have time for any more adventurous detours today." He hoists himself up and sticks out his hand. "Come along, then, Kara."

I grab his hand, and after he pulls me up, I tuck the feather safely in my knapsack. *Kaaw, kauwww,* calls a silver-winged bird floating in the wind above us. We hurry along, and out of the corner of my eye, I see a flash of light. It's quickly getting darker now, and I begin to see them more and more all around us. The high, rhythmic notes strum in my head. I feel myself getting sleepy and peaceful. I want to sit down and rest for a moment. I look at Dominic, and he sees it in my eyes.

"Let's talk," he says. "What would you like to talk about?"

"Honestly, I don't feel much like talking now. I'm very tired."

"Tell me about your family. I've just seen glimpses of them at different moments in your life. Tell me what they're like."

"Well, my mom is great. She's kind, understanding, and a good listener, though I had to get past my teenage years to realize that. My dad is hardworking, generous, and mostly kind. His temper can be quite a sight, but he's mellowed a lot as he's gotten older. He didn't approve of most of the boys I wanted to go out with when I was in high school. I was fearful of his temper as a child, so I tried not to do anything that would make him angry. My sister, on the other hand, she knew how to push his buttons and ended up getting in trouble a lot. I hated to witness that and would try to mediate between the two, but it usually didn't help much. To this day, I cringe when I hear a parent yell at their child in anger."

He raises an eyebrow and looks at me. "I see, and what about your sister? Are the two of you very close?"

"We used to be when we were younger. I still love her very much, but things have changed between us. Most of the time now, she just treats me with contempt. Lately, I just try to avoid being around her so we don't get into another argument." I kick a pinecone across the path.

"Did something happen to her? Why is she so angry with you?"

"She's angry at everyone but mostly seems to direct it toward me. I'm a few years older. Maybe it's because I ignored her a lot when she wanted to tag along with me and my friends. I should have included her more and considered her feelings. I know she had a tough time in middle school. Also, I dated a guy that I found out later she really liked, and that added fuel to the fire. She befriended this girl named Marly, who didn't like me for some reason, and it was like they teamed up in their hatred of me." Dominic nods, listening intently. "I don't think she really hates me. I guess she's just going through a hard time right now."

"What do you mean by that?"

"Well, she's been depressed and angry. Then she started drinking a lot. She'd come in the door at night with Marly, very drunk, stumbling, laughing, and falling down. If I said anything to confront them, it never turned out well."

"What about your parents? Didn't they see all this happening as well?"

"No. They go to bed early and slept right through those episodes. I finally tried to talk to my mom about it, but when she spoke with Julia about it later, she just said I was exaggerating. She admitted to drinking but said she wasn't really drunk and that it wouldn't happen again. My mom believed her."

"I see."

"She has been a little nicer to me since I broke up with Tom. Also, she's taking medication for the depression now, so that might be helping too."

"Well, that's good. Hopefully she's on the path to recovery, then?"

"I guess so. Sometimes she still has these episodes of being extremely angry, and she still drinks—I don't think as much as before, but I really don't know, because she's out a lot. I worry about her."

"I can see that." Dominic nods, slowing his pace a bit. I continue with my pinecone kicking along the dusty path.

"The scariest time was when I came home from work late one night. Dad and Mom were out of town at one of his work conferences. I walked in the kitchen, and Julia was sitting on the counter cross-legged, with her little switchblade in her hand. She was clicking it open and close, open and close, and staring into space with a glassy look in her eyes. There was an almost-empty wine bottle next to her on the counter. Then she took the knife and started scraping it up and down her arm. She didn't see me standing there in disbelief."

"Good heavens! What did you do?"

"As calmly as I could, I asked her to put the knife down. She just stared at me with this vacant look and then laughed, but she did put it down, next to her, on the counter."

"What happened next?"

"I asked her if she was okay, if there was anything I could do for her, a glass of water, anything?" I close my eyes for a moment, remembering…

"Julia, do you want to talk? I'm here for you."

"Ha!" she laughs with a smirk. "No, I don't need anything from you, Ms. Perfect."

"I'm not perfect. I just want to help you!"

"You can't!" she yells. Then, as she stares at me with pain in her eyes, silent tears begin to trickle down her face.

"Julia, you're my sister, and I love you! Let me help you. Don't shut me out!" I reach for her, and she lets me hold her for a moment. I say a quiet prayer for her, and she sits there stiffly, tears sliding down her face. She says nothing else. I kiss the top of her head and ask, "Do you want to stay up and watch a movie together?"

She straightens and pushes me back. "No, I'm fine now. I'm going to bed." Not knowing what else to say or do, I watch her quickly retreat back to her room.

I feel tears sting my eyes at the memory. "It's like we're strangers instead of sisters living in the same house. She rarely speaks to me anymore and treats me like I'm her enemy. I feel so helpless. I can't pull her out of that dark place."

"But there is one who can," says Dominic gently.

"Who?" I look at him. "Oh, you mean God."

"Yes, the Ancient One himself has a healing balm for all sicknesses, even of the heart."

"Yes, I know. And I've prayed and prayed for her, but nothing good ever seems to happen."

"Oh, you shouldn't say such things!"

"What?" I exclaim. "It's the truth!" Dominic walks on quietly, saying nothing. "Where is this Ancient One, and why doesn't he hear my prayers?"

"He hears you, Kara. Why do you think you are here?"

"I don't know! You're the one who keeps telling me I have some kind of assignment. I don't see how being here is the answer to my prayers!"

"You must be patient and have faith."

"Faith in what?"

"Faith in the one who can see your whole story from beginning to end. The one who is outside of time itself." He stops for a moment and puts his hand on my shoulders. "Kara, can you trust me?"

I look up at him. "What other choice do I have?" I whisper. He gives a little smile and nods with understanding.

Hoo hoo! Whoo hoo!

"What is that?" I say with a start. Looking up, I see a large owl settle on a wooden post up ahead.

"That is the lamppost at the start of the bridge. Come on, we're almost there."

The lights still flit and flicker around us, but I no longer feel sleepy.

"Is that really an owl?" I say as we get closer to the large bird sitting perfectly still and watching us.

"I think so, but stay alert," he says as he picks up a long walking stick off the ground. I follow his lead and grab a smaller one and hold it ready.

The owl merely watches us as we walk by, his head turning as we go past. I hear the water of the river close by.

"Sometimes there is a guard at the entrance to the bridge. We may have to pay a toll to cross over. Just follow my lead."

"Okay, but I don't see anyone there."

Suddenly, a dark figure rises up from under the start of the bridge. He is cloaked in a long gray robe with a hood and a black leather belt around his waist. He appears to be holding a long spear of some kind with a curved blade at the tip.

"Halt! Who goes there?" he calls out in a low, gravelly voice.

"We are two travelers on our way to Averton."

The menacing guard straightens to his full height and holds out a pale hand, palm up. "You must pay the toll to cross over. Three silver coins."

Dominic pulls out his coin pouch. "I only have two silver, but here is one gold piece instead. That should be more than enough."

The cloaked stranger closes his fingers over the coins and eyes us both with eerie silence. "I will take that feather instead," he says, pointing at me.

I look down and realize that the tip of the brilliant plume is sticking out of the top of my knapsack. I quickly push it back down. "That is just part of my cap, my clothing," I stammer. "It is of no value to you."

"Nevertheless, since you are lacking the third silver coin, I require that as payment."

I look at Dominic, not wanting to give it up but unsure how to proceed. There is a cold chill in the air, and I feel myself shiver.

"I have given you more than enough with the gold piece! We are on errand for King Vespes! You must let us pass!"

A raspy laugh escapes the guard's throat. "Very well, then. But I cannot guarantee your safety."

What does that mean? I think to myself with growing alarm.

He pauses for a moment longer and then slowly steps aside. Dominic raises his walking stick, and we step forward together, watching the guard and keeping ourselves on alert.

He stays facing outward, with his back to us, as we begin our ascent up the bridge.

The bridge itself is made of old worn-out timbers and curves high in an arch above the rushing water below. There are gaps and holes in places, and we are stepping carefully in the dark. As we walk, I feel a vibration under my feet. The bridge itself begins to bump and rattle.

"Hurry!" says Dominic just as a spiky claw thrusts up through a hole in the wood and grabs Dominic by the ankle. I hear myself screaming, and then we both start beating at it with our sticks. There is a fierce, growling noise, but it refuses to let him go.

"What is it?" I yell in panic as the bridge continues to shake.

"It's a river troll. You must let me handle it. Take my bag and run to the Averton Inn. The path will lead you there. Go!"

"No! I'm going to help you. I'm not leaving you!"

The thumping beneath my feet is getting stronger and knocks me to my side. I catch a glimpse under the bridge and see a large dark spiny animal. It continues thrashing upward in the water, pushing against the wood and trying to break all the way through. It still has a grip on Dominic's ankle.

"Kara, you must go! I will find you. Go now!"

The guard speaks without turning. "My name is Keor. I have the power to call it off. Simply give me the feather and I will do so." He then turns and stares at me coldly. "Otherwise, both of you shall die."

"No, Kara! Don't listen to him! Take our bags and go! Don't look back."

The monster is still gripping his leg, and I can see he is grimacing in pain. Another board cracks, and both claws push through and take ahold of Dominic, pulling him down farther as he yells out in fear. I grab the feather and pull it out, holding it up high above my head. "Call it off! I have the feather. Call it off now!"

Keor looks at me and calls out, "Rigort, hent!"

The beast lets go of its hold on Dominic, removing one claw and then the other as Dominic gasps in relief. The beast falls back into the water, snorting with tension.

"Hand it over," demands Keor, holding out his ashen palm toward me.

Dominic looks up at me as I take a step forward and then, with a sudden jerk upward, thrusts his bag at me and jumps to the side into the river, yelling, "Go, Kara! Run!"

It all feels like it's happening in slow motion. I watch as he swims frantically away.

"Hand me the feather now, or your friend will be torn apart!"

In a crazy moment of panic, I obey Dominic's request, and grabbing his sack, I half-leap, half-run down the bridge away from Keor. I hear the troll thrash in the water behind me as Keor yells, "Rigort, belot! Belot!"

The beast propels itself toward my fleeing friend. I am running desperately toward the woods opposite of where I think Dominic is headed. I am running, running, listening for sounds of Dominic or the troll, but I hear nothing. Nothing but the beat of my feet on the woodland floor and my gasps for air.

A root sticking out of the ground trips me, and I stumble and fall. I lie there stunned for a moment, then anxiously peer through the brush toward the river. I hear nothing except the rush of the water. Staying low, I crawl quietly closer to the water. I find a sheltered spot close to the water's edge and look up and down the river. Nothing.

"Where is he? Where is the troll?" It's too quiet, eerily so.

Crawling on my stomach under the brush, I look back over at the bridge. There is no sign of Keor either. "What is happening? I can't be alone in this place. What's happened to Dominic?"

"What have I done? I should have just handed over the feather! What's wrong with me?" I feel frozen with fear and regret and realize I am shivering again. "What if that creature is tracking me right now? I need to be really still and think. I need a plan. God, help me!" I whisper.

The thrum of the crickets and vayaklos song begins again, and as I look around, the flickering lights are all around me, rising above me and into the branches of the trees. I look up at the one I'm leaning against. I should climb up it for safety from the troll and to get a better view while I figure out what to do next.

I look for a branch to pull up on. There, to my right. With a deep breath, I lunge for it and begin to climb. My boots grip into the trunk, and I feel my adrenaline kick in again as I hear a noise to my left. A growling sound—the troll!

I climb faster as high as I can. Finally, I can go no further, as the branches are becoming too thin. Sitting precariously in a thick curved branch, I quiet myself and listen.

There is a rustling sound, and then I see it. Down below and over to my left, the creature is emerging from the brush and heading back into the water. There is no sign of Dominic anywhere. "Please, God, let him be alive," I whisper. "Help me to find him."

As I sit there, squinting in the darkness, something wet drips into my eye. I brush it away and see blood on my hand. Gingerly I touch my forehead and flinch at the sting of it. There seems to be a gash there, probably from when I tripped and fell.

It's fairly bright out, with both moons glowing in the night sky above me. The lights of the vayaklos continue to flicker around me in the trees, and I stop and stare at the beauty of it.

Kya-kya! An eagle with tawny golden wings suddenly appears and perches on a branch not far from me. It seems to be looking directly at me. *Kya!* it calls out.

"Hello, there," I say quietly. I've never seen an eagle up close before, and I stare at it in amazement. I don't feel so alone now, and a sense of peace and rest begins to wash over me. Feeling sleepy, I close my eyes for a moment and realize I need to get some sleep and regain my strength. But I can't sleep here. I've got to climb back down and find a safe spot. Opening my eyes, I see the eagle flying off deeper into the woods.

I begin my descent down the rough bark of the tree. As I gently plant my feet on the ground, I look around carefully and listen for any signs of movement.

Kya-kya! It's the eagle again. I can't see it now, but I hear it calling to me from farther in the forest. I decide to head toward it. The brush and trees are thicker now, and I'm continually pushing back branches out of my face. I don't know why I'm following the eagle, but inside it feels like the right thing to do.

My eyelids are heavy with sleep now, and I just want to lie down. Maybe I should just sit and rest for a moment. *Kya!* I see the eagle again. It's perched high up in a tree not too far away. I press on, making my way toward it.

"Where are you leading me, Mr. Eagle?"

When I am almost to its tree, it takes off again, gliding through the trees with graceful ease. I hurry through the dark woods after it and come to some sort of clearing. It lands gently on a rooftop, peeking through the branches. I step out a little farther and see it's a small cottage by itself. Actually, it's more like a log cabin, rustic and alone, with a small light glowing in one of the windows.

I pause, wondering who might live here in a place so isolated. Maybe I should stay hidden close by and see who comes out in the light of day. I look around to see where I might be able to lie down and sleep for a bit, hidden from view.

There is a pile of chopped wood to the side of the cabin, and as I inch a bit closer, I can see a small ax lying on the ground next to it. I should grab that for protection, I think. Whoever is inside is probably asleep anyway, so I carefully step up to the weapon. I crouch down for a moment behind the pile of wood and assess my situation.

Okay, I think. *At least I have a weapon now.* I look back behind the cabin, where there is a small backyard with a few tall thin trees and a path leading back into the thick woods. I quietly head back there and take the path to find a place to lay my head down and rest for a few hours. Looking back, I see the majestic eagle still perched on the roof, watching me silently. A little way down this narrow path, I see a large old tree with a wide trunk to my right. Walking behind it, there is a soft pallet of leaves I settle down on, the brush around me a good cover. As I pull my cloak around me for warmth, I feel sleep come quickly as I relax onto the cool, dark earth.

On to Averton

> "Weeping may endure for a night, But joy comes in the morning" (Ps. 30:5 NKJV).

I hear these words echo in my head as I awaken from a dreamless sleep. Light is streaming through the branches above me, and squinting, I take in my surroundings. Birds are singing all around me, and I see a squirrel hopping from branch to branch in a nearby tree. It's quite scenic and peaceful, and for a moment, I lie still in nature's calming embrace.

Then I remember I am alone. Feelings of fear and regret creep up on me as I think of Dominic. "Where is he? How will I find him?"

I remember the cabin. Whoever lives there must be up by now. I must go and check it out. Brushing leaves from my clothes, I rise up, flinching at a stinging pain in my leg. I raise my skirt and see a cut on my leg just above my boot crusted with dried blood. My face has stopped bleeding too, but I must look a mess. I smooth my hair down around my head, raking through the tangles with my fingers. I realize I am also extremely thirsty. Maybe there's a stream nearby. My little canteen is nearly empty. "No, I should check out the cabin first. If it's a friendly stranger, they will have water to share."

I head back through the trees up the path to the cabin. I don't hear any noise, but I stay just to the side of the path to keep hidden. I am clutching the small ax as I approach and then decide to hide it in my knapsack instead. I can always pull it out if I need to.

At the edge of the backyard, no one is in sight. I hesitate, trying to decide if I should peek in a window or just head straight for the door and knock. I decide to go to the door.

The old wooden stairs creak as I go up to knock. Before I can even raise my hand to the door, it opens abruptly, and I stand there face-to-face with an old, grumpy-looking man with a scraggly gray beard. He's wearing a black woolen cap.

"Who's trespassing on my property?" he demands.

"Pardon me, sir. I was just in need of a drink of water."

He squints his eyes and looks me up and down. "What's a young person like you doing out here in these woods, anyway? Are you lost or something?"

I don't know what to say. "I...I'm looking for my friend. We were out walking and got separated."

"Lost your friend, you say?" He suddenly looks a bit kinder. "Here, sit down on this chair here. You're bleeding." I touch my forehead and feel the crusted wound.

"Yes, thank you," I say, sitting down on the small wooden bench on the porch.

"I'll get you some water...and a bandage." He turns around, and I peer into the cabin as he shuffles back inside. It's sparse, not many furnishings, a faded rug on the floor. There's a gun mounted on the wall over a small fireplace.

I won't go in, I think. *I'll just get some water and then find my way to town, to the inn Dominic told me about. What was the name of it? Aver...Averly?* I struggle to remember. *I've got to get there, so he can find me.*

A moment later, the hermit man is back at the door, holding a cup of water in one hand and some white strips of cloth in the other, along with a tin of some type of ointment.

"Here you are." He hands me the water and puts the ointment down on the bench beside me. "You can put some of this medicine on that cut."

I comply, grateful for this kindness but still wary of this stranger. He stands there, arms crossed, watching me. "You'd best be on your way now. I don't take in strangers."

I nod and hand him back the empty cup.

"Could I have one more drink before I go, please?"

Grunting, he grabs the cup and steps back inside. I quickly apply more ointment to the gash on my leg as well before he returns.

"Here," he says gruffly, handing me the cup again. "And you can take this piece of bread with you, but I can't give you no more. Now, be on your way!"

I rise up at his command and gratefully take the bread. "Thank you for your kindness." I begin to step down off the porch and head back toward the forest.

"Wait, where are you headed?"

"To the town of Averly," I respond.

"You mean Averton? It's southeast of here. Follow that narrow path through the woods to your left. And don't look back—these woods are not safe! Just look at you...," he continues grumbling under his breath, shaking his head and heading back inside his cabin.

"Thank you!" I call out as he slams the door behind him. Taking a deep breath, I head toward the path he pointed out to me. It's hardly a path at all, branches sticking out everywhere. I shield my face and press on, to Averton. Hopefully, Dominic will find me there. Or maybe I'm on my own now. Time will tell.

As I walk on, the night before seems like a bad dream. My mind keeps replaying the events over in my head. I see the troll creature, thrashing around in the river, all gray and spiny and fierce. I see Dominic swimming for his life, racing to the shore. Did he make it? I feel a stray tear slide down my cheek. I wipe it away, then pause, remembering I still have the hermit's ax in my knapsack. I should probably just keep it. "I need it more than he does," I reason. But I also realize I don't want to steal from him. He did me no harm, and he gave me water and a salve for my cuts. I turn around and quickly head back. "I won't knock. I'll just leave it by his front steps."

Back at the cabin, I lay it on the ground. Turning, I set my face forward and head back to the trail. I feel strangely better, even though the logical side of my brain is calling me stupid for not keeping it.

The air is cold as I press on through the bristly trail. I hear the scurrying sound of small animals about me as I walk on. Just when I start wondering when this trail is going to start thinning out and where it is leading me, I hear something. It sounds like a cow. There must be a farm close by. I feel a spark of hope. "If there's a farm, there's people, a town. Averton! I must be getting closer."

"But what will I do when I get there? I've no money—wait! Yes, I do. Dominic threw me his sack before he jumped into the water. Do I have it?" I throw down my knapsack and begin to dig through it.

"Yes! His brown bag is there with his food, jacket, and coins—gold and silver coins! And food! How did I forget about this? Thank you, God," I whisper with a sigh of relief.

I sit down for a moment and pull out the bread the hermit gave me. I was going to ration it, but now that I see I have supplies, I hungrily devour it. "Now, I just need to find a stream to refill my canteen, and life will be good. I'll keep heading toward the farm. There must be water there or a brook along the way." I finish the last of the crumbs, thinking that must have been the best-tasting bread I've ever had.

The path is opening up before me now as I walk along, and I feel my strength returning. I suddenly hear the sound of water and head toward it through the brush. A little off to my left, I see it, a small running brook.

I hurry over to it and dip my canteen into the cool, clear water. I drink it down and fill it again. "So good, so good! Thank You, God!" I breathe in, resting for a moment on a large flat rock. I pull my boots off and rub my tired feet. Then, deciding I should clean myself up a bit, I splash the cold water on my face and skin. I spend the next few minutes shivering, but overall, I feel better. *Town must not be far away,* I think hopefully.

The sun is high in the sky, and I lie back on the rock and soak in the warmth. It feels glorious. Closing my eyes, I hear birds all around me. A soft wind is stirring the leaves in the trees, and I relax and just breathe for a moment. I realize I have not thought of my family or Tom or anything else in my own world for quite some time, and it's actually a relief. I don't have any cares right now except for what I'm facing here.

I open my eyes and see one of the large silver crane birds up high in the branches above me. The sky is a brilliant blue, and it strikes me how similar this is to my getaway pond back home. Except that this world is more colorful and mysterious and dangerous. "Maybe if I fall asleep now, thinking about home, I'll wake up there, back in Sonia's living room."

I close my eyes again and entertain this notion. "Back home, back to my miserable job and back to the emptiness without Tom. Back to the painful relationship with my sister. Back to…my mom. I miss my parents, especially my mom. I know I have their love, even in this strange place. And Sonia, my dear friend…" I feel darkness and loneliness creeping back upon me. "I'm not needed there. Life will go on just fine without me. Tom is gone."

I feel the pain in my heart seep out once more. I push a stray tear off my face. Maybe I don't need to get back. I see my mom's face in my mind's eye, speaking words of encouragement to me. "I know it hurts now, Kara, but you'll find someone better. Someone who truly loves you, and you will be happy again."

The familiar pang of sorrow returns, and I let it simmer there for a moment, just inside my chest. *Let it go*, I think. *Who needs love, anyway? Love is pain.* My heart feels cold now, like the stone I am lying upon. The sun has slipped behind a cloud, and I sit up, wiping my eyes. *I'm wasting time.*

Pushing dark thoughts down, I pull my boots back on. "Averton could be just ahead—time to continue this journey…"

I go up and down another gentle hill as the space between the trees widens. I hear more animals now, cows and goats bleating in the distance. As I crest the next hill, I see barns, red and white, nestled in the valley below. There are cows on one hill and sheep and goats on another. I see a man walking in the distance, his dog by his side. They are heading away from the sheep toward a quaint-looking farmhouse.

The path transforms into a wider dirt road now, and I walk on, hoping this is the way to Averton. As I pass the farmhouse, I see the road splits up ahead. I don't see any signs. "Maybe I should stop here and ask for directions. This place looks safe enough."

I pause for a moment and then head cautiously to the front door. As I get closer, I hear the dog barking, announcing my arrival. A man opens the door and steps out, shutting the dog inside.

"Can I help you?"

"Yes," I say. "I was wondering if you could tell me which road to take to get to Averton?"

He gives me a curious look. "Are you traveling there alone? On foot?"

"Yes, I'm meeting a friend there. I just want to make sure I'm on the right road."

"Who is it, Lawrence?" a short sturdy-looking woman comes to the door.

"This young woman is traveling to Averton and needs directions."

"Oh, my dear, that's quite a ways down the road. Won't you come in and get something to eat before you head over there?"

"Oh, no, thank you, I couldn't intrude. I really must get going."

"Well, at least take some food with you for the road. Let me get you something." She turns and hurries back inside. The farmer smiles at me and shrugs his shoulders.

"Would you like to sit for a moment?" He gestures to a chair on the front porch.

"Okay." I sit and look out at the road. "How long do you think it will take me to walk there from here?"

"I'd say it's probably about a four-hour walk. Not terribly far. I'd offer you a ride in my horse cart, but the wheel just broke off it this morning and I need to fix it."

"I don't mind walking." I smile back convincingly.

"All right, then, you just follow this road to the split and then take the fork to the right—that will lead you straight to town. There are a few other little roads along the way, but the road to Averton is the widest and most well-trodden."

I nod and smile again. "Thanks. That helps a lot."

"Name's Greely, Lawrence Greely," he says, sticking out his hand.

"I'm Kara. Nice to meet you."

"And I'm JoAnna," says his wife, returning with a bowl of something hot and steamy. "Would you like some hot soup before you go?"

"Sure," I say politely, holding out my hands to receive it.

"It's chicken soup. I just made it this morning. Strength for your walk." She smiles at me as I dig in gratefully. It's very good, and I finish every last drop as I listen to her tell me about their farm.

"It's a busy life with a farm like this, but we enjoy it. My children, Ky and Kelly, help us with the animals, mainly the sheep, goats, and chickens. Lawrence tends to the cows. We deliver milk to Averton and the nearby towns. Would you like some fresh milk?"

"Yes, I would." I surprise myself with my response since I don't usually drink milk. For some reason, it sounds really good to me right now. She brings me a brimming cupful. I drink it down and find it to be amazingly good. "Thank you so much!"

"Would you like to take a jug along with you? I can cap it up tight so it won't spill."

"I would love that."

She smiles at me and heads back inside.

"Well, you'll have to excuse me now." Greely tips his hat. "I've got to head off to the barn and see to that wheel."

"Of course, thank you again, and it was nice to meet you."

JoAnna returns with a small jug of milk and some bread wrapped in a cloth. "Here, my dear. For your journey."

I rise up and gratefully accept the gifts. "Thank you for your kindness. I should be getting along now."

"All right, love. Come back to see us anytime."

I manage to fit the jug and bread into my knapsack and head back toward the road. I see two children running up on the sheep hill. *That must be Ky and Kelly,* I think to myself.

It looks like they are playing a game of tag, with Kelly darting in and out of the groups of sheep, shrieking in delight as her brother fails to catch her.

I remember playing freeze tag outside with my sister, Julia, and the neighborhood kids. We would stay out till way after dark, running and playing until we wore ourselves out. "Red rover, red rover, let Cindy come over!" we would chant, shouting with our arms linked tight as she would try to break our blockade. And then all of us would fall to the ground, laughing. Those innocent, carefree moments are gone now. Julia and I barely speak these days. I miss our friendship. I miss those times.

We are very different, Julia and I. She is extroverted and social. I am more of an introvert and need lots of time to myself. Julia is good at crafts and baking things. I'm more into reading, writing, and drawing. I am neat and orderly and do not like to make a mess. Messes do not seem to bother Julia in the slightest, which is one reason we did not do well sharing a room. But she'll always be my little sister. I've teased her, ignored her, fought with her, played with her. And now I miss her very much. *Does she miss me?* I wonder.

I look around at the fields around me. There are rows of corn to my right and grassy fields to my left, with a few horses grazing on a distant hill. It's hard to believe this peaceful panorama is so close to the dark swamp.

It's beautiful but lonely as I walk on down the road by myself. "Dominic, please be okay! Please come find me! I've got to be strong. I might be on my own now for a while." I look up to the sky and see a break in the clouds with a prism of rainbow light shining through. God is watching over me. I hold on to this.

The road curves and bends through the hills. There are scattered homes, with different crops and farm animals all around. The sun is low in the sky, and I've been passed by numerous people on horseback and those with horse-drawn carts. A band of gypsies stops and asks if I want to ride along with them. I politely decline. They continue to ride along beside me for a while, offering many different wares for me to buy. I finally agree to purchase a small dagger in a leather pouch, and also some ointment for my cuts and scrapes. I give them a gold coin, and they throw in a necklace pendant for good measure. A young girl with a long black braid sitting on the back of the cart tosses me something, and I catch it in the air. It's a shiny red apple.

"Thank you!" I call out. She smiles and waves as their horse quickens its pace and they move on ahead down the road.

I rub the apple on my cloak and take a bite. It's very good, and I'm grateful for it. *How much farther?* I wonder as I continue my march. My feet feel pinched and tired, and I want out of these

THE LEAF KEY

walking boots. I look around, searching for another cool stream to refresh myself.

As I come over another hill, I see another fork in the road at the bottom. This time I see a small wooden sign with markers on it. Forgetting my weariness, I jog down to it and read, "Averton [with an arrow pointing south] 2 miles, and Redmonton [with an arrow pointing east] 10 miles."

"Redmonton. What was it Dominic had said about it? Something about ponies…oh, yes, he told those hunters we encountered that I worked there with the pull-ponies, to explain my strange manner of dress to them. I should remember that if people start asking me questions about myself." I am somewhat familiar with horses, briefly owning one during my teenage years.

I throw the apple core out into a field and keep walking. It encourages me to see the signs and know I only have two miles to go. I will get there before nightfall. No stream in sight, I walk on amid a growing number of houses around me and in the hills about. I see smoke coming from chimneys. People are preparing their dinners, and I can smell meat being roasted. My stomach growls in response, but I ignore it, walking steadily on.

Feeling hopeful, I quicken my pace again. "I wish I knew what this inn looked like. I can always ask someone in town." As I walk on, I see a young woman walking up ahead of me. She has a rod perched on her shoulders that she is balancing with two pails, one on each side, filled with some sort of liquid that is sloshing out a bit from under the lids. She hears me approaching and glances back.

"Hello." I wave with a smile.

"Hello, yourself!" she answers back. "Where are you off to?"

"I'm heading to the inn at Averton. Have you ever been there?"

"No, I've not stayed there. But I've seen it often enough. Are you visiting someone, or do you have work in town?"

"Visiting," I say and leave it at that.

"Oh, well, I've heard it's not fancy, but comfortable. And besides that, it's the only inn in town."

"Do you know where it's located once I get to town?"

"You just stay on this main road, and when you get to town, you can't miss it. It's on the right-hand side of the road and painted dark blue with white shutters. And there's a big sign out front too."

"Thanks! And where are you going?"

"Oh, I'm delivering this apple cider to a home about a mile down this road. I'd be glad for company if you want to walk together and have a chat."

"I'd be happy to." I smile, glad to have someone to talk to for a while.

"Do you have an apple orchard?" I ask.

"Well, we have apple trees, pear trees, and a vegetable garden too. We eat from it and sell some to the locals around here."

"That sounds nice. Is it a lot of work?"

"It can be, but we have a large family, so there's lots of us to help. It's good when the weather cooperates as well."

"Yes, and it's a beautiful day today," I say with a smile. "My name is Kara. What's yours?"

"I'm Goldie. My home is just back over that hill. Where do you live?"

"Redmonton," I say quickly. "I'm just visiting a friend in Averton. How many are in your family?" I ask, hoping to change the topic back to her.

"There are seven of us altogether. I have two brothers and two sisters. I'm the eldest of the girls. What about you?"

"Oh, I just have one sister, Julia. She's two years younger than me."

"How old are you?"

"I'm twenty-three. And you?"

"Eighteen. I just had my birthday last week."

"Oh, happy birthday, then!"

"Thank you." She grins and shifts the weight of the pails on her shoulders.

"Do you need help with that?'

"Oh, no. I just keep shifting the weight a bit as I walk. It's really not that heavy. I've carried six pails at a time, but that is a bit much. It gives me a backache."

"You're very strong."

"No, I'm just used to it. I actually enjoy walking and making deliveries."

"Doesn't your family have a horse and cart?"

"Yes, but my older brother's using it for deliveries farther out today. What are you and your friend planning to do while in Averton? If you don't mind my asking."

"Oh, we just have a lot to catch up on. We're actually planning to travel on to Silvenia together."

"You're going to the kingdom of Silvenia? I would love to go there someday."

"Why is that?" I ask.

"I've heard it's a beautiful kingdom with a huge palace and lots of Cordelia blossom trees all over the place. They bloom year-round with bright-pink- and violet-colored petals that are always floating through the air when the wind blows. At least that's what my mother tells me—she's from there."

"Why did she leave?"

"She met my father when he was working there as a young man. His home was out here, so when they got married, she came here to live in the country with him."

"Doesn't her family still live there? Couldn't you visit them?"

"No, her parents moved out here to the country as well. They live just over that other hill there." She points to the west.

"Oh, I see."

"Father did say that after I turned eighteen, he would take me there for the Harvest Moon Festival in September. I've heard it's a lot of fun," she says, smiling.

"What do they do at the festival?"

"Well, people and woodfolk come from all over, as well as royalty with their guards and gentry to celebrate the Fall harvest. Sometimes even the windfolk from up in the mountains make an appearance."

"The windfolk? Who are they?"

"They are the mystical people that live up high in the mountains. And that is where they usually stay, so to see them among regular folk is quite unusual. Haven't you ever heard of them before?"

"Just a little. I don't know much about them. Why do you call them mystical?"

"Probably because people don't know much about them and they seem so distant and mysterious. Some say they are very ancient and wise and others say they are angels sent from God to watch over our world, but whether they are good or evil, I do not know. Most people just stare and observe them from a distance when they see them at the festivals."

"Have you ever seen such a one?"

"Not among people. But once, when my sisters and I were hiking on a path through the woods together, we thought we saw a group of three of them riding on horseback. They were very tall and kind of, I don't know, regal-looking, I guess. There was a glowing light around them. It may have just been the sunlight through the trees, but it stayed on them as they went along."

"Did they see you?"

"I don't know. But they didn't come over to us. They were traveling away from our path, deep into the woods. We were tempted to follow—very intrigued we were—but the woods were thick and we didn't want to get lost."

"How interesting. I hope I get to see them someday."

She smiles at me. "It's been great talking with you, Kara. This is my turnoff, so I'm going to have to say goodbye for now."

"It was wonderful meeting you. Maybe I'll see you when I pass by this way again."

"Yes, I hope so. My home is just back over that first hill we came down. It's gray stone with a grassy roof, and there are apple trees to the side of it. Till we meet again!" She waves, shifting her load a bit and heading down a dirt path toward a small cottage.

"Goodbye!" I wave.

My thoughts are now filled with images of the mysterious windfolk. I remember Dominic telling me about Lady Vallora, the keeper of the keys, and how she can communicate with the animals. I think about the messenger birds that brought my key to me. What were they called? Oh, yes, the starlings. "They bring the leaves from the sacred forest to her, and some of them are keys for specific people. And one of them is me."

I look around me in wonder, thinking on these things. "Why was there a key for me to come here? What's so important about me?" I walk on, deep in my thoughts.

King Vespes

King Vespes

Meanwhile, at the Silver Palace, things were heating up at the dinner table, and I don't mean the food. "Blast this tiring business of being king, with all its rules, formalities, and bothersome people and advisers to deal with every day! I just want to eat my dinner in peace, not hear any more about the affairs of the kingdom and how I really should meet with the countess of Kentwallace, who would surely be the best choice for marriage, not to mention a beneficial alignment of our territories and noble families. I'm so sick of it!"

"Get out! Everyone out! I am the king, am I not? I am the law here and now, so out!" Vespes glances at Trea, who is also pushing her chair back. "Except you, Trea. Of course you can stay. But everyone else, out!"

All is silent now, except for the sound of chairs moving and people somberly departing. No one dares to argue with Vespes, especially when he is in one of these moods, which lately has become more frequent. Best to make a quick departure until things cool down.

"Why don't you want to get married?" asks Trea innocently.

Vespes sighs and cuts into his steak. "I'm sure I'll marry eventually, but it will be on my terms, not theirs."

"But you had Delvana marry King Greffen!" She glares at him. "I miss her!"

"Ughh, do we have to go over that again? I told you, it was the best thing for her. King Greffen is a noble king, with a prosperous kingdom."

"But it's so far away! And we don't even know much about him. What if he's cruel to her? And he's old!"

"Ha!" he laughed. "Thirty-five is not old. And he seems to me a very gentle and proper king. I'm sure Della will be very happy with him. She is a queen now, with a vast kingdom to rule with her husband. What more could she want?"

"Oh, Vespes! You know nothing about women. What about love?"

"She will grow to love him."

"Listen to yourself! You sound just like your own advisers, whom you just dismissed. I feel like I don't even know you anymore." Sighing, she pushes her chair back. "I'm not hungry," she says, turning to leave.

"Trea," he says. "I miss her too."

She casts him a sorrowful glance and then quickly walks out of the room. Vespes picks up his wineglass, takes a sip, and then roughly flings it against the wall, shattering it. A minute later, a servant peeks into the room. "Did I call for you?" Vespes shouts angrily.

"No, my lord."

"Then leave it be!"

"Yes, Your Majesty," he says, hastily retreating.

The king rubs his forehead and groans. He looks around at the unfinished steak and potato dinners and feels some regret for his quick temper. "Why does it seem like no one is on my side anymore? I've only been king for a few months, and I'm loathing all these new responsibilities. How did Father make it look so easy?"

"Ah-hem, excuse me, Your Majesty," says Erol, the butler, standing solemnly in the doorway. "I have a letter for you delivered from the empress of Icelandia. Would you like to see it now, or should I put it on your desk?"

"I'll take it," says Vespes, holding out his hand.

Erol hands him the letter and pauses. "Is there anything else you need right now, sir?"

"No, thank you."

Erol bows briefly and heads back out the door. Vespes stares at the letter in his hand. It looks like some kind of formal document, sealed with a golden seal of wax. He opens it with curiosity, having never spoken with anyone from this country before. "What's in Icelandia? What riches lie there?"

He scans over the handwritten note inside. It is a request for the empress's daughter, the princess Mira, to visit Silvenia along with her court and discuss a possible alliance with Icelandia for mutual benefit. It's signed by Celia, empress of Icelandia.

"Sounds like more husband-hunting business to me. Why can't they leave me alone? I'm just beginning to learn how to be a king. I'm not ready to be married." Vespes sits on the edge of the table, chewing on his thumbnail. "On the other hand, what is it I'm so afraid of? It's not like I have to marry her just because she's coming to visit our kingdom. And I'm sure she'll be bringing along gifts from there. Of course I'll have to present gifts from Silvenia as well. But maybe it wouldn't hurt to learn more about Icelandia."

The more he holds the letter in his hand, the more the idea appeals to him. "Erol!" he calls out.

"Yes, my lord?" he responds, appearing quickly at the door.

"Get a paper and some ink. I need to respond to this letter."

"Of course, sir."

Vespes stuffs the letter inside his vest pocket and paces the floor, considering the right words to respond with.

"Ready, sir," Erol says, sitting at the table, preparing to write.

"Take this down."

To Celia, empress of Icelandia,

It would please me greatly to welcome your daughter, the princess Mira, along with her royal court, to our kingdom of Silvenia. Please ask her to come as soon as she is able. We eagerly look forward to this favorable meeting.

With respect,
Vespes, king of Silvenia

"How does that sound to you, Erol?"

"Very fine, sir. A distinguished invitation."

"Good. Give it to Arnie and have him deliver it right away."

"Yes, my lord." Erol gives a quick bow and exits the room.

Satisfied yet feeling a bit weak now for some reason, Vespes sits down and rings the servant bell. A young servant girl named Jenny appears at the door and curtsies. "Yes, my lord? How can I be of assistance?" she asks with a slight tremor in her voice.

"Bring me some hot tea, please. Have it brought up to my room."

"Yes, my lord."

"Maybe I just need to rest for a while." He heads back up to his bedroom, the letter feeling heavy in his pocket.

Lady Vallora

The sun is high in the sky, and the water in the forest brook is shimmering with light. It's midday, and Lady Vallora is looking for Sabine, her sister and keeper of the starlings. Her steps are calm and steady, even with her growing sense of unease.

This morning, like most mornings, Vallora rose early just before sunrise, to be silent and hear from the Ancient One as she sat by the pool of Miron. On this day, it was revealed to her that Dominic, a trustworthy and loyal guide, has gotten lost in the underground. Vallora is now beginning to see the urgency of this mission and is seeking counsel with her sister on how to proceed. "He must be found, for Kara's sake and for the well-being of all Paredonia." She finds Sabine under a dogwood tree, tending to a bird with an injured wing.

"My sister, I need to speak with you."

"Yes, of course. I'm just putting this little one down to rest for a while. There you go." She places him in a small nest of twigs and down. It settles down comfortably. Sabine looks up at her sister, who is pacing quietly back and forth.

"What's the matter? You look troubled. Please sit down." She pats a spot on the bench next to her.

Vallora sits. "Kara is here, and Dominic, her guide, is now missing. I perceive that he has slipped into the underground, and his fate is unclear to me. Mercurio is aware of the girl's presence in this world. He is trying to stop her, but I'm not sure if he knows where Dominic is. We must send help to rescue him, and Kara needs protection."

"Perhaps we should inform the elders and come up with a plan together."

"Yes, that would be wise. I was thinking that perhaps you should send out some of the starlings first, to see where Kara is and that she is safe."

"Good idea. I just need to find Kara's starling so she can lead the others. I will do that at once."

"I'll speak with Cardone and ask him to invite the rest of the elders to meet with us at the garden pillar court within the hour."

Sabine nods and heads off into the forest, calling for the starlings as she goes. She sings out a high, clear note that rises and falls, birdlike in sound. Many birds begin to fill the air above her and circle down like a swirling blanket around her into the trees below.

"Where is Perk?" she asks, looking around at them. The starlings are chirping and flitting around the branches, and then one of them flies directly to Sabine and alights on her extended arm.

"Hello, Perk. I need you to find Kara for me again. Bring some of your best flyers and search along the road to Averton, by way of the swamp. I need to know where she is and that she is safe. Can you do that for me?"

Perk chirps in response and tilts his head, almost like a nod, and then flies back up into a tree branch. Then, jetting himself up into the sky, he calls out a melodic message as other birds join him. They form a flock of about twenty birds and head off over the tops of trees to the south.

"Thank you, my loves," Sabine calls out after them, and then she heads back toward the forest garden.

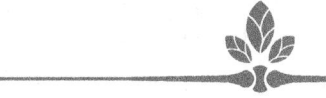

Dominic

Dominic lifts the moon rock close to his face and peers around the dark cave, blinking his eyes to adjust to the damp darkness. The only sound is the steady dripping of water through cracks from the surface running down in small streams to the pools below. Covered in mud, he considers this good camouflage as he quietly makes his way through the underground caverns.

It is completely dark, except for a small shaft of light every now and then from cracks in the surface of the cave. The moon rock was a gift to him from his mother before he went on one of his journeys to become a guide. She had bought it from a traveler who had been up to the Northern Isles. These rocks contain a mineral that absorbs the light from the sun and the moon and glows in the dark. It was a rare gift, and he was glad to have it now.

So far, his journey below has been uneventful. He has not come across any distasteful creatures yet, and he is glad to have escaped from the fearsome river troll. Unsure about the circle of liquid mud next to the riverbank, he had taken a chance and jumped in feet first, narrowly missing the extended claws of the troll.

The creature had shrunk back from the dark hole as Dominic swirled and sloshed down the muddy chute, landing finally on his bottom after a long slide down to the cold, dark cave floor. With his arrival there seemingly unknown, he had hurriedly crawled through the narrow tunnel to a wider cave with many curves and openings. He hid behind a spiky stalagmite wall to gather his thoughts and catch his breath.

Clutching the moon rock to his chest, he closes his eyes. He envisions his mom.

"Wherever this journey takes you, you've got everything you need to accomplish your task on the inside of you. Have faith, be brave, and remember, I'll always be praying for you. The Ancient One watches over you, and you'll never be alone."

"I'm not alone," he says softly to the darkness around him.

"You're my brave soldier," he hears on the inside.

Clearing his throat, he straightens his shoulders and says with a firm voice, "I am strong, brave, and courageous. Nothing frightens me. The Holy One is on my side, and I will complete every assignment with good success!"

Blinking in the darkness, he looks around him and listens. Silence echoes through the walls, except for the water dripping. Taking a deep breath, he pushes off the floor. "Okay, now to find my way out of here."

He feels his way along the cave wall and comes to a divided path, two openings into more darkness. Closing his eyes, he questions for a moment which way to go. Relying on instinct, he proceeds to the left, which also seems to be a more uphill route.

He continues the gradual climb up under the damp earth, longing to see the sky and feel the sunshine on his face again. "I will surely find my way back," he encourages himself. "I can't lose hope, for Kara's sake as well as my own." He presses on.

Up ahead, the path rises up considerably, and the air feels a bit different. There seems to be a hint of light, but it's coming from below, not from cracks in the ceiling. He proceeds carefully up the small curve of the path and stops suddenly as he realizes the path has come to an end. The air is cold and dark and vacant. He looks below and sees a great drop-off, with what appears to be water below. The light is coming from a lantern in a small boat in the water. He can just make out three dark figures in the vessel. They seem to be handling a large net, pulling it up into the boat.

Dominic lies down on his stomach and peers over the edge to the sight below. He strains to listen, hoping to catch some of the conversation between them. Are they agents of Mercurio? Or absconders like him?

Staring down into the gloom, Dominic sees there are three men, and one of them is holding a small fish up in the air now.

"I've got one!" he says.

One of the others tries to grab it away, and the third one sits down abruptly, grumbling something. They talk low among themselves for a moment, seemingly deciding what to do with one small fish between the three of them.

Dominic can feel the tension between them and wonders for a moment if they're going to fight one another for it. Arguing, they begin conversing in increasingly hostile whispers. The hissing voices echo in the cave, and while this is going on, Dominic hears another sound, like scratching, coming from the walls close by him. The dirt wall beside him begins to crumble, and a hole begins to form as two claws and a grayish snout pokes through the mud.

It appears to be a large kind of mole or rat that has broken through and is now very rapidly approaching the landing where Dominic is frozen still. It comes straight for him, showing jagged teeth in front. Dominic rolls over, instinctively shielding his face with his arms. When it jumps on his chest, adrenaline kicks in and Dominic grabs it with both arms and hurls it over his head into the waters below. It lands in the water with a loud thunk! All three men look out into the water and then up toward the ledge. Dominic is crouched down low and out of sight.

"Who's up there?" the one who tried to snatch the fish calls out.

Dominic lies perfectly still, not making a sound.

"There's no one there!" grumbles the one sitting down. "It's just something in the water."

"I thought I saw something fall from up above," says the one holding the fish.

"Hey!" he calls out. "Is someone there? We need help to get out of this place!"

"Stop yelling!" says the one sitting down. "We need to be quiet!"

Dominic lies silent, not feeling comfortable about these three strangers. He determines he will find the way out on his own. The men sit quietly for a moment in the boat, staring out into the darkness.

"There's no one there," says the third man. "Let's just try to catch some more fish and then head out. Come on, hand me that net."

Dominic looks up at the hole the mole has pushed through. There are small rays of light filtering through. "Maybe that's a way back up to the surface! I need to see if I am small enough to squeeze into it."

He quietly gets up and begins to insert himself into the tunnel opening, but it is very narrow. He clears away more mud and debris with his hands and tries again. He is now able to get in, but moving forward will be quite difficult because it is so narrow. He'll have to crawl extremely slow in darkness, not knowing where it's leading. "And what if I get stuck in there? Or another mole creature starts to come through?" He shudders at the thought.

He sits there for a moment, staring at the small beams of light. They seem to beckon him.

"What now, my Lord?"

He hears nothing, but the urge to go forward is strong, so he climbs in. He continues to work quietly with his hands, pulling dirt out and clearing it out of his way to get through this detestable and narrow way of escape. He feels his emotions waver back and forth between hope and fear, questioning and resolve. His arms are caked with mud, and every now and then, he pulls out crawling bugs and worms along with the dirt. He decides quickly not to focus on that and presses on with diligence and determination.

A New Friend

The starlings are swift in flight, and soon they are over the town of Averton. They are flying low over the streets and rooftops, searching eagerly for the young woman named Kara. By instinct, they seem to know she is somewhere close by now, here in this busy little town.

*****

    It is early afternoon, and the street peddlers are calling out their wares for sale. People are walking to and fro, mothers with their children, people on horses, donkeys pulling carts. I have just emerged from the Averton Inn to explore my surroundings.

    Finding the inn last night was a huge relief, and it was just as Goldie had described. A tall dark-blue building with white shutters. The innkeeper is a middle-aged man with small round glasses, squinty eyes, and a friendly manner. He provided me with a comfortable room on the second floor with a small bed next to a window. Out the window I can see there is a brook behind the inn and plenty of tall shady trees. I found it quiet and comforting to be in a room by myself with a soft bed to settle into for the night. I enjoyed a good night's sleep full of dreams, but they disappeared quickly with the morning light.

    I survey the sights on this main street of town with curiosity. I've had breakfast at the inn, so I'm not hungry. I quicken my step as I walk past the peddlers selling food. I'm looking for a place that sells combs or brushes; my hair has gotten quite tangled on this journey. I see a shop ahead that has women's hats and dresses in the window. Perhaps they'll have what I'm looking for.

As I walk toward it, I feel the rush of a bird's wings zoom past me in flight. Instinctively, I put my arm up over my head. "What in the world?" I quicken my steps toward the shop, thinking it to be a mother bird protecting its baby that I have gotten too close to.

It only happens once, and as I enter the doorway of the shop, I look out and up. There is a small flock of birds that have landed on the roof across from where I am. I look to see if there are any baby birds on the sidewalk that may have fallen from a nest. Seeing nothing, I shrug and turn my attention back to the store.

The store is filled with women's jewelry and apparel, and there are three women in there besides me looking around. One of them is speaking with the shop owner. "Do you have any other skirts in this color with pockets?" He nods and heads toward the back of the store, where there are many other fabrics piled together. "I can make you whatever kind of skirt you would like. Would you like to look through our fabric assortment?" She smiles and nods, heading over to it.

I am looking at a table set to the side with jewelry and other small items on it. I see a small silver comb and brush set. The man sees me looking with interest and walks over. "Can I help you with something?"

"Yes. How much is this comb and brush set?"

"That would be ten copper gildens, my dear."

I look in Dominic's bag and fish out what looks like copper to me. He takes it with a smile. "Is there anything else you need while you're here? Perhaps a new dress?"

"No, thank you. This is all I need right now," I say, smiling back at him.

"Very well. Let me know if you change your mind." He walks back over to the other lady still searching through the pile of cloths. I start to head back out the door and remember the bird. I look up to the roof across the street. The flock of birds are gone now.

As I step out, the suns feels warm on my face, and I drink it in. "Where to now?" I look up ahead and see more shops and residences. People are walking with purpose in their steps, and a small group of teenagers are running and laughing on the other side of the street. I follow their gaze and see they are chasing a dog. It runs into an alley, and they turn and run after it.

He looked frightened. I stop in my tracks and decide to investigate. Turning back, I head toward the alley with quickening steps. As I approach, I hear boys laughing, and I turn down the alley with haste.

The dog is cornered at a dead end and barking at them. One of them picks up a rock. "Throw it!" yells one of the others with a laugh.

"Stop!" I yell, barely controlling my anger. "Get away from him! That's my dog!" I find myself saying. A group of five young teenage boys turn and look my way.

"He's not your dog!" yells one of them. "He's a thieving stray! He steals from the back of our store, and we're making sure he stays away." He takes a step closer to me with a challenging glare. I glare back at him, feeling a fierceness rise up in me.

"No! He's mine. Get away from him, all of you, or I'll yell for help!" I walk closer to the group of them. The dog is pacing nervously back and forth at the dead end, looking for a way of escape.

"Fine, lady. You can have him. Just don't let him come near our store no more!"

"Don't you threaten me, young man," I hear myself saying as I slowly approach the dog. "Go on home now, all of you!"

They shuffle about, one of them defiantly staring me down, refusing to budge.

"Come on, Mitch," says one of the others. "Let's go."

"I just want to make sure she gets her dog," he says with a smirk.

This is not going as well as I had hoped. *Why did I get myself into this?* I think regrettably. *Because I care about helpless, innocent animals, that's why.* I look at the mutt, muddy and shrinking away from me as I approach him.

"Come here, Buddy," I cajole. "Time to go home now." I try crouching down lower so as not to appear like a menacing stranger. He looks at me, sizing me up with his eyes.

"What's wrong with your dog, lady? You need some help?" he taunts me.

"No!" I say firmly. "Go away—you're scaring him!"

"Mitch! Let's go," says a younger boy, pulling on his arm.

"Fine! I'm coming. Relax."

I watch them with what I'm hoping is a fearsome glare, commanding them to leave. They finally saunter off in the direction they came from. I look back at the dog. He is watching me closely.

"I wish I had a treat to give you. But I don't." He looks at me and whimpers. "Do you want to come with me? I don't have a home for you, but we could be homeless together. What do you say?"

I reach out my hand to him. He decides to come closer and cautiously sniffs my hand. When I try to reach with my other hand to pet him, he quickly backs off again. "Look, if you want help, you're going to have to trust me." I reach out again. "Come here, Buddy."

He stares at me, unmoving. "All right, then, I've got to get back. You can follow me if you like." I start to head back out of the alley. I look back at him and smile, and he begins to follow. As I head down the road again, I see a street vendor selling sausages and jerky. I buy him a sausage, and he stays closer to me now.

What am I doing? I think to myself. *I barely know what I'm doing in this land, and now I'm taking on the care of a strange dog? Very smart, Kara.* I crouch down and watch him as he devours this special treat. *I think I have a new friend.*

I pat him on the head, and he eagerly comes up to me now. "Okay, okay, let's head back to where I'm staying and figure out our plan." He wags his tail and follows me as I head back toward the inn. I stuff the rest of the sausage into my bag, and we trek down the road together.

"How am I going to get him into my room? Maybe the owner doesn't allow dogs." I look at him with concern. "I'll just ask nicely, and if he says no, I'll have to figure something out."

Soon we are back at the inn and I walk up to the owner, who is sitting behind the front desk, reading.

"Excuse me, sir. Would you allow me to take my dog up to my room with me?" I ask with a pleading smile.

He looks at me and then looks down at the dog. "I don't usually allow pets. However, if you pay double for your room, he can stay with you."

"You have a deal! Thank you!"

"You're welcome. Just take him in the back first by the brook and clean him up a bit. There's a servant back there who will have some towels…and soap!" He frowns to himself and then goes back to his reading.

I hurry to the back with Buddy and look for a servant to help us. I see a lady sitting at a table, folding napkins. "Excuse me, ma'am. Are there some soap and towels here somewhere I could use? The owner told me to ask."

Without hesitating, she calls out, "Mary! Bring out some soap and towels, please!"

"Thank you," I say, looking down at Buddy, who is sniffing at my bag, which I put on the ground.

"You're welcome," she says, continuing with her folding.

Soon another servant girl comes out the door with a bar of soap and two towels.

"Here you are, madame."

"Thank you so much," I say.

She quickly heads back inside, and I turn toward the brook, calling Buddy to follow. He trots along with me, fearless now. "Do you like the water? Come on, boy!" He sniffs around at the edge and then starts to attack the bubbling water by a stone, barking and lapping it up.

Laughing at him, I splash some water on him and try to get him to come in a little deeper. "Come on, boy, come to me!" He jumps in and starts swimming around frantically. I help him up onto a low rock and manage to get some soap on him as he wiggles around, shaking his wet fur all over me. "Well, I guess we both needed a bath, huh?"

I back up again, shivering in the cool water, and call to him. He readily jumps in and swims to me. "All right, we're clean enough. And I'm freezing! Let's go inside and get warm." I head back up to where I laid the towels and dry us both off. He follows me back inside, and we go up to my room together.

He makes himself at home by jumping up on my bed and settling down on the blankets. I look at him in amusement. "I guess we'll be sharing things for a while." I pat him on the head and change into some warm, dry clothes. I lie down next to him on the bed and relax for a moment.

Hearing a soft bump at the window, I look up and see a bird on the windowsill looking in the glass. "How odd. I feel like it's watching us," I tell Buddy. He ignores me and closes his eyes, quite comfortable. I get up slowly to walk over and take a closer look.

Seeing my approach, he takes off in flight and I watch him fly back over toward the trees. He disappears into the branches, and I shrug it off. "I guess I scared him off. I do wish Dominic would show up here. How much longer should we stay here, Buddy? What do you think?"

He opens his eyes and looks at me briefly, thumping his tail. "I hope he's okay. I don't want to think otherwise. We'll give it a few more days and see what happens," I tell him. Sitting back down on the bed, I decide to go back downstairs to get us some dinner. "Wait here, boy. I'm going to fetch our supper." He watches me head out the door, and as I close it, I listen for a moment to make sure he doesn't bark. There is quiet. I quickly head down the stairs to the food area. I realize it's nice having someone to return to.

The Windfolk

Perk and ten of his fellow starlings rush back to the mountains to inform their mistresses of Kara's whereabouts. Dominic has still not been found, but they will receive new instructions before heading out again. The other starlings have stayed behind to keep a watch on Kara.

They fly swiftly, against the wind, focused on their task. Meanwhile, back in the forest garden, Lady Vallora, Sabine, and the other elders are discussing things.

"We must not lose her. Or Dominic. When did you find out they were missing?" asks Jodir, a tall elder with long silver hair. He is one of the oldest of the windfolk, having lived in the mountains of Shazir for hundreds of years, and is respected for his wise counsel. He also uses few words and speaks slowly, his very tone commanding respect.

"Only this morning, I was made aware of this," said Vallora.

"I have sent the starlings to search along their path. They took the one by the swamp, heading toward Averton," offers Sabine.

"That is good. Let us hope they return to us soon with good news."

"Perk is swift and has a sharp eye. He will find them," assures Sabine with confidence.

Vallora begins to pace again, a thoughtful look in her eye. "Why did he take her by way of the swamp? Surely, he knows the dangers of that place."

"Perhaps he doesn't know of the safer route through the forest?"

"No, he's been trained well. I think probably he just wanted to keep her as far away from the empress as possible. He was instructed to keep her safe at all costs."

"Should we inform the king of this incident?"

"The king is still unaware of the crisis altogether. He is still learning how to be a king, and I fear that he is not ready for the dangers that lie ahead. The empress Celia has already approached him with an offer, and I have learned he has accepted. No doubt her evil influence has begun affecting him already. I don't know if he is strong enough to stand up against her dark powers."

"Nevertheless, he is the king. He is in place for this time and this season. We cannot see what lies ahead and what decisions he will make, but we must trust the Ancient One and His wisdom. He has sent Kara here to help, we know that. And we know that He will not fail," Jodir continues.

"Let us join together now and seek His face. Let us pray for them to be found safe."

Vallora, Sabine, and all the elders gather closer in and form a circle in the midst of the garden. They continue in prayer for some time until Sabine suddenly looks up. "They are returning."

As she is speaking, the starlings approach, calling out a melody as they descend toward the garden. Sabine smiles at them and holds out her arm, where Perk alights. They listen as he communicates with them by his song. Sabine looks at Vallora, and she nods, taking in their report as well.

"Kara is in Averton. She is alone, except for a dog that she has taken in." Apathoc, one of the other elders, frowns and shakes his head. "That is well," asserts Vallora. "She is comforted, and the Ancient One has provided for her."

"Where is Dominic?" questions Apathoc. "Why has he not been found?" He looks at Sabine.

Sabine questions Perk, and he responds. "They do not know. There are tracks of both of them seen up until the place close to the river bridge. The flock continued on from there and found Kara in Averton, and half of the flock have stayed behind to keep watch over her."

Jodir closes his eyes for a moment and then speaks. "They must be sent back now to keep watch over the swamp for Dominic. There are trees there that have roots that go down deep into the underground. There are many that have the life of His light still in them. They can communicate what they know to the starlings."

Sabine nods and communicates this to Perk. He eagerly flies up again toward the tops of the trees and calls his flock together. About ten more join them in this new task.

"Go, my dear ones. Make haste and find Dominic!"

They soar upward together in rank, Perk leading the way. Over the trees and back down through the mountainside, they fly with purpose and a joyful energy. Sabine smiles to herself, knowing Perk to be one of her most faithful and enduring birds with a keen eye.

Vallora sits down again by her sister. "The trees in that area, are not most of them poisoned and dull, unable to communicate?"

Jodir responds, "There are many there that still receive His light and drink it in. They communicate quite well with the birds of the air. You must have faith, Vallora."

"Yes, you are right. Let us pray together now in faith and hope the starlings return to us soon with good news. Kara is safe in Averton for now, with her dog and the starlings watching over her. Let us remain in peace, trusting in the Ancient One for help." At her word, they lift their voices together in the language of the wind and pray.

The Alliance

Celia Tremonde

Celia sits on her marble throne, tapping her icy fingers together. "We must get the princess packed quickly and ready to travel by tomorrow morning," she informs her servant, Hilio. "Go see to her at once. Tell her I need to speak with her urgently, and have the others help you pack her things."

"Yes, my queen," he bows and exits quickly.

"The enchantment I have on that letter will only last so long. But I am glad he is so easily persuaded," she says to herself with a wicked smile. "Once I have the kingdom of Silvenia, the others will follow right along. Mercurio took care of King Rufus for me. Now I will finish the job."

She peers down the hall impatiently. "Where is Mira? What is taking her so long?"

Around the corner, Hilio returns to the throne room.

"Hilio! Where is my daughter?"

"She is coming, my queen. She was out in the field, practicing with her bow. She is coming along now."

The empress frowns and sits back on her marble throne, tapping her fingers on the stone. "Are her bags being packed?"

"Yes, my queen. As we speak."

"Have Arten lead the entourage and bring five royal guards and one of her maidservants as well. Pack five extra packs with the silver and gems I will gather from our treasury. They are to be presented to King Vespes upon arrival along with a letter I will prepare for him. Do you understand?"

"Yes, I will inform him immediately. Do I have your leave to inform the servants now as well?"

"Yes, go." She waves him off.

As he departs, Mira enters the room. "What is it, Mother? I was in the middle of my archery lesson."

The empress fixes her gaze on Mira. "My charming daughter, you'll have plenty of time to practice with your bow later. Right now, we have urgent business to attend to."

"What do you mean?"

"King Vespes of Silvenia has invited you to come visit his kingdom. He has heard of your charm and beauty and longs to meet with you and hear of our kingdom as well. He wants to arrange an alliance with us for the benefit of both our kingdoms. I am arranging to send you at once with a royal entourage. Arten will be leading it, and you may bring one of your maidservants along with you."

"An alliance? Does this alliance involve my betrothal to him?"

"Possibly. But you will do what is necessary for the good of our kingdom. We have discussed this before, Mira. Don't test me."

Mira stares at her mother, feeling confused and angry at her indifference. She knows better than to argue with the empress, however. "Do I have to leave right away?"

"You will depart in the morning, at first light, because the road is long. Don't worry, my darling," she says, touching her daughter's cheek. "I will make sure you have everything you need. Now, why don't you go to bed early so you can be well rested for the journey ahead?"

"What is he like, the king?"

"King Vespes is young, handsome, and foolish. He will be easily won over by your enchanting qualities."

Mira's thoughts go to Arten. She is glad he will be coming with her. Her mother looks at her, discerning her thoughts.

"You may have to leave Arten behind. He is a good trainer, that is all. He is loyal to me, so don't get any silly ideas."

"Of course not, Mother. What other instructions do you have for me?"

Celia eyes her daughter warily. "Do you understand this is for your benefit as well as mine? We will take over the lower kingdoms and rule the land without interference. All will be ours. You can choose any man you like at that point. But first, you must win over King Vespes and get him to do as we say. He will ask for your hand in marriage, and then we can claim Silvenia as our own. The lesser kingdoms will then have to bow to our power."

"What about Mercurio? Doesn't he lay claim to these lands as well?"

"I will deal with Mercurio. He trusts me. I am in contact with him regarding our plans. He applauds my endeavors and looks forward to sharing in the spoils. I am sure he will assist us as needed."

"How benevolent of him."

"Enough talking! Go and speak with your maids and make your preparations. I will see you off in the morning with further instructions."

Mira turns abruptly at her mother's harsh tone and heads back out of the grand hall. *At least I will be traveling with Arten,* she thinks again to herself. *I am sure he cares for me. He will protect me.*

She quickens her pace back to her room, not noticing her mother's watchful eyes upon her back.

As soon as Mira is out of sight, Celia walks over to a window by her throne and reaches behind the long velvet curtain and pulls a cord. The wall behind the throne opens with a narrow panel, and she walks over to it and pulls open a hidden door. Stepping in, she closes it quickly behind her and descends a stone stairway to her secret room.

It's a small cellar of a room, with no windows. She locks the door behind her and heads for a wooden chest in the corner. Out of it she pulls a vial of some sort of dark liquid and places it on the table before her. She then takes some parchment paper out of a drawer along with a long quill pen. She dips the quill into the open vial and begins to write. When it is transferred onto the paper, it turns to a dark black ink. She is writing the instructions for her daughter to follow once she arrives in Silvenia.

"You will follow this to the letter, my daughter," she says commandingly to the air around her. She feels a chill in the atmosphere around her and feels strangely empowered. She trembles without warning, feeling for a moment like she is the one being controlled.

She shakes off that thought and stands erect, holding the paper like a scroll before her. "I will take the land and the people for Mercurio and my father, Danere. We will not be stopped! He will give me many kingdoms to rule over and subdue. It has already begun! The people will worship me!" She stops suddenly, fearing her rantings will be heard somehow.

"Never mind all that now," she says to herself. "My instructions are ready." She closes up the vial and puts away the parchment. She opens the door to the stairway and feels the cold draft as she heads back up to her throne room in the dark.

Mira

Arten is adjusting the packs on the horses when Mira walks into the stables. He looks up at her and smiles. "Did you pack your bow, Princess?"

"Of course I did," she says, returning his smile. "I need to practice, don't I?"

"You need lots of practice, that's for sure," he says teasingly.

"I always hit the target!" she protests.

"Just hitting the target isn't the goal. It's hitting the mark that counts."

She ignores his insult and drops her bags on the ground in front of him. "When are we to leave? I am ready now."

"Be patient. We are waiting on the empress to give us her final instructions before we can depart. In fact, we should head over to the palace hall now."

"Yes, of course."

Mira follows reluctantly at a slower pace behind him. He looks back at her. "Come, Princess. We mustn't keep the empress waiting."

"I'm coming, I'm coming!"

As they enter the great hall, Celia is sitting on her throne, looking a bit impatient. "I assume you are now ready, Arten? Is everything in order?"

"Yes, my queen. All is ready for departure."

"Very good." Then, turning to Mira, she says, "I have instructions for you, my daughter, written on this parchment. Keep it close so you can refer to it often. It will be very helpful for you." She hands Mira the scroll.

Mira takes it and holds it to her side. She suddenly feels a bit sick, a little light-headed, and takes a step back.

"What is it, Mira? Are you well?"

"I…I'm fine. I guess I'm tired. I didn't sleep much last night."

"I'm sure that's all it is. Arten, be sure to look well after my daughter. Make sure she has plenty to drink and time to rest at night. It is a four-day journey through deep woods and water. Don't get distracted and get off course. The king is expecting her."

"Yes, my queen. I will do as you say."

"Come, Mira. Let me look at you."

Mira steps forward and feels her mother's cool hand on her cheek for a moment. "I know you won't let me down," she says. "Goodbye, Mira. Embrace this time, and you will share the reward with me." She then turns to Arten. "Send me word when you safely arrive." He bows quickly and turns to go.

Mira straightens her shoulders, feeling a bit numb, but steady. *What is going on with me? I felt fine earlier.* Mira tries to pinpoint the problem but then decides she is too tired to care. *Why do we have to leave right now? I wish I could just go lie back down.* She follows behind Arten, wrapping her hunting cloak around her arms.

Soon they are on the road leading to the great Icelandia forest. Their group includes Mira; Arten; Julias and Jude, brothers and tower guards; Vico, a skilled hunter; Kurt, who keeps the treasury chest and gifts; and Ceyla, Mira's handmaid. Seven of them on this journey to Silvenia.

Their horses keep a steady pace down the icy path to the woods. It is always cold here, but it is what they are used to. Mira has never been out of Icelandia, and she is quite curious about what it is going to be like in Silvenia. She feels the freedom of being away from her mother's grasp and breathes in the cold air deeply. She is starting to wake up now, especially with the cold wind in her face.

"How far do you think we will get today?" she asks Arten.

"We will be well into the forest and will camp there for the night. The next day we will have to cross the river."

She looks at him. "Is it a deep river?"

"It can be, in places, if you don't know where to cross."

"That sounds a bit frightening," she says. "Will the horses know what to do?"

"Yes. They are seasoned travelers. Don't worry, Princess, we will keep you safe."

She stares at the tall trees ahead in the distance and feels a mixture of excitement and apprehension. She has been in the woods close to the castle many times, by herself and with Arten, learning to use the bow and arrow and to practice her riding skills. *I won't be afraid,* she thinks to herself. *This is going to be a grand adventure. I will make it so!*

They set camp later that evening as the sun is going down in a leafy clearing close to the river. Vico and Julias catch some fish in the river, which is shared by all. They also have some carrots and potatoes that were brought along in their sacks.

"We must eat it all and burn any scraps. There are still bear and wild boar in these parts. We don't want to attract any unwelcome visitors."

Mira eats the dinner gladly, quite hungry now. The rest of the group joins in as well, grateful to eat and rest. With the sun almost completely down, soon the only light will be from the moons through the trees. The woods are thick, and it is hard to even see the sky except for a few openings here and there.

"I hear there are vayaklos lights in the south," says Ceyla, sitting back and eyeing her surroundings.

"Yes, farther south, where it's a bit warmer," says Vico.

"What are vayaklos?" asks Mira.

"Mischievous little creatures that come out at night with the second moon's glow. They usually live deep in the forest."

"Oh, I hope we see some!"

"You will. But mind you, they like bright and shiny things and may steal a button or two off you."

Mira subconsciously puts her hand over her jeweled pendant, which she is wearing at that moment.

Arten notices. "Yes, you will want to tuck that away for sure, milady."

Mira slips it under her collar. Ceyla glances down at the silver buttons on her waistcoat, wondering if she needs to be concerned.

"We shouldn't come across any of those for a while yet. Don't worry, ladies, we'll keep a watch out." Kurt grins. He throws another log on the fire, and it crackles and spits.

"We should get ready for sleep now. Jude, you take the first watch. I'll go after you. Ladies, we bid you good night," says Arten, tipping his cap.

Mira and Ceyla get up together and head for the smaller tent. "Do we have to retire so early? I want to walk down by the river."

Arten sighs. "Fine, I'll take you ladies on a quick walk, and then it's off to bed. We must leave at daybreak to make the most of our time. We mustn't keep your king waiting," he says with sarcasm in his voice.

Mira looks at him with interest. "You sound like you're jealous of him. Are you?"

"Not at all. I just want to complete this assignment and fulfill the wishes of the empress." They begin to walk down a small hill toward the river.

Mira gives him a sideways glance. "Can we practice with the bow tomorrow before we leave?"

He looks at her, considering. "All right, but be ready bright and early. We can't take too much time, but maybe we can hunt something for our dinner."

Mira nods and walks on ahead. The sound of the rushing water beckons. "Where are we going to cross?"

"You see over there, where the river narrows?" He points to the south. "That's the best spot, and it's more shallow there as well."

She squints and looks in that direction. "Okay, if you say so. It's hard to tell in the dark."

"Just stay on your horse, that water is icy cold." He kicks at a stone and it topples down the bank into the water.

"Won't our legs get wet?" asks Ceyla.

"Yes, but we'll build a fire after we cross and dry ourselves before we head on."

The first moon is beginning to glow in the sky, and they spy a beaver in the water farther upstream pushing a stick through the water. Mira turns and finds Arten staring at her. He looks away quickly, picks up a rock, and throws it into the water. She smiles inwardly and keeps it to herself as they walk quietly now by the edge of the churning river.

The Tunnel

Dominic pulls forward with his fingers, gripping the wet dirt and grabbing ahold of it. He is in a dark, narrow tunnel, and the progress has been slow. Feeling claustrophobic, he finds it hard to breathe now. *Rest for a moment,* he hears on the inside and stops struggling.

He forces himself to draw a deep breath and then exhale slowly. He does it again and feels his muscles relax a bit. *Now go!* He heeds this inner voice and pulls forward again, squeezing his body through a little at a time. It seems to be getting darker now. *Where are those rays of light I saw before?* he wonders. *Lord, how much farther? Please, help me!*

He reaches forward again and continues to pull himself along, bit by bit. Now, reaching, he grabs a rock and is able to get a firm grasp and pull further. Pull, wiggle, push with the legs, repeat. Over and over, he continues for what seems like hours; he has no idea how long he has been at this, but it seems like forever.

Suddenly, he sees a ray of light before him, dust particles in it dancing before his eyes. Hope surges, and he pulls himself forward again and again. More rays appear, and he realizes he must be getting close to the surface. He ignores the bugs and the worms he is pushing past and presses on with diligence, tears wetting his face as he struggles on.

Light beams through a curve in the tunnel just ahead. With renewed strength, he pushes hard and reaches the opening to the outside. As he pulls himself up, his head and shoulders break through an opening of leaves, mud, and twigs. He gulps in the sunlight and fresh air with joy.

"Thank you, Lord!" He pulls the rest of his body out with ease now and falls onto the surface of the earth in relief. He hears birds crying out above him and looks up. There is a flock of birds circling just above him. One of the birds flies to the ground and lands right in front of him, watching him.

"Hello," he says wearily. "It's good to see you."

The bird cocks his head to the side and makes a sound. Then it flies back up into the trees and disappears. Dominic pushes up to a sitting position, too tired to get up and move yet. He breathes deeply and looks at the woods around him, trying to get his bearings.

Suddenly, the bird is back. It flies up in front of him and drops something into his lap and then flies off into the trees. Looking down, he sees it is some berries on a branch. It looks like raspberries. He looks up for the bird but can't find it.

"Thank you!" he calls out. He eats them with a grateful heart. It gives him some strength, but he really needs some water. Looking around, he sees the swampy water close by. That won't do; he'll have to keep looking. There must be brooks leading up to the river.

The bird swoops down again and sings a song as it circles above him. Then it perches on a branch and watches.

"Are you trying to tell me something?"

The bird circles above him again, then flies to a tree farther out and sings again.

"Do you want me to follow you?"

He slowly pushes himself off the ground and steadies himself. "Strengthen the weak hands, and make firm the feeble knees" (Isa. 35:3 NKJV). He recalls this verse from his childhood. His mother was teaching him the Word of God. Feeling some strength returning, he walks forward, following the bird.

He walks for a while, following diligently, and then he hears it. The sound of rushing water over rocks comes to his ears. Smiling, he sees it up ahead and speeds his pace. Bowing low, he drinks in the cool water until he is satisfied.

He looks up to thank the little bird, but it is gone again. He puts his hands together and says a quiet prayer of thanks to the Ancient One, who has taken care of him yet again. He looks around. *Where exactly am I? How long was I even down there?* Being in the dark has caused him to lose all track of time.

He is obviously still close to the swamp, but this clear brook must lead back to the river. *I've got to cross over the river another way and try to find Kara.* He looks down at his clothes and realizes he is covered in mud. He decides to just lie down in the brook to get clean.

The cold water rushes over him and jolts him awake. As he lies there in the water, staring up at the sky, a whole flock of birds flies in circles above him. They are descending. He sits ups and looks around him. They have settled in tree branches all around him and appear to be watching him. Then, one by one, they fly before him and drop more fruit branches in his lap.

"Miraculous!" he exclaims, gathering all the branches together. "Thank you very much!" He looks around at them, and they chirp with a joyful sound and together fly upward into the sky. He waves as they fly off again, up above the trees. Two of them circle back and descend back into the trees above him, keeping watch.

After eating more of the berries, he hunts around for some dry twigs and finds a flint rock. It takes him a little while, but he finally manages to start a fire and dry himself off a bit, hanging his wet clothes from a tree limb close to the fire. He huddles down close to the fire. The sun is low in the sky, and he sits down to think.

"Kara must have made it down the path to safety. The troll was after me when she ran, and I don't think a water troll would travel far from the river. I will follow the brook back to the river but stay away from the bridge. There's got to be another place I can cross safely. I will pray for guidance."

As he kneels, praying, the flock of starlings is flying fast over the trees back up to the mountains of Shazir.

The White Wolves

I wake up to numbness and tingling in my leg. I try to move it and realize that the dog is lying on me. "Buddy, move over!" He grunts and lifts his head for a moment, tail thumping. "Move over, please!" I push him a bit, and he gets up, circles again, and settles down onto the bed.

I straighten my leg and stretch, yawning. "I wonder what time it is." I glance up at the window, and sunlight is pouring in. My stomach growls. "I guess it's time for breakfast," I say, getting up and walking to the window. Opening the shutters fully, I look out to the brook below. There are two squirrels chasing each other up a tree.

I wonder about Dominic and try to push negative thoughts from my mind. "It's been close to a week now. I may have to face the fact that he may be gone." She looks at her peaceful dog on the bed. "We may have to find our way to Silvenia on our own, Buddy. What do you think? Are you up for this?"

He raises his head, tail thumping.

"All I know is I'm supposed to meet with the king. He has some kind of assignment for me. And then hopefully, he can help me get back home. I'm glad I have you with me now on this journey."

He barks at her.

"Oh, yeah, breakfast. Come on, let's go downstairs and find some." He follows her readily, then passes her, going swiftly down the stairs. At the bottom, they almost run into the cook, who is putting out some hot oat bread and honey.

"Pardon us!" I exclaim as we head quickly to the back porch. A young servant girl is there, wiping down the tables.

"Would you like something to drink?" she asks.

"Yes, please. Something hot?"

"We have tea. And shall I bring you some breakfast as well?"

"That would be perfect. Thank you so much!"

I sit at a small round table while Buddy runs down to the brook. I watch him run around and roll on his back in the grass. It gladdens my heart for a moment. Two starlings watch from the trees above as I enjoy my breakfast, which I share with the dog, now back at my feet. He snaps up a link of sausage with delight. I am enjoying some eggs and toast. Looking at the birds, I throw out some crumbs for them as well.

Without hesitation, the birds join each other on the ground and have their snack. Then, retreating back up into the trees, they continue to wait and watch for others of their flock to return. They will keep watch over Kara until then.

As Buddy and I take our daily walk through the town, I make the decision to wait one more day for Dominic. "And then we will take our journey together," I say, looking down at my fluffy friend.

Meanwhile, Perk and his flock have returned to the mountains. Lady Vallora and Sabine reveal to the elders that Dominic has been found safe close to the river. Sabine is relaying the details to Jodir.

"They found him emerging from a small hole in the ground and brought him food for his strength. Then they successfully led him to a nearby brook, where the water revived him. Two of the flock also stayed behind with him to keep watch. He must be on his way back to cross over the river by now."

"The trees informed them of his location, to be sure," says Jodir thoughtfully. "He must get across the water safely this time."

"How can we help him?" asks another.

Vallora steps in. "I can send the forest wolves to protect him. They will listen to me."

Jodir nods in agreement. "Yes, that is a good plan. But you must urge them to return as soon as he crosses over, to keep them safe as well from the hunters. Their pelt is highly sought after, and their primary purpose is to protect our borders from Mercurio's dark agents at this time. You know this."

"Yes, they are our fierce allies. I should send them at once. They are swift runners, but it will still take them at least a day and night before they reach that area."

"They can get there that fast?" asks Sabine.

"Yes. They have a straight path down the mountains that is a shortcut for wolves. Man does not travel on it—it is too steep for them."

"You have my leave to do as you see fit," says Jodir.

Vallora bows gracefully and turns to leave.

"What about Kara?" asks Cardone.

"She is still in Averton, staying at the inn," Sabine replies. "The starlings are keeping watch, and they will send Swift to inform us if she departs from there."

"Very good. Then we can be about our work here while we wait."

The group of elders bows respectfully to one another in honor and separate. Sabine watches Lady Vallora disappear deep into the forest, looking for the wolf pack. She locates them an hour later deep in the upper regions of the mountain, where snow is still on the ground. She knows them each by name.

Aro, the leader, approaches her first, welcoming her with a friendly howl announcing her welcome. The others follow behind him, eyes alert. The pups play and frolic off to the side, and two of them break away and curiously come up to her ankles, sniffing.

A bark from Aro, and they quickly retreat, running back to their playmates in the snow. Shealti, his mate, is by his side, and they sit silently before Vallora, offering a lick to her outstretched hand.

"It is so good to see you, Aro, Shealti, all of you. I come with urgency, asking for your help." She spends the next few minutes explaining about Dominic and where he is located. With responding yelps and barks, Aro and his pack enthusiastically agree to take on this mission of protection.

"You must leave as soon as you can. He is in grave danger and must get across the river safely as soon as possible. Do you understand?"

Aro howls his understanding and circles his pack, barking his instructions to them. The pups will stay behind with their mothers, and two of the beta males as well. The rest of them go bounding through the forest at top speed, with Aro in the lead, snow spraying behind them.

"Thank you, my noble friends!" calls Vallora after them, lifting her hand in fond farewell as they race off through the trees. Gravity increases their speed as they tear down the side of the mountain together. They are prepared to take down the troll if necessary, with all its spiny fur and sharp claws. Hopefully, that will not be the case, but they will do whatever it takes to fulfill their mission to protect Dominic and their land.

As they race on, Dominic makes his own way through the forest quietly, believing the brook is leading him toward the river. His clothes are dry now, and he feels stronger, although he finds his one ankle is a bit sore. He must have wrenched it in his underground travels. Favoring his right foot, he makes his way through the thick brush slowly, hoping he is heading in the right direction.

The sun is setting, and he will have to find a place to sleep for the night that is safe. He would like to keep going but realizes that will not be wise, as he needs to keep up his strength. His thoughts travel to Kara. *Is she waiting for me in Averton? Or has she traveled on to Silvenia without me? Most importantly, is she safe?*

He whispers a prayer for both of their safety and that they will be reunited soon. He knows they are being watched over, and he feels a subtle sense of peace even with all the uncertainty surrounding him.

As he walks on, he sees a rocky overhang ahead with a small sheltered spot underneath. It's not a cave but can be a good shelter for the night. He heads over to it. "This will work," he says to himself. He starts to gather soft leaves and spreads them out for bedding.

"I sure do miss my cloak, but maybe I can just hunker down in this pile of leaves to keep warm tonight." He looks up at the rising moon softly glowing through the trees, and he is so glad to see it.

Preparations

Vespes awakens to a dull pain in his forehead. Opening his eyes, he rubs his temples and looks toward the window. The sky is gray and filled with clouds. "Just like my head," he mumbles. Slowly he rises from his bed and reaches for the bell cord. There is a knock on his door.

"You may come in," he says with effort.

"Yes, my lord?"

"Erol, please bring me my tea and breakfast up in my room today. You can serve it on the balcony."

"Of course, and would you like me to bring up your appointment schedule for today?"

"Yes, I suppose I have to look at that as well," he says with resignation. He thinks for a moment. "When is my first meeting today?"

"Ten o' clock, sir."

He groans. "Reschedule that one for tomorrow. I am not feeling up to it this morning."

"Yes, sir. Anything else?"

"No, that will be all. Thank you."

Erol bows and retreats, shutting the door quietly behind him. Vespes begins to lay out his clothes for the day and sees the letter from the empress still sitting on his bedside table from a few days ago. He remembers responding to her request, asking her to send her daughter as soon as possible. "What was I thinking?" he mutters, picking up the parchment. His head feels cloudy and uncertain. "Well, it's too late to back out now. I must prepare for her arrival."

There is another knock on the door.

"Come in," he calls, setting the letter down on his pillow. Trea enters, holding her cat, Mirabelle, who is purring. He starts to protest the entrance of the cat but bites his tongue instead. He doesn't want to be at odds with his sister today.

"Are you okay? Erol said you weren't coming down for breakfast."

"I'm fine. Just a headache, that's all."

"Would you like some of my willow bark tea? I can make it for you."

He looks at her. "Sure, that would be nice." He realizes he is going to have to tell her about the impending visit from the princess. "Um, there's something I need to tell you. We're going to have a royal guest coming to stay with us for a little while."

She looks at him with interest, her eyes widening. "Who?"

"It's nothing to get excited about. The empress of Icelandia sent a letter stating she wanted to discuss some political matters that would be beneficial to us, and she is sending her daughter, the princess Mira. They should be arriving soon…any day now, in fact."

"Oh my goodness! What brought this about? I thought you were against meeting any royal women right now and didn't even want to think about marriage?"

"Who says this has to do with marriage? We will discuss political benefits and a possible alliance."

"Alliance? What do you mean?"

"I've said too much already. I don't even know if anything will come of it. But I've already sent the invitation, and there's no backing out now. To be honest, I'm not even sure why I sent it. It was like a compulsion or an automatic response. Maybe I just felt pressured with all the flack I've been getting from our advisers around here. Anyway, I must ask you to help me out with her. If this turns out to be a big mistake, please help me keep her entertained until I can arrange for her departure back to her country." He says all this while nervously shaking his leg back and forth.

She smiles at him. "You're nervous! Don't be. She's just another girl, like me. And you are a smart and respected king. I'm sure she will be impressed."

He rubs his head again, frowning. "Could I please have that tea now? I really need to clear my head."

"Sure!" She jumps up. "I'll go get it ready." She bounds back out the door, bringing her gray cat with her.

Vespes is just finishing getting dressed when Erol returns with his breakfast. He lays it out on the small round table on the balcony. Vespes steps out to thank him and sees his schedule lying on the table by his plate.

"Shall I set a place for Princess Trea as well? She informed me she will be preparing your tea this morning."

"Yes, thank you. That will be fine. I should be ready for my next appointment." He glances at his schedule. "By 11:00 a.m."

Erol nods with understanding and departs with a small bow. Vespes is just about to bite into his toast when Trea returns with his tea.

"Did you say grace?" she says, grinning. He frowns at her again but bows his head for a moment.

"There, are you happy now?" He picks up his toast again and takes a bite. "Erol is bringing your breakfast up shortly."

"I know. I passed him on the stairs. Now, tell me more about this princess and where she is from."

"Just a minute. Let me look at my schedule for the day." He picks it up and reads through it speedily. He's aware of most of the meetings but has to make sure nothing else has been added on that he isn't ready for. He takes a few moments longer, stalling for time.

"Do you have a lot going on today?" she asks, wanting him to get to on to her question.

"Not too much. Just the usual briefings with the advisers with their updates and questions. Also some locals who need more supplies, and questions from the staff regarding how to prepare for our guest."

Her ears perk up. "Yes, our guest! Do tell me more about her now."

"I really don't know much about her at all. Or her country. Which is why we're having this meeting. The empress has stated that an alliance between our two countries could be very beneficial and she will be bringing proof of this with gifts and information for me to consider. Her daughter is merely the courier of this information, and I am being hospitable in considering this offer. If it turns out to be not for our benefit, we will wrap this up quickly and be none the worse except for some wasted time, and hopefully, we will receive some beneficial gifts and she will leave here with favor and a good report of our wonderful hospitality and treatment of Her Royal Highness." He says all this while buttering his next piece of toast with multiple layers of butter.

"I see," Trea responds. "Will she be staying in the guest room on the third floor? The one right down the hall from me?"

"Yes, the blue room. I expect the servants are already preparing it. You will have a new friend to visit with for a time. That should make you happy."

"I am looking forward to it," she says, looking up at the door as Erol knocks with her tray in his hands.

"Thank you, Erol," she says gratefully, spooning cinnamon onto her oatmeal.

"You are quite welcome. Will there be anything else?"

"That is all for now, Erol," Vespes says, looking out at the billowy gray and white clouds.

"What are you looking at?' says Trea.

"Just at all the clouds. It looks like it might rain. I was hoping to go out riding today."

"Oh, if you do, can I come with you?"

He looks at her, regretting he mentioned it, as he was hoping to get away from everyone for a while. "Sure. That is, if it doesn't rain. Anyway, I need to prepare for this first meeting, so I'm going downstairs to my office now. Enjoy your breakfast," he says, pushing back from the table briskly.

"Already?" She frowns. "Well, that's all right. I'll see you later today, then."

"Right." He smiles, heading out the door. He is glad to be on good terms with his sister again. "But why are women so clingy sometimes?" he mutters to himself as he heads down the stairs. Since his father's accident, Trea has been his closest companion, a true comfort at times, and a real nuisance at others. "Probably because she knows me so well and then wants to talk about everything. Maybe this royal guest will be a blessing in disguise. They can have long talks about everything under the sun, and I can get more time to myself!"

He sits at his desk, organizing his papers, waiting now for his 11:00 a.m. meeting. "I should be done all this by 3:00 p.m." He sighs to himself. "Let's get this over with."

Time to Leave

I am dreaming again. A pack of white wolves runs through the forest at top speed. They are graceful and fierce, running with force and determination. They are running toward someone. Someone who is lost in the woods. I am running, tripping, falling, and getting back up and running some more. Too scared to look back. I hear something chasing me, branches cracking, leaves crunching. I've got to get away! It's almost upon me. "Nooo!" I yell out, flailing with my arms, only to find out I am in the bed at the inn, with Buddy at my feet.

He whimpers, then thumps his tail, looking up at me.

"Oh, Buddy, I'm so glad you're here," I say, patting his head for a moment and then lying back down. "I was dreaming about wolves running through the forest. Maybe it's because I have a dog as my companion now. It was just so vivid and real. But it was just a dream. We are safe."

"Here, come closer." I pat the spot next to me. He moves up next to me, circles again, and settles down by my side. I put my arm around his fur and close my eyes again. "Keep us safe, Lord."

Drifting back to sleep, I try to picture happy thoughts in my mind and let myself slip away again. The dream returns, and I see the wolves again running in a pack. Then I see a woman's face, pale and beautiful. She is speaking to the wolves, urging them on. I am running again. I trip and fall, falling down a steep hill. There are rocks tumbling down around me. I am spinning fast, dark colors and sounds surrounding me. "Stop!" I yell out.

Buddy jumps up and barks.

"Oh, Buddy. I'm sorry, I did it again. I didn't mean to frighten you too." I pat his head, and he licks my face. "Okay, okay, I'm fine now. It was just another crazy dream." I sit up now and see sunlight streaming in the window. "I think maybe it's time to leave this place."

I begin to pack up my few belongings and look around the room a final time. "Come on, Buddy. Let's get some breakfast and then hit the road. Maybe the innkeeper will know where I can get a map with directions to Silvenia." We tromp down the wooden stairs together, an aroma of bacon and sausage in the air. The innkeeper is sitting at the front desk, finishing his own breakfast and reading over some papers.

I decide not to interrupt his breakfast and sit down at my usual little table on the back deck. Buddy immediately runs down to the brook and sits by the edge, watching the little fish dart around in the water. I hear the birds singing in the trees above me. "It's another beautiful day here in Averton," I comment to myself.

"Can I help you, miss?" asks the servant girl politely. "Would you like the same for breakfast today?"

"Yes, please. And can I get an extra plate for the road? I plan to check out today, and I want to bring some of your delicious food with me."

"Of course, I will go get that for you."

"Thank you so much," I say. I look out at Buddy, and he's perched on a rock, looking like he's about to jump in. "Buddy! Don't jump!" I start to get up to try to stop him, and he starts barking repeatedly at something in the water. I run down to take a look.

He is still barking as I approach. "What is it, boy?" I look in the water and see there is a snake, long and green, slithering on top of the water. It's headed our direction and doesn't look frightened by my barking dog.

Without hesitating, I grab Buddy under his belly and hoist him up. Then I half-run, half-stumble back up the hill toward the inn. When we reach the deck, I look back. No sign of it. "Good! It's probably still in the water." Still, I look around for something to smash it with if it decides to venture up the hill after us.

There's a large rock to my right on the ground. I pick it up and put it close to where I'm sitting. Then I glance back down at the brook. I see no sign of it, but I keep alert. It is as green as the grass before us, and I don't want that thing sneaking up on us. I've been holding on to Buddy's fur this whole time, and I find myself wishing I could have a leash or rope of some kind to keep him up here by me. I look at him.

"I don't think I can trust you to stay right here beside me the whole time. I don't want you to get bitten." I head back inside with him and walk over to the servant girl, who is filling cups with tea.

"Excuse me, is it possible that you could find me some rope? I just saw a snake down by the brook, and my dog wants to attack it. I need to keep him by me, and I thought maybe somewhere in this inn there is some rope I could use as a leash?"

"A snake! What did it look like? Where is it?"

"Oh, it's all the way down the hill in the brook. You don't need to worry. It was a green snake."

"Was it bright green? Like the color of grass?"

"Yes, I think so."

"Those are very poisonous. They are usually only found in the swamplands. Are you sure it wasn't just a common brown one?"

"It definitely looked green to me."

She pauses for a moment. "Okay, I'll look for some rope for you, but first, I must tell the innkeeper. If it's a green snake, someone needs to go down there and get rid of it."

"Okay, thank you," I say as she hurries off to speak with him.

"We'll just have to stay put in here until then, Buddy." I look out the back window and see two birds flying over the brook, circling and swooping low over the area where the snake was. "How curious. I haven't seen birds do that with a snake before. I wonder if it's close to a nest of theirs."

The snake has raised its head up out of the water and is planning to slither up the bank to the grass. The two birds swoop low in front of it, attempting to block its path. One dive after another, they take turns annoying the snake, distracting it for the moment.

Finally, it gives up and turns back the other direction into the water and slithers away. The birds pause, watching from a tree above. It glides on top of the water, heading slowly downstream. Then it slides up the other side of the bank and is soon hidden behind a rock.

The innkeeper strides out the back door with a shovel in his hand and a focused look on his face. I watch from the safety of the windows, with Buddy at my side. He walks up and down the length of the property by the brook with no success. It's hidden safely on the other side, curled up behind a boulder.

He comes back in a few moments later and shrugs. "I don't see it now. It probably was scared off by the dog. Still, I would think it's better if you eat your breakfast inside today." He looks down at Buddy.

"Yes, that's what we'll do. Thank you," I say. "Also, I'll be checking out after breakfast today."

"Right, then. Just come to see me after you're finished, and we'll wrap things up."

"I was wondering, Do you know where I can get a map to Silvenia?"

"Is that where you're heading? I can draw you some directions from here, or you can get an actual map at the merchant shop down the street."

"That's very kind of you. I would appreciate the directions, if you don't mind."

"I'll get it ready for you while you have your breakfast." He smiles and heads back over to his desk, stowing the shovel in a closet on the way.

I take my seat by the window, and Buddy lies down on the floor beside me. Soon we are enjoying a nice, warm breakfast, and I have an extra portion wrapped up in a little sack for the road.

After I pay what is owed for the room and board, we head out together onto the streets of Averton, feeling well-fed and ready for what lies ahead. There are a few clouds in the sky overhead, just enough to protect us from the steady heat of the sun. My water container is full, and I head over toward the merchants to find a map. The innkeeper has drawn out some directions for me, but I'm thinking it will be good to have a map as well. Also, I'm looking for a good walking stick to bring along. There's probably some down by the brook, but after the snake episode this morning, I'm going to keep my distance from there for a little while.

I pass cottages and shops of all sorts, still heading down the main street through town. Finally, I see a little shop that looks promising and head inside. I have Buddy on a rope leash now and tie him safely to a post outside the door. He sits down and looks at me. "Stay here for a moment. I'll be right back," I tell him.

Inside, there are books and scrolls and parchments all over the place. I head over to the desk at the side and inquire, "Hello, do you have any maps for sale here?"

The tall skinny salesman with spectacles on the end of his nose looks up at me. "Yes, we do. What sort of map are you looking for?"

"Just one of this area, and Silvenia too."

He scratches his head. "Okay, over here to my left are the maps. Let me see if we can find what you're looking for." He walks over to a table with many papers on it and pulls out a scroll. After he has unfolded it, we look at it together. It has *Paredonia* in large letters across the top. Below that is a diagram of roads, towns, and cities, rivers, and bridges. I see *Silvenia* in large letters to the left. The river Baton comes down from the upper right corner and cuts the map in half, with Averton on the right side of it. Looking closer, I see the Baton Bridge, where we had so much trouble. I bite my lip subconsciously, thinking of Dominic.

There are many other kingdoms listed there, as well as other towns and cities. In the upper right corner, it shows the location of the mountains of Shazir. I find myself wanting to study every section of this map. "Yes, this is the map I want. How much is it?"

"Five copper gildens. Will you be needing anything else while you're here? We have many interesting books. Perhaps you'd like to take your time and look around."

I take a moment and consider. "I would like to take a look at them, but I have a dog waiting for me outside, and I don't want to leave him out there too long by himself."

"Oh, that's no problem. You can bring him inside with you while you take your time and look."

I like this idea. "That's very kind of you. Thank you. I will do that."

"Wonderful! I'll hold your map for you right over here by me."

I thank him again and head over to get Buddy and bring him inside. He thumps his tail at me as I approach. "What a good dog you are!" I exclaim. I lead him into the store and head toward the bookshelves.

I've always loved to read, and I'm curious as to what sort of books are in this world. It's very different here and yet, in many ways, the same. Like going back in time. I pull out a thick book with a dark cover. It looks very old, and I blow the dust off the top of it before I open it. It's a book about sword fighting and ancient battles. I put that one back and pull down another, a dark-green book with *Elmwood* printed across the top cover.

As I flip through the pages, I see there are pictures of large elm trees and forests of green and gold. It is very beautiful, and I admire the amazing pictures. They appear to be drawn and painted by hand, and there are stories about a place called Elmwood, with interesting-looking characters interspersed on the pages. As I read on, I find there is a character named Willa, and her brothers, Pont and Marcus. There are interesting animals as well, depicted in scenes throughout. I keep this one in my hand as I continue to look around.

There are books on hunting, sewing, farming, many instructional books. As I keep looking, I see a large book with a black cover on a top shelf and pull it down. My eyes widen. "It's a Bible! They have the Bible here!" I decide to hold on to that as well.

Buddy is wagging his tail at every person who comes in and is pulling on the leash now to sniff around a corner. I hold the two books in my hand, feeling the weight that I will be carrying with me. I have to decide. I flip open the Bible and read where it falls open to: "Your word is a lamp to my feet And a light to my path" (Ps. 119:105 NKJV).

The words seem to jump off the page at me. I know I have to bring it with me. I close it and look at the other book. "I will bring that one too, and perhaps it will also tell me more about the mysteries of this place."

So heading over to the bookseller, I pay for the map and the two books. I notice there are tables to the side of the store where people are sitting and reading. I should sit down for a moment and study this map as well.

I pull up a stool and open the scroll before me.

Image of Map of Paredonia

It's a detailed map of Paredonia, and I look it over with great interest. I can see the path we came down on, from the Oakendale Forest to Vicor and through the swamplands. I see Averton and Redmonton, and a little town called Bakersville—that must be where the farms were.

I see Silvenia to the far west. "I wonder how far it actually is. What did Dominic say again? I wish I could remember. That seems so long ago now." I pause and picture Dominic in my head again.

"He can't be gone. I refuse to accept that. He's probably figuring out how to find me, or getting help, or gathering some supplies. Maybe he's here right now in town, looking for me!" I look up from the scroll with hope, scanning my surroundings.

"Wishful thinking. I must focus on the journey before me now. I've got to find Silvenia, complete my task, and find my way back home. I won't focus on the things I have no control over. God, please direct my steps," I whisper under my breath as I look back down at the map. Buddy lies down at my feet now and settles in, putting his head down.

From what I can tell, it looks like I need to head south on the road toward the kingdom of Rondival, perhaps staying there for a night, and then head west toward the river again. There is another bridge, called Blain Bridge, where I can cross to head over to Silvenia. I shudder, thinking of my last bridge crossing.

"I will plan to cross with other people this time. I won't try it alone, although this bridge is probably more traversed than the smaller Baton Bridge." I look down at Buddy lying peacefully on the floor. "We'll do this together," I say quietly, patting him on the head. "And I won't let anything happen to you." He thumps his tail in response, and once again I am glad he is with me.

I rise to my feet, and Buddy follows my lead. Together we head toward the door and I wave my thanks to the bookseller as we exit. Out on the street, there are people walking about and talking with street vendors. I look up and down the road, searching for Dominic.

No sign of him. I sigh, heading out onto the street. "Come on, Buddy. It's time to go."

The Crossing

Dominic is awakened in the morning by the sound of the wolves breathing hard all around him. He jumps up, startled at the sight, looking for a tree he can climb up to escape. They circle him, panting. Then, one by one, they sit or lie down all around him.

He looks into the eyes of the leader. It approaches him and bows its head in submission. Slowly, Dominic musters up his courage and reaches out for the animal. It licks his hand, and he feels a surge of relief.

Calming himself down, he asks aloud, "Are you here to help me?"

The leader raises his head and gazes at him.

"I'll take that as a yes! In that case, I'm so glad to see you. I need to get across the river safely. Can you help me do that?"

The wolves, mostly white, some gray and white, jump to their feet and stand, waiting. Slowly, Dominic stands up and stretches his legs. The leader looks at him, then purposely begins to head back into the woods, the others following.

"I guess you know the way," he concedes and begins to follow as well. As they go along, two of the wolves flank him on each side, and two walk behind. He feels strangely peaceful, and they proceed together through the forest at an even pace.

He looks at them as they walk along. They are large and beautiful, yet also fierce and noble-looking. They must be from the northern mountains. *What are they doing down here? Were they sent all this way to help me?* Dominic ponders this in silence, grateful for the protection. He would not have to worry about the troll in their company.

Thinking about it, he has no idea which side of the river he may have come up on. Maybe he is already on the other side. But then, why are the wolves here? *Maybe they're leading me into a trap. Could they be agents for the other side?* He studies them again. *No, surely these are the white wolves from the mountains of Shazir.* He closes his eyes for a moment and whispers another prayer. "Lord, be a shield around me."

He hears the sound of water. Looking up, he sees the river ahead. No sign of a bridge. *That's good. I want to stay far away from there. They must know another way to cross.*

They stop together as a group at the riverbank. It's fairly wide across and no telling how deep. There are rocks and a few swirling areas that could be trouble. "I guess we're swimming across?" he questions aloud. The leader looks at him and then proceeds into the water; the other wolves begin to follow, and the two that have been flanking him draw in close to his side. He walks forward with them, bracing himself for the cold rush of water.

It slopes down quickly, and soon his feet can no longer reach the bottom. He begins to swim, but there is a strong current and he feels it pull him to the right. He bumps into the wolf on his right, and it keeps swimming steadily beside him. They are about halfway across when he gets pushed by the current into a slippery boulder. Bouncing off that, he is pulled under in a whirlpool of water and his arms flail, reaching for something to hold on to. His fingers feel wet fur, and he grabs ahold. At the same time, he feels a tugging on his shirt behind his head and is pulled up by the teeth of a wolf. Reaching the surface again, he inhales sharply and lets himself be pulled along by his canine companions.

Soon they are close to the other side, and he hits the bottom with his feet. They scramble up the bank together, with a few stumbling steps on the slippery rocks. The wolves pace back and forth now, the leader coming up to Dominic and licking his face.

"We made it! Thank you so much, my noble friends. I wish you could accompany me the whole way, but I can see you are eager to return."

Without any hesitation, the wolves turn back and head into the river again, following their leader. He watches them for a few minutes, then realizes it's probably not wise to stay so close to the river now. He turns into the forest and looks for a path. Looking up, he says with hope, "It's just You and me now, Lord. You've gotten me this far. I know You won't let me down. Please help me find Kara. Protect her like You've been protecting me. And thank You!" He smiles up at the sky and walks on, pushing branches back and stepping over rocks.

He walks on for about another hour, then begins to feel tired and weak. He realizes how hungry he is. "I've got to find something to eat." He begins to search the trees and bushes around him, looking for fruit or berries. "What I wouldn't give for some of my mother's beef stew right about now," he says to himself. "Or her sourdough bread, warm from the oven!"

"I am the bread of life." He hears this on the inside and remembers his mother teaching him from the Ancient Book. "He who comes to Me shall never hunger, and he who believes in Me shall never thirst" (John 6:35 NKJV). "Jesus said this." He remembers.

"I'm hungry now, Father. What do I do?" He hears his voice, empty in the wind around him. He hears nothing else. "What was it my mother told me to do? Oh, right, repeat the Word, let it sink in."

He repeats this verse over and over as he walks along. "I am the bread of life, whoever comes to Me"—he breathes in—"will never go hungry. Whoever believes in Me will never be thirsty." Over and over he repeats these words, pressing forward. He feels steadier now, like a second wind. Step by step, he keeps moving forward.

After about three hours, he notices the trees are more spread out and he sees a clearing up ahead. He increases his speed and soon is upon a path to an area of hills where he can see farmhouses in the distance.

Heaving a sigh of relief, he sits down to catch his breath for a moment. As he sits, he sees some wild strawberries around him on the ground and offers his thanks for this supply. He also finds a patch of mushrooms that he is pretty sure are safe to eat. He enjoys these as well, then gets up to head toward the farmland down the hill.

Walking down, he sees a sign up ahead that says "Bakersville, 2 miles."

"Averton is just a few miles south of there. I'm on my way, Kara!"

Arten

Mira hears a horn blast. It startles her awake and then blasts again. Ceyla is next to her, peeking out the door of the tent.

"What's all the commotion about?" says Mira.

"Not sure, milady. I don't see the men, but I hear the horn coming from the hill by the river."

Mira quickly grabs her bow and pulls on her boots. "I'll go see what I can find out."

Ceyla looks up at her. "I'll go with you!"

Mira doesn't answer and quickly heads out of the tent, Ceyla following close behind. She looks over at the men's tent and sees it is torn on one side. She peers into it; no one is there. Her head whips around. "Where are they?"

Ceyla steps up close beside her. "I think it must have been a wild animal of some kind." She looks at Mira, trembling at the thought.

"Here, take this." She picks up one of the men's swords from inside the tent and hands it to Ceyla. She grips it tightly, and both of them begin to search around. They get to the top of the hill, and still there is no sign of them.

"How could we not hear anything?" she asks Ceyla with amazement.

"I don't know. I was sound asleep until I heard that horn blow."

"I know. Me too. And it sounded like it was coming from up here, didn't it?"

"I'm not sure. I was half-asleep when I heard it."

Suddenly, they hear noises, men running and shouting, a loud groaning and snorting sound. Then they see it, a large brown bear running in their direction. It has an arrow in its side and is headed straight toward them. The men are giving chase.

Ceyla screams and runs back toward the tent area. Mira grabs an arrow and steadies herself. She feels her legs wanting to bolt and run, but she stands her ground and aims. It's very close now, and she tries to focus. She lets go, the arrow hitting him in the neck, and he stumbles to the side, skidding to a stop a few feet away from her.

Arten runs up from behind and delivers a final blow with his sword. The danger is over. Mira's legs finally give way, and she drops to the ground. Arten runs up to her and picks her up. "You got it! I've trained you well!" He smiles and begins to carry her back toward the tents.

"I'm all right. You can put me down," she protests. Ceyla is hiding in their tent, tears still on her face from the fright of it all. He puts Mira down and stands close beside her.

"It's okay, Ceyla, it's dead," she says, comforting her. Then, turning back to Arten, she adds, "When did it come upon your tent? We didn't hear a thing until your horn blast."

"It was shortly before dawn. It pawed into our tent, and we came at it with swords. Vico managed to chase it off into the woods, and we wanted to make sure it didn't return. When we wounded it, it turned back toward the camp and we blew the horn to alert you."

Mira takes a deep breath, relieved that it is over.

"That was some shot you took, Princess Mira," says Jude.

Mira smiles up at him and notices Arten watching her closely. She likes noticing this and has a warm feeling inside, along with a bit of nervousness. She realizes she is falling for him. She wonders if he is feeling this way too, or if it is just her imagination running wild.

"Well, we should pack up camp now and head across the river. The day is getting away from us," he says. With that said, they all begin to pack up and get ready.

"What about breakfast?" Julias asks.

"We'll see to that when we get to the other side and light the fire. And we've got plenty of bear meat to bring along. Let's get to it!"

Vico and Jude see to the bear, while the others pack up and get ready to cross. Finally, after what seems like a long time, they are ready to go. Mounting the horses, they begin the journey across.

They head to the shallow spot Arten had pointed out the other night. The horses seem to know the way and confidently push through the water. Ceyla's horse stops to drink for a while, and she kicks him repeatedly to move on. She doesn't want to be left behind. Finally, it stops drinking and follows along a few paces behind the others.

"Ceyla, you doing all right back there?" yells Arten.

"Yes, we're coming. He's just a bit stubborn, that's all."

Soon the water is deep enough that the horses begin swimming. "Don't try to control them now!" yells Vico. "They know what to do. Just let them do it!"

Ceyla's horse is still dragging behind the others, and she is panicking a bit, kicking his side and pulling tighter on the reins.

"Relax, Ceyla. Let her do the work now. I'll wait for you," says Vico, beckoning her with his hand.

Slowly her horse treads the water, moving toward Vico and his horse. "Why is he so slow?" she says, her eyes widening at the swirling water around them.

"Just take it easy, that's it." Soon she is right beside him and he nudges her horse with his, guiding them along. It thrashes a bit in the deep water, and Ceyla starts to slide off the saddle. Vico grabs her by the arm and pulls her over to him. "I've got you now. Just slide up here beside me."

She grabs onto him and pulls up behind him on his horse in the water. Then he reaches over and grabs the reins of her horse and leads it up to shore. Ceyla rests her head on his back, and then he lifts her down to the ground.

"Thank you!" she says gratefully. "Sorry I was so much trouble."

"No trouble at all." He tips his hat and hands back her horse's reins. She grabs it reluctantly, and they join the rest of the group.

"Ceyla, are you all right?" asks Mira.

"Yes, I just think that's enough excitement for me today. As long as we don't have to cross any more rivers or kill any more bears, I think I'll be just fine!"

After a hearty meal by the fire, they are ready to travel farther south. Mounting their horses, they carry on through the thick woods. Mira rides next to Arten, with Ceyla on her other side. Julias, Jude, Vico, and Kurt follow along from behind.

Mira is thinking about how Arten carried her after the bear episode. *He must feel something for me. I know he must.* She studies him as they go along. He is riding quietly now; in fact, everyone in the group is quiet at the moment. *It must be from all the excitement this morning,* she thinks to herself.

"I wonder what this king of Silvenia is like," she says aloud.

No one says anything at first. Then Kurt offers, "I hear he has a prosperous kingdom."

"But what is he like? How do the people of his kingdom regard him?" She eyes Arten from the side, but he says nothing.

"He is a new king. His father, King Rufus, is more well-known," says Julias from behind.

"Is he dead?"

"No, but he had a serious injury of some kind and is not able to rule the kingdom anymore. King Vespes was just recently crowned king a few months ago."

"I see. Well, I guess I'll find out more about him when we meet. How much farther do we have to go?"

"We will camp in the forest again tonight, and then it should be just a few more days if we keep on at a good pace," says Arten.

Mira takes this in. *A few more days of freedom,* she thinks to herself. *I haven't even read over my mother's instructions yet. I guess I better take a look at that soon.* She feels for the scroll in her cloak pocket to make sure it's still there. A thin paper scroll, it crinkles under her fingers, and she pats it in place.

As she rides on, she feels that same unsettled feeling in her stomach again. She's not sure she wants to read what's on that scroll but knows she has to. She has no choice. She must obey her mother's wishes. She is not free to do as she pleases. This has been ingrained into her.

When I am queen, the thought comes to her, *then I can make the rules and people will have to do what I say. I will have the power over my own destiny then. But until then, I must obey. I must pass the test.*

Later that evening, when they are all settled down for the night in their tents, Mira gets up to go outside and look at the stars. She has read the instructions from her mother, and the words are circling around in her head like birds of prey. She needs to walk and think.

She heads past the other tent and begins to walk through the trees, looking up at the stars. Up ahead, she sees an open patch where there aren't many trees. She heads there. *Why does my mother want me to do this? Isn't her kingdom grand enough? Why does she want Silvenia too?*

The instructions are painfully clear. She must convince the king to marry her and then poison him slowly to his death with the vial of dark liquid her mother has included inside the scroll. Then she is supposed to take control of the kingdom and give it over to her mother. In return, her mother will then give her rule over a lesser kingdom in that territory, and she will be free to rule that one as she pleases. And she can marry, if she chooses to then, whomever she wants.

And she wants Arten.

"You shouldn't be wandering about in the dark by yourself, Princess."

She looks up and sees Arten walking toward her.

"I wasn't going far. I just needed to think, and I felt cooped up in the tent."

"I see. And what is it you're thinking about?" he asks, getting closer to her face.

"Nothing, nothing important. I just wanted to clear my head."

"Were you thinking about me? I was hoping you were." He puts his hands behind her back and pulls her close. Her legs feel shaky as she looks up at him.

"Maybe I was."

He kisses her without warning, and she doesn't resist. Her emotions reel inside her. She feels like she doesn't ever want it to end, but she stops him.

"Arten, my mother wants me to marry the king. What am I going to do?" She feels breathless and leans against him for support.

"Don't. You can't marry him."

"I have to! I have no choice! You know her—she will have her way. Once she decides on something, no one can stop her, not even me. You know how powerful she is."

He looks down at the ground. "Yes, I do." He steps back from her for a moment, pacing around.

"Let's run away, Arten! You and I, we could do it!" She walks up to him. "Do you love me?"

He begins to kiss her again, and they stay wrapped in embrace for a while, losing track of time. Finally, she pushes him back again and looks into his eyes. "Arten, will you help me escape?"

"I will figure out something," he replies.

They stay together for most of the night, until dawn is about to break. Then, realizing they have fallen asleep together on the ground, they hurry back before they are discovered.

As Mira enters her tent, Ceyla is just beginning to stir. "Ah, what time is it? Is it morning already?" she asks sleepily.

"Yes, the sun has just come up. Not everyone is awake yet." Mira climbs back onto her pallet and lies down to rest for a moment.

"What were you doing up so early?"

"I just had to relieve myself. I think I'll lie down for a few more minutes until everyone has awakened."

Ceyla nods. "Yes, that's a good idea. I'll be right back as well." She heads out of the tent, and Mira is left alone with her thoughts for a moment. Her heart feels warm, and she tingles with excitement. She thinks about Arten. *He loves me! He's going to help me escape.* She ponders this thought for a moment. *But how? How can we escape my mother's grasp? She is so powerful! But she is not all-powerful. We will get away. We can make a life for ourselves without her interference.* She feels no love for her mother, no remorse, just a small tinge of fear.

Her mother could be very cold and unrelenting toward her enemies. She had seen it firsthand. There was the killing of an entire village by her army in the small town of Freiden to the east. Arten had told her about this. They had dared to oppose her by not turning over to her someone she considered a traitor, and they had paid the penalty. Freiden was gone—not even the children were left. No survivors. She shuddered thinking about it.

But this is my mother. She wouldn't kill her own daughter, her only daughter! Mira thinks of her father. She had never known him; her mother said that he had died when she was a baby in a battle with another kingdom. She wonders at times if that is indeed the truth. There are rumors, murmurings that he was murdered by the empress herself. *Could those rumors be true? And if they are, even more the reason that I should escape with Arten.*

I will be brave. I must get away from her. And I love him. I will trust him to find a way for us. She feels her body relaxing into sleep again. She lets go and sleeps until she is gently shaken awake by Ceyla.

"Milady, they are saying it is time to get ready to go."

She pushes up from the mat, rubbing sleep from her eyes. "Yes, of course. I am coming."

Silvenia

The servants are talking among themselves as they straighten the guest room together. "Who is she?" asks Marta, the youngest of the maids.

"Some princess from up in one of the Northern Kingdoms. I hear her mother is an empress," offers Talia, a kitchen maid. They are laying out the clean bedding, dusting and folding extra quilts as they talk.

"When is she arriving?"

"I hear any day now. Jenny is to be her personal maidservant while she is here, unless she brings her own maidservant with her."

Jenny looks up from her dusting. "That's right. I hope she is nice and not too demanding. I remember the last visitor, Madame Tussalt from Esckestan. She was frightful!"

"Positively horrid!" exclaims Talia. "She made me clean off her shoes immediately every time she came in from outside. And if I wasn't there fast enough, she would report me to Cora! At least Cora knew better than to listen to all her blustering. She would tell her that it would be dealt with immediately and then would call me aside and scold me mildly, and that was the end of it."

"Thank heavens for Cora."

"Yes, we servants have to stick together!" Jenny says with a grin. As she smooths out the bedspread, Erol appears in the doorway.

"The princess Mira has arrived! Everyone hurry now to the entrance to greet her properly. I will inform the king." He walks off in a hurry, and the women look at one another with wide eyes.

"Let's go!" says Jenny, fixing a flyaway hair in the mirror and smoothing her apron. Talia leads the way down the stairs, and they all follow with haste. Soon they are lined up at the entrance outside, with Cora at the head of their group. Erol and the other menservants are lined up as well, and they are all watching the royal group approach on their horses.

King Vespes has just stepped outside himself, with Trea close by his side. He looks serious and a bit nervous, Trea notices. She puts her focus on the visitors now in clear view. There are seven of them on horseback, five men and two women. The woman in the middle must be the princess. She has an elegant riding dress on, pale green, and a dark-green riding bonnet with jewels on it. Her hat sparkles in the sunlight.

Trea studies her—long dark-brown hair, almost black, and striking, light-colored eyes. They look green, like her dress. She carries herself high in her saddle; she actually seems a bit stiff, and her smile looks forced. *Maybe she's nervous too,* thinks Trea. *I will have to help put her at ease.*

The leader of the group, a tall man with blond hair and beard, dismounts and speaks. "May I present to you, Princess Mira, daughter of Celia, empress of Icelandia." He bows and walks over to her to help her dismount gracefully.

Vespes walks up to her and bows. "We are so happy you have come. I am King Vespes, and this is my sister, Princess Trea. Please let us escort you in and help you get comfortable. I'm sure your journey has been long." He offers his arm to her, and she takes it, glancing at Arten fleetingly. He is looking straight ahead and doesn't seem to notice.

The group heads inside, and the servants get to work, offering hospitality to the highest degree. The princess's bags are taken up to the blue room, and Ceyla's to the room next to that, which is a smaller guest room painted pink.

The men are all stationed on the other side of the castle, Julias and Jude in one large bedroom with two beds, and Vico and Kurt in another. Arten has his own room across from them.

After they are given a small tour, the king offers them time to rest from their journey and suggests they gather together again at dinner around 6:00 p.m. in the main dining room. They agree to this, and Erol advises he will come and let them know when dinner is ready to be served.

Jenny is stationed in the small servant's room across from the blue room and lets the princess know she is also available for assistance. She shows her the bell in her bedroom that she can ring for service.

Mira, looking a bit distracted, responds with a weak smile, tells her she's feeling very tired now, and shuts her door. Jenny retreats back to her spot across the hall. All is quiet in the castle again.

Trea, who has been trying to engage the princess in conversation while they tour the castle, is downstairs now in the kitchen, talking to Cora, the head cook. "She seems kind of quiet," she says, munching on a piece of celery left on the counter. "I don't know what to think about her yet."

"She looks very elegant and refined to me," says Cora. "She is probably just getting adjusted to her new surroundings and has been trained to be more formal with strangers. We are all still strangers to her right now." She smiles at Trea. "But don't worry, I'm sure you will make her feel right at home, and then she won't seem so distant. You'll have a new friend!"

"Yes, and she's right down the hall from me!" She pauses for a moment. "Maybe I should check on her and make sure she's settling in okay."

"She probably just needs a little time to rest first. Give her a good hour or so, I think."

"You're right, of course. I guess I'm just so ready for some new female companionship around here. I really have been missing Delvana a lot."

"I know. We all miss her. I do hope she will be able to visit us soon."

"Yes, well, I think I'll go walk to the stables and visit with the horses for a while. Maybe I'll go for a ride to the pond."

"Good idea. It's a beautiful day, and the sun is shining. Go enjoy yourself!"

Trea smiles and heads outside, taking the walkway to the stables.

Meanwhile, Mira is up in her room, reclining on the big sleigh bed and thinking of Arten. She thinks of their evening together last night, how he promised to find a way for them to be together. She thinks of his passionate embrace, his strong arms holding her close, and she feels light-headed again. She has never felt this way before, and her emotions rise and fall inside of her. Her mind is so full of him she can't seem to focus on anything else.

Is he thinking about me right now? she wonders. She gets up and paces across the room. Looking out the window, she sees the king's sister walking up a path toward what looks like the royal stables. *She's a talkative one. At least I don't feel like I have to do all the talking around here.*

She looks into the closet next to where the servants have already hung up her clothing along with her cape. She glances again at her cape and reaches in to pull out the scroll from her mother. Holding it in her hand, she walks back over to the bed and sits down to unfurl it. She frowns as she reads the writing once again:

My daughter,

These are the things you must do while in the kingdom of Silvenia:

1. *You must win over the affections of the king and his royal family. I know this will not be difficult for you with your great beauty and charm, which you have inherited from our royal bloodline. Your influence there will be great. I have seen to it.*
2. *You must marry the king. He will no doubt propose to you very quickly, and you must accept and prepare the wedding plans with haste. I will come down to attend the royal wedding and will assist you in preparations for taking over the kingdom.*

3. *The kingdom shall prosper under my rule, and I will prepare a second, smaller kingdom close by for you to rule over, with any husband you should choose. Men are not really necessary, in my opinion, but can be quite useful at times. You are free to do as you please in your own kingdom, of course.*
4. *As soon as you are betrothed to the king, you must give him one drop from the vial I have enclosed every day in his drink. It will ensure my reign over his kingdom and success for the both of us. Don't trouble yourself about what is in it. Trust in my skill and wisdom as an empress and as your mother. I will be queen over all this land, and you will rule after me. You will see all this has to be.*
5. *Read over these instructions every day and carry them with you everywhere. This is very important. You must follow my instructions to the letter. To be a queen, you must pass the test.*

*With affection,
Your mother, Celia Tremonde,
empress of Icelandia*

Mira drops the scroll down on the bed and stares at her fingers. They are smeared with the black ink. She feels sick. "I must obey her. She will suspect if I try to betray her and get away. I know she will!" A sinking feeling stirs in the pit of her stomach. She lies back on the bed and shuts her eyes. Her determination from a moment ago feels lost.

"I'm just going to rest for a moment," she mutters, feeling cold and sleepy. Her body drifts into sleep.

The next moment, she is awakened abruptly by a rap on the door.

"Who is it?" she calls out wearily.

"Princess Mira, dinner is about to be served." It's the butler.

How can it be time for dinner already? she thinks. *I just lay down a few minutes ago!* She sits up and calls out, "I'll be out in just a few minutes."

"Yes, Princess," he replies, and she hears him walk off down the corridor.

Sighing, she rises up and steadies herself for a moment by the bedpost. She moves slowly to the mirror and stares at her reflection. Her eyes look dark, and her skin pale. She splashes some water on her face from the pitcher on the nightstand and brushes her hair. Then she pinches her cheeks and looks again. "That's a little better," she murmurs and heads over to the door to go down for the dinner.

Arten is probably waiting for me, she thinks to herself, but when she opens the door, she sees Trea, the king's sister, waiting for her to come out.

"I thought I'd walk with you down to the dining room," she says, smiling. "Did you have a good rest?"

"Yes, thank you. To be honest, I still feel a bit tired. I probably just need a good nights' sleep."

"Of course. Did you find your room comfortable? It's the nicest guest room in the castle. And I'm just down the hall from you, in that room there." She points. "If you need anything at all, or just someone to talk to, feel free to come find me."

"That's very kind of you. Thank you." Mira looks over the bannister as they descend, searching for Arten. Finally, they enter a large ornate room with a long dining table at the center. Everyone is already seated at the table. Apparently, she is the last one down.

"Princess Mira!" King Vespes rises up and escorts her to her chair, which is right beside him. She looks at his face.

He is pleasant-looking enough, but he's not Arten. He's just a silly young king who is looking for a bride. Someone he can rule over and display on his arm at royal events. Someone who can bear him royal children. Well, it's not going to be me!

She looks over at Arten and tries to catch his eye. Suddenly, there is silence, and everyone is looking at her. "Princess?" says the king, pausing. She realizes he has been speaking to her, and she has no idea what he just said.

"Oh, I'm sorry. I was distracted. What did you say?"

"I was asking how you liked your room."

"Oh, I like it! Very lovely, and quite comfortable." She stares down at her plate as a servant girl places a bowl of soup in front of her. She forces herself to smile at the king and picks up her soup-spoon. "This looks delicious. What kind of soup is it?"

"It's pumpkin soup with sour cream, my favorite!" says Trea from across the table.

"It's very good," says Mira truthfully as she takes another spoonful.

The king tries again, "Tell me about your country. What sort of foods do you enjoy in your kingdom?"

Mira sits, thinking for a moment. "Well, we eat venison stew a lot, and we have a dish I like called potato pie." She looks around her and notices everyone is listening. "It's just a pie crust filled with potatoes, rice, and some vegetables and seasonings."

The king smiles at her. "That sounds very good. Perhaps we can have Cora try out that recipe while you're here."

She looks up at his face. "I'd be happy to help her with that. I don't remember the exact ingredients, but I think we could figure it out together."

"I will be happy to help too," adds Trea, liking the idea. Mira smiles at her. "That would be perfect."

Glancing around the table, she notices Arten is talking quietly with Vico. *Why won't he look at me?* she wonders.

"I was thinking we could take a tour through the main village in the kingdom tomorrow, if you're up for it. Or did you want to get right to discussing the briefing from your mother, the empress? I am completely flexible and at your service."

Trea looks at her brother. *He sure is laying on the charm. The princess really is quite beautiful. I guess I shouldn't be surprised.* She chews on a biscuit, watching the two of them, trying to picture them together as a couple.

"I would love a tour through your kingdom. From what I have seen so far, it is quite lovely."

"Then that is what we shall do. After breakfast tomorrow."

She nods in agreement, and they continue on with small talk and conversations throughout the table about the people and customs of Silvenia. Trea notices she doesn't offer too much information about Icelandia but keeps directing the conversation back to their kingdom with her questions. *And Vespes is going on and on. What has made him so talkative all of a sudden? This is a whole new side of him I have not seen before.*

After dinner, they rise to take a short walk together through the rose garden in the courtyard. Mira looks with longing toward Arten, but he excuses himself early, along with the other men, saying it's been a long day and they need to head back to their rooms. *He's probably jealous,* thinks Mira to herself. *Surely, he knows I can't be rude to the king and ignore his attention to me. Maybe he will sneak over to my room tonight and then we can be alone and finally have a moment to talk. He's probably just trying to figure out a plan for us to escape.*

Trea starts to excuse herself as well, and Mira interjects, "Don't leave yet. I'm just getting to know all of you. Please stay." Trea nods willingly and walks along beside her, with the king on her other side. They walk together through the courtyard, with Trea pointing out her favorite types of roses and asking Mira her opinion.

"I like the blue ones."

"Oh, then we shall cut a small bouquet for your room so you can enjoy them all the time! Jenny! Please cut off some and put it in a vase for the princess."

"Yes, milady." Jenny curtsies from behind and hurries off to complete her task.

Mira finds herself distracted again with thoughts of Arten. "You know, I think I really am feeling quite tired now. Would you mind if I headed up to bed now? I want to be well rested for our tour tomorrow."

"Of course, let me escort you up," says Vespes, turning back toward the castle door.

Soon she is back in her room, with a vase of blue roses on her bedside table now. She sits on her bed quietly to listen. All is still. Her fingers press against the blanket on her bed, and it crinkles. She remembers she left the scroll on her bed. *No one must see this! How could I be so careless?*

She looks around the room, wondering if any of the servants might have seen it. *No, my bedsheets are just like when I left the room, and the scroll is hidden under the folds of this blanket. No one has touched it.* She breathes out a nervous sigh.

As she lies in bed, the burden of the scroll feels like it is pressing down on her chest. She tries taking a deep breath and forces her mind to think of something else. Arten. *Where is he? Why has he not sought me out yet? Surely, he could make up some excuse to come and speak with me.* Her heart feels sick with longing for him. *He will find a way, if not tonight, then tomorrow for sure.*

The room feels dark and empty. She closes her eyes and tries to let sleep come. Her thoughts drift back to the other night, when she was alone with him, and she comforts herself with these images as her eyelids get heavy. Soon she is fast asleep.

She is awakened by a soft tapping on the door. *Arten!* Her heart leaps. She gets up quickly and sees the sunlight streaming through the window onto her face as she glances in the mirror. It is morning already. She smooths her hair in place and sits on a soft chair by the bed. "You may enter," she calls out.

The door opens quietly, and she sees Jenny, the servant girl. "Good morning, Princess. I was just seeing if you would like me to bring you some hot tea? Also, breakfast is almost ready in the dining room."

"Oh, is it breakfast time already? I just need to get dressed before I come down. Some hot tea would be lovely, thank you."

"Yes, milady." She curtsies and departs the room quickly.

Mira sighs with some disappointment. "Well, at least I'll see him at breakfast. I will make it a point to speak to him."

She gets ready with haste, putting on a dark-pink-and-red dress with navy undertones. One that is suitable for riding as well, since they are planning on some type of tour today. It will be interesting to see more of this kingdom outside these castle walls.

Trea is waiting for her again as she steps out of her room. "Good morning, Princess!"

"Please call me Mira."

"Mira." She smiles. "We can head down to breakfast together. The men have already eaten and are out preparing the horses and coach for the tour today."

"Oh! I must have slept in late, then. I do apologize."

"It's perfectly fine. We wanted you to get your rest after your long journey here. And the men said they wanted to get an early start on their journey back."

"Pardon? What did you say?"

"I said the men wanted to get an early start—"

"For their journey back? Back where?"

"Well, back to Icelandia, of course. I figured they had discussed all that with you. I'm sure they wouldn't depart without your instructions."

"Of course," replies Mira, trying to push down the shock. "Did they say anything else to you before they left?"

"Just that they had an errand for the empress they had to attend to that couldn't wait and they would be back as soon as possible."

"Right. Yes, thank you." She feels the room closing in on her but keeps walking.

"Are you all right? You look a bit pale all of a sudden."

"No, I'm fine. I think I just need to eat something." She forces herself to calmly walk to the dining table and sit down.

"Me too. I'm starving!" Trea sits across from her and rings the servant bell.

During the rest of the mealtime, Mira somehow makes small talk with Trea, although she doesn't remember later what they've talked about. When they finish eating, the king enters and escorts them to the royal coach, which is parked out in front of the castle.

"Would you prefer to ride on horseback or in the coach?" he asks.

She looks up at him. "In the coach, I think."

Weakly, she sits down beside him and the tour of the kingdom begins.

The Road to Rondival

Walking through the busy little town, Buddy and I keep pace together down the dusty road. One starling follows along from up above, the other one now headed back to alert the others of their departure from Averton. We've passed all the little shops along the main street now, and the houses are becoming more spread out.

"I guess we just follow this main path out of town and watch for the signs headed south to Rondival," I say to Buddy. "It doesn't look very far, from what I can tell on this map." I pull it out again and glance at it. Buddy stops, panting and waiting patiently for me.

We continue walking for about an hour, and then we notice a sign up ahead tacked to a tree. As we get closer, we see it has two arrows on it: "Kingdom of Rondival, 8 miles, and Blain Bridge, 11 miles."

"I guess we should probably spend the night in Rondival. I don't want to wear us out, and you look pretty tired already. Here's some water." I reach down and pour some water into a small cup I've brought. He drinks it readily, and I drink some from the flask myself. "Don't worry, I'm sure we'll be able to get a good dinner in the city."

We continue south, down the dirt road, until there are just trees and fields around us on both sides. Looking at the scenery around me makes me think of my childhood home in the countryside of New Jersey. I remember riding my horse through the trees, playing in the cornfields with my sister, games of hide-and-seek, and climbing trees. A memory pops into my head.

Julia is trying to reach a branch to climb up the tree on our back hill. "Give me a boost. I can't reach it."

"Okay," I reply. "Hop up!" I link my fingers together to let her step up. She presses down on my palms with her shoe, and I've got her

full weight as she reaches for the branch. "Just a little higher," *she says, reaching up.*

"You're too heavy now. I can't lift you any higher. I need to put you down."

"Wait, just a little higher. I can almost reach it."

"Hurry up! I can't hold you!"

She pushes up with the sole of her foot, and my hands break apart. I watch—it feels like in slow motion—as she falls and slides down the hill, headfirst. There are some large rocks at the bottom, and she is headed straight toward them. It happens so fast all I can do is watch, with shock spreading through my body.

She comes to a stop right where the rocks are and lies there for a moment.

"Julia, are you okay? Julia!"

She pushes herself up, with tears on her face, then runs inside, yelling, "You almost killed me! How could you just drop me like that?"

"Julia, I'm sorry! Please, wait!"

She runs inside to Mom, and I follow, feeling guilty and wanting to kick myself for dropping her. At the same time, I'm also extremely relieved that she is okay, and I want to protest that nothing serious happened and defend myself to my parents.

Why am I reliving that painful memory? I think to myself. *We were just kids, probably about ten and twelve years of age. It was just an accident, anyway.* I feel my heart long to see Julia again, and my mom and dad too. Again, I wonder if they are looking for me. *Do they think I'm missing or, worse, dead?*

I am pulled to a stop by Buddy. He has lain down on the ground to rest, panting. "Are you okay, Buddy? Need some more water?" I pour him another cupful, and he drinks a few gulps and then just lies there. "I guess you're just tired. I know we've been walking a lot today. I'll sit with you for a few minutes, and then we should keep going to get to Rondival before dark." I take a seat on the ground next to him and pet his head. He thumps his tail in approval and lays his head down on his paws.

I close my eyes. In my mind's eye, I see Julia. She is lying on her bed, facedown, one arm hanging off the side. Her room is in its normal disarray, random piles of clothes, papers, and pictures everywhere. I can hear her breathing.

I feel the cold air in the room. "Julia? Can you hear me?" I move closer to her still form lying on the bed, asleep. *Am I really here?* I think, keeping my eyes clamped shut. "Julia?" I look down at her arm. There's a dark-red stain on the floor by the bed. "Is that blood? No, there's an empty red wine bottle tipped over, and it has leaked some onto the carpet." I put my hand on Julia's back. "Julia, wake up. I'm here." I feel something wet on my arm and open my eyes.

Buddy is licking me and thumping his tail. "Oh, Buddy. I forgot you were there for a minute." I feel lost in the moment. Closing my eyes again, I try to see Julia again. Nothing. Blackness. I look at Buddy and feel a tear run down my cheek. Wiping it away, I rise up. "Come on, Buddy. We can't sit here all day. We've got to get to Rondival!"

He jumps up with me, and we continue on.

I try to push anxious feelings about Julia out of my head. *Why was I seeing that? Is my imagination just running wild? Was that really her?* I walk faster, passion and determination to get back home growing within me.

"What does it matter if I get back to her? She doesn't listen to me anyway," I say out loud into the open air. Buddy barks at me. I look at him and shush him. "I can't fix her!" I whisper with anger and frustration. "I can't bring her back."

Buddy barks again. "What, are you trying to tell me something, boy?" He barks again. "I wish I could understand what you're saying."

We've been walking at a quicker pace, and soon, I begin to see more people and houses along the road. After about another half-hour, I see some sort of tower up ahead in the distance. As we get closer, I see a large stone wall surrounding it and other homes and buildings all about.

"This must be it, the kingdom of Rondival. It certainly is bigger and grander than the town of Averton."

People are all around now, passing us on horses and in carts and carriages. There is a large gate up ahead that leads into the city. We head toward it along with many others who are entering as well. The tower is connected to a castle, which appears to be in the center of the city, homes and shops encircling it. It is on a hill, and everything else is in lower descending order. The farthest streets outside of the castle lead to numerous farms of different sorts, spread out on the hills about them.

As we enter the kingdom, there are merchants everywhere, calling out their wares and holding them up as we pass by. We pass by a merchant selling sausages and meats of all kinds, and I stop to buy some for Buddy. "Good sir, do you know of an inn close by where we could stay for the night?"

He smiles at me. "Of course I do! There are two right up this main street here, if you just keep heading toward the castle. The closer you get to the castle, the more they charge you. The first one is the Gleaming Gables, and the second one is Rafter Point. I've stayed at both places, and they're first rate."

"Thank you very much! I appreciate your help," I say while paying him for the food. He tips his hat, and we move on. I take in all the new sights with interest, while looking for the Gleaming Gables Inn. The clouds are getting thicker now, and the air is cooler as well. I wrap my cloak around me and press on through the crowd. I am feeling extra hungry now, but I decide to wait until we find the inn to settle down and eat something.

A lone starling watches from above, gliding in wide circles above Kara and her dog. The other starling should have gotten the word out by now of Kara's whereabouts and will head back soon. For now, she will continue her watch alone, singing out a clear melody of notes as she glides in the sky above.

Julia

Julia stirs in her bed. Her head is pounding. "Ohhh, why did I drink all that horrible wine? I need some aspirin." She pushes herself up and heads to the bathroom, barely making it there in time to vomit in the commode. She rests her head on the cold rim for a moment, and then vomits again. There's a knock on the bathroom door. "Go away, Kara! Leave me alone!"

"It's me, Mom. Are you all right? You don't sound like yourself."

"Oh, yeah, I'm fine, Mom. Just some kind of stomach bug."

"Can I do anything to help?"

"Nope. I just need to rest for a while. Thanks."

"Okay." She hears her slowly retreating from the door. Her angry stomach is calmer now, and she lies full out on the bathroom tile, her head pulsing with pain. She wants some aspirin but feels too weary to get up and retrieve it. Moaning, she buries her head in her arm. Then, forcing herself up, she reaches into the medicine cabinet, but the aspirin is not there.

She sticks her head out into the hallway. "Kara!" she calls out. "Did you take the aspirin? I need it." No response. "Mom?"

"Yes, dear. I'm down here in the kitchen. Did you need something?"

"I need aspirin. It's usually in this bathroom, but someone moved it. Do you know where it is?"

"It's here in the kitchen cabinet, dear. That's where I usually keep it. Here, I'll bring it up to you."

She hurries up the stairs with a concerned look on her face. Julia groans inwardly. "I'm fine, Mom. Don't worry about me."

"It's just that I thought I heard you calling out for Kara. You know she's not here, right?"

"What do you mean? Is she at Sonia's house?"

"No, Julia. I mean she's not here. You know she's been at the hospital. We just went to see her the other day." She pauses, a mixture of weariness and concern in her eyes. "Maybe we should set up another appointment for you today with Dr. Clair."

"What? No! Kara was just in my room. She was leaning over me as I was waking up. I know she was." She looks at her mother, her thoughts jumbled and lost.

"You must have been dreaming again. Remember, you were talking about your nightmares with Dr. Clair. Maybe we should ask her about a different medication to help you sleep better."

Julia presses her throbbing head with her palm. Her mind feels numb. "Why is Kara in the hospital?"

"She's in a coma. The doctors think it was caused by an aneurysm in her brain. Can't you remember?"

She searches her thoughts. "What do you mean a coma? She can't be in a coma. We were just talking yesterday about going to look for Percy together. We were going to search the neighborhood on our bikes."

"Okay, Julia, just go lie back down. I'm going to call Dr. Clair and see if she could come by today and help us sort through this. You're not thinking straight. It must be from the medication."

"No, Mom! I don't want to see a doctor! Take me to Kara right now!" She feels a hot tear run down her face. Her mom puts a hand on her shoulder and gently steers her back toward her room.

"Okay, dear. Just let me get your father first. We'll take you to see Kara. Calm down, it's going to be all right." Julia sits down on her bed and stares at her mom in disbelief. "Now, just stay right here. I'll be right back." She heads out of the room and down the hall.

Rising, Julia gets up and listens quietly in the doorway. She hears her mother on the phone. "No, Ed, she's not herself. You better come home right away." Julia goes back over and sits on her bed.

She thinks back to her last memory with Kara. Kara had just walked in her bedroom yesterday and asked if she had seen Percy lately.

"I haven't seen him in a few days. I think he might be missing."

"He probably just has a new girlfriend. We could get on our bikes tomorrow and go looking around the neighborhood if you want."

"Yeah, let's do that." Kara smiles, with a look of hope in her eyes. Julia isn't sure if that is for the cat or because she has finally agreed to do something with her.

"Julia," her mom interjects, "Dad's on his way home now, and then we can go to see Kara with him at the hospital."

Julia looks up at her, not sure what to say. "Okay, I think I'll just lie down for a while until it's time to go."

"Okay, dear. Would you like me to bring you some water or ginger ale for your stomach?" She eyes the empty wine bottle on the floor.

"No, I'm fine. Just need to rest," she says, turning over with her face to the wall.

"All right." She hears her mother go out and head back down the stairs. Lifting herself up quietly, she heads over to Kara's room. Once inside, she looks around. Her bed is made—that's typical. Nothing seems out of place. She walks over to her dresser. There are her books on top, some pens, and a notepad. A necklace. There's a leaf. It's pretty, vibrant and colorful. Kara must have found it and brought it home to save it for a scrapbook or something.

She picks it up and studies it. Then she hears her mom coming back up the stairs. Stuffing it in her pocket, she heads back over to her room and lies down. Her mom peeks in her room but doesn't say anything. Julia lies still, her eyes closed.

Why can't I remember what happened? I know Mom wouldn't lie to me. This is like a bad dream. Maybe Mom's right. Maybe this is one of those nightmares she was talking about. She pinches her arm. "Ow! Okay, not dreaming." *Think, think. Surely, I can remember seeing her at the hospital. Mom says we just went there the other day. How many days has she been there?*

She closes her eyes and lets her mind wander. A scene flashes into her mind. They had another conversation.

"Are you ready to go with me now to find Percy?" she asks.

"What? Oh, right, you mentioned that yesterday. I don't feel like it right now."

"It's really nice out. Come on, it might do you good to get outside. We could head to the pond, then circle back opposite ways to look for him."

"No, Kara! Not right now. I'm tired."

"Okay, I'll go on my own, then. I miss spending time with you, Julia."

"Don't get all dramatic on me. I'm just tired right now. I'll go later."

"Yeah, okay." She leaves then.

"Was that our last conversation? Then what? Why don't I remember her being in the hospital?" she says out loud.

"Because you were in the hospital yourself," says her dad, standing in the doorway. "Dr. Clair just released you yesterday to come home. You've been at Sheltered Elm Hospital for the past three weeks, for almost drinking yourself to death. After you heard about Kara, you went on a binge. You were passed out from the alcohol mixed with your meds. They've been treating you for that and counseling you for depression. We talked about all this in length yesterday. Don't you remember?"

Julia closes her eyes. It's all coming back to her now. The clinical smell, the dirty white walls, the bruises on her arms from the IVs. She opens her eyes and looks at her arms. The yellow-brown spots are fading now. She feels weak. "I…I had forgotten. But I remember now." Tears spill down her face.

"It's okay, honey." Her dad and mom come closer. They sit on each side of her.

"I was so mean to her! I need another chance to talk to her. Can we go see Kara now?"

"Of course we can," says her mom.

Her dad looks at her. "Are you sure you're feeling up to that right now? You could rest and get a good night's sleep first, and then we could go see her right after breakfast in the morning. Dr. Clair said it was important to let you rest. You haven't been sleeping well at night."

"Mom, you said we went to see her the other day. Why can't I remember?"

Her mom looks at her lovingly. "That was on the way home from your hospital. You kept asking to see Kara, over and over. We couldn't deny you that, even though you were still weak from what happened to you. We went in and saw her only for a few minutes since it was past visiting hours and they were making an exception for us. You fell asleep in the car on the way home."

Julia searches her mind for this memory, but all she can recall now is the sterile white room she has stayed in herself, apparently for the past three weeks. "I want to go see her now." She looks at her parents pleadingly. "Please."

"Of course, yes, let me go pull the car around," says her father, getting up to go.

"Thank you," Julia says, getting up and pulling on her shoes. "Come on, Mom. Let's go."

Goldie

Dominic walks on for many miles. Realizing he has no money with him now, he looks for an opportunity to be of assistance, repairing a fence, helping someone with digging or painting. There are numerous farms around him now, and he's been asking at most of them along the way. So far, no one has needed his help, but one kind lady did offer him some food for the road, and he accepted it gratefully.

He is not far from Averton now; perhaps he can get a quick job in town and search for Kara while he is staying there. "I wish I knew someone in town. I will just have to make myself useful and get some money for the road." His ankle is still a bit sore, but it's not as swollen as it looked before. "The cool water from the river probably helped some. I could use some more cool water to drink right about now."

He looks around. There's no sign of a brook or a well, but there is another farmhouse up on the right. "I'll try there." He walks up to the little gray house and knocks on the door. He notices an apple orchard to the side of the house.

A young man answers the door. "Hi. Can I help you?" He looks to be in his early twenties, tall, with sun-freckled skin and reddish-blond hair.

"Hello! My name is Dominic. I'm on my way to Averton, and sorry to say, I've lost my coin pouch on the journey. I was wondering if you needed some help with your apple orchard, or if there was something here that I could repair for you? I'm good at fixing things," he says with a hopeful smile.

"Oh, I see. Um, well, I think we have all the help we need right now, with my brother and sisters here, but let me go check with my dad and make sure. Please wait here." He turns and heads back inside. Dominic waits patiently on the porch. He turns and looks at the numerous apple trees full of fruit and ready to be picked.

A few minutes later, a tall older man appears and greets him. "Hello, I'm Ray. My son tells me you're looking for work? I could use someone just for today to help me pick and load some crates with apples for delivery. We can always use an extra hand, but I can only offer you twenty gildens for today." He looks Dominic over, noticing his short stature.

"Oh, don't worry about my size. I'm stronger than I look!" He smiles. "And twenty gildens would be perfect! Just one thing, Could I get a cup of water before we begin? I've been walking for a while, and I'm quite thirsty."

"Of course! Here, come into the kitchen with me and we'll get you all set up." He heads through the living room toward a kitchen painted bright yellow. In the kitchen, there is a young woman sitting at the table, peeling potatoes. "This is my daughter Goldie. Goldie, this man will be helping us with the picking today. Could you get us both some cold water? We're heading outside to get started. And send your brothers out too."

"Yes, Pa." She stops what she's doing and gets up to get the drinks for them. Dominic smiles at her.

"Nice to meet you, Goldie. You remind me of a friend of mine."

"Oh? Who's that?

"Her name is Kara. Your face reminds me of her. She gets that same focused look of concentration when she's working on something."

"Kara—I know someone by that name. Met her on the road the other day, and I remember because I haven't heard of that name before. She was traveling to Averton."

Dominic's eyes widen. "Yes! That might have been her. We were supposed to meet there, but I was delayed in my travels. Did she have on a red cloak? Brown hair with blue eyes, and freckles?" He's excited now, and the words tumble out of him unchecked.

She closes her eyes to think. "Yes, brown hair and freckles. Not sure what color her cloak was though. It's been about a week since I saw her. I remember she was very nice. She asked me about getting to Averton."

"That's wonderful news! Thank you for telling me. I was worried about her finding her way. I'm sure she's safely there by now and just waiting for me to arrive."

"Well, we better get started, then, so you can continue with your journey," says Ray. "Come on, I'll show you around the orchard." He heads out to the back, and Dominic follows, bowing politely at Goldie.

"I'll be right behind you with those waters!" she calls out.

They head out to the orchard and are soon joined by Goldie and her brothers, Jared and Owen. Goldie hands them two brimming cups of water and puts a pitcher down on an overturned basket. Dominic downs his in a few seconds, and she pours him some more.

"Wow, you were really thirsty!"

"Yes! Thank you so much. I'm ready to work now."

Goldie turns to her father. "Do you want me to help out here now too? I'm just about finished in the kitchen."

"Why don't you finish up in there first? And you and Ma can fix us some lunch as well. If you want to help us after lunch, that would be fine."

"Okay," she says, slightly disappointed. She wants to ask more about Kara, but she can do that later. They have a full day's work ahead of them and many baskets to fill.

Dominic helps them load up basket after basket, which they then load up on a cart. Goldie brings them some sandwiches, then stays and helps sort the apples, pulling out ones that aren't good. While they work, she asks him more questions about Kara.

"I remember she asked me a bunch of questions about the kingdom of Silvenia. I told her about the festivals they have there, and about the windfolk. She was really interested in hearing more about them. How did you two become friends?"

"Well, I knew her family and met her when she was a little girl. I'm like her adoptive uncle, I guess you could say." He smiles and carries out another basket full of apples.

"Where does her family live?"

"Oh, way out near Redmonton. But we're meeting up in Averton to travel on to Silvenia together."

"What are you going to do in Silvenia?"

"Goldie, you shouldn't pry him with so many questions. He is trying to work," reminds her father.

"Oh, it's all right," Dominic replies. "I was also interested in hearing about how Kara was doing, since I missed out on traveling with her."

"She seemed just fine. She chatted with me all the way to my last delivery, and I told her to be sure and stop by and see me the next time she was passing through."

"I'm glad to hear it. And when we pass through here on our way back, we'll be sure to stop by and say hello. I really do appreciate this job today. Thank you again," he says to Ray.

"Well, we appreciate the help. Now, let's head over to the pear trees and see what progress we can make over there as well." He gestures toward another grove of trees in the back. "Goldie, find your sister and have her come help as well. She can help you sort and divide what we gather into the baskets."

"Yes, Pa." Goldie rises up and heads back toward the house.

The men carry on, moving ladders, climbing up to hard-to-reach spots, which Dominic finds he is especially good at, and lifting crates of apples onto the carts. Jared has brought over a new cart now and parked it in front of the pear trees.

By evening, the whole family, along with Dominic, has worked for hours and made a lot of progress. They stop for dinner when Goldie's mother calls out that it's time from the kitchen door.

"I'm so ready to eat," says Jared.

"Yes, I think we've all worked up a good appetite. That's enough work for today. Let's go enjoy some good food and relax. We're pleased to have you as our guest, Dominic. You helped us more than you know."

"Very glad to be of service. And thank you so much for the dinner invitation as well."

"You definitely earned it! Honestly, I don't know how you got up so high on some of those branches. It made me a bit nervous watching you."

"I've always loved to climb, ever since I was little. It's good to know I still can!"

Heading inside, they smell a delicious beef stew, the steam from it rising from the table. There are buttermilk biscuits and butter with honey and what looks like a fresh apple pie warm from the wood-burning stove.

"This looks amazing! I can't thank you enough for your kindness and hospitality."

"It's our pleasure," says Margaret, Goldie's mother.

Everyone digs in heartily, and soon they are leaning back in their chairs, smiles on their faces.

"Pa, when will I get to go to Silvenia? Remember you promised to take me to the Harvest Moon Festival after I turned eighteen?"

"Right, and I am a man of my word. But you just turned eighteen, and we do have to finish with the harvest right now. You will have to be patient just a little bit longer."

"We still have a few months until the festival," interjects her mother. "We'll have to discuss the details of who will go and who will stay and look after things here." She looks at Ray, and he nods.

"Yes, we will discuss all that in the weeks after the harvesting is done, and the new planting that needs to be done is accomplished as well." He clears his throat and looks at Dominic. "So would you like to stay another day and help some more, or do you need to go and meet your friend now over in Averton?"

Dominic pauses for a moment, considering. "I would really like to stay, but I am a bit concerned that she is waiting for me."

"We will pay you another twenty gildens, and five more. I could use another day of progress like we had today."

"Your friend is not in any danger, is she? Are you concerned about her well-being?" says Margaret. Goldie looks up at him with this question hanging in the air.

"No, I'm sure she is getting along fine. She has a good head on her shoulders. I will stay one more day to help."

"If you could just stay until after lunch tomorrow, that would be perfect, then you will still have plenty of time to get to Averton by suppertime and meet your friend."

"That sounds perfect," Dominic says, enjoying his last bite of pie. "I must say, you are an amazing cook, Ms. Margaret!"

"Thank you." She smiles at him. "I will make up a sleeping place for you in the living room. You just make yourself at home."

They all rise from the table, and Goldie grabs him by the arm and ushers him into the living room. "Would you like to see our books? We have a whole little library in here!"

"Absolutely! I love to read."

"Me too. Does Kara?"

"Yes, I know that for a fact."

"Let me show you my favorites. I've read them over and over. I really do need some new ones to add to our collection."

Dominic looks around the living room. It is warm and inviting, a fireplace to one side, with bookshelves on both sides of it. There is a multicolored woven rug on the floor, and soft, cushioned chairs positioned around it, and there is a chest in the middle full of extra quilts. Margaret is arranging a pallet for him close to the warmth of the fire.

"I hope you will be comfortable here. There are extra blankets in the trunk if you get cold."

"This is perfect. Thank you so much."

Goldie has pulled down a couple of books to share with him, and Greta, her sister, steps out of the kitchen. "Mom, tell Goldie it's her turn to clean up the kitchen. I did it yesterday."

"She's right, Goldie. And we need to let Dominic get some rest as well. There'll be more time to visit tomorrow at breakfast." She turns to him. "We'll have breakfast ready at 7:00 a.m., so we can get an early start before you need to leave."

"That sounds good. I'm an early riser, anyway." He looks at Goldie, who is slowly heading back toward the kitchen. "I'll be happy to help with the dishes. It's the least I can do after such a fantastic meal!"

Margaret starts to object, but he has already headed into the kitchen and grabbed a towel. "Mr. Dominic, there is no need for you—"

"It's my pleasure, and I'm happy to help!"

Goldie smiles, grabs the bucket of water, and begins washing off the plates.

"Well, all right," says Margaret. "I've got to put some laundry away, and then I'm off to bed. Don't stay up too late talking—Goldie, I mean you!"

"Don't worry, Mom," she responds with a grin.

After the dishes are done, they head back into the living room. Greta is reclining on a large overstuffed chair by the bookshelves, the book she is reading on her lap, facedown, and her eyes are closed. Goldie touches her arm. "Greta, why don't you head up to bed now? You're tired."

She looks up with a start. "What? Oh, yes, I'm about to head upstairs." Goldie walks over to the shelves and pulls out another book to show Dominic.

"Have you ever read *The Golden Cup*? It's one of my favorites."

"Can't say that I have."

"Here, take a look at it. You can take it with you, if you like, and then you could return it on your way back with Kara. That way, you won't forget to stop by."

"We won't forget." He smiles. "But I am not sure when exactly that will be."

"That's okay. I've read it many times and would like to share it. That's what good stories are for!"

"Then I will take it along. And thank you!"

They continue on, talking and looking at books for another hour. Goldie looks over at her sister in the chair, slumped over in sleep again. "I better help get her up to bed now. I've enjoyed talking with you. See you in the morning!" She taps her sister on the shoulder, and she startles awake. "Come on, sleepyhead. Let's go up to bed."

They head up the wooden staircase together, and Dominic settles down on his pallet by the fire. The fire crackles and flickers, and he stares into it, feeling warm and tired. He thinks of Kara and whispers a prayer for her safety and protection. "Hopefully, I will be back with her by tomorrow evening. Lord, please help me find her quickly. And thank you for this job and the money for the journey. You always take care of me."

He smiles to himself, and a sense of peace washes over him. "Everything's going to be okay," he whispers to himself, drifting off into sleep.

The Scroll

Vespes steals a glance at Mira's face as she sits beside him in the coach, while Trea talks about the scenery in the kingdom around them. She has been doing most of the talking, and Vespes is grateful to have her along, especially since he feels at a loss for words. He is captivated by Mira's beauty and wishes he could think of something interesting to say, but he feels weak and foolish.

"And this is the Royal Bakery, where they make the very best bread in the kingdom. Would you like to go in for a treat? They usually have warm tarts on display." She looks at Mira, who is trying her best to look interested, but her mind is somewhere else.

"Actually, I'm still quite full from breakfast. Maybe we could stop by there on the way back."

"Of course! That's a much better idea. Now, over here to the left is Windmere Park. It has many lovely flowering trees and walking paths. We should go walking there one day while you are here with us. There's a large waterbird area with Germanian peacocks. They fly freely all around the park and are quite beautiful. Some people say that even sterradors have been spotted there. Though I've never seen one, as they are quite rare."

"Yes, I've heard of them but never seen one myself. I would be happy to go walking there with you. It sounds like a lovely place." Mira smiles weakly, but it takes a lot of effort. All she wants to do is think about Arten and figure out why he left so suddenly with the others. *It doesn't make sense! He loves me. Or does he? Maybe all these strong feelings I have are not shared by him. Was he just using me? Toying with me for his own pleasure?* She feels a hot surge of anger flare up inside her.

"Princess?" Vespes begins.

"Please, call me Mira. There is no need for us to be so formal. And may I call you Vespes?"

"Of course, I would like that. I was thinking that after lunch we could go riding together on the grounds behind the castle. What do you think?"

"Actually, I would like to practice with my bow and arrow some. Could we go to a place where we could do that?"

"Absolutely. There are many good trails in the woods on the castle grounds. I'll bring my bow as well, and we can practice together." He shifts his weight, and his arm brushes against hers. She seems to notice and pulls her cloak around her, moving her arm away.

"Are we heading back to the castle now?" she asks, looking out the window.

"Yes, we are." He can't think of anything else intelligent to say. He looks at Trea, hoping she'll jump in.

Trea smiles at him knowingly. "Mira, I asked Cora, our cook, if she knew how to make that potato pie you talked about. She said she has an old recipe that she thought would do—she's making it for our lunch today!"

"That's wonderful," she says with some effort, turning back to look at Trea. "I'm feeling quite hungry again."

Later, after a satisfying lunch, Mira speaks up. "That was the best potato pie I've ever tasted. It's honestly way better than what we have at home. You must tell Cora she did an amazing job."

"I will." Trea smiles. She starts to ask if she can go along on the riding excursion with them, then reconsiders. *I'll let them have some time alone together,* she thinks to herself.

"Do you need some time to recharge before we go out riding?" says Vespes, trying to be considerate.

"Yes, I think I'll just head up to my room for a little while before we go."

"Perfect. Let me escort you up." He pushes his chair back and offers his arm to her, trying not to seem overeager.

Mira enters her room and quickly shuts the door. Vespes feels an electric sensation on his arm from her touch. He feels unsteady, smitten. *What is wrong with me? I need to get ahold of myself. But all*

I want to do is be with her. He heads back over to his office and sits down at his desk, putting his head in his hands. Trea enters.

"Vespes! How are you doing? Isn't she amazing?"

He looks up at her, not sure if he should share what he has been feeling.

"What is it?" she asks.

"Nothing. I mean, of course, she's great."

"That's it? She's great? I think you're feeling more than you're saying."

"I'm just beginning to get to know her, just like you."

"Don't you think she is beautiful?"

"She is stunning." He lets the words slip out. "Half the time I don't know what to say around her."

Trea smiles. "Just be yourself. The words will come."

"Easy for you to say. You never seem to be short on words."

"I guess it's just my natural talent. Honestly, though, it is so nice to have another woman to talk to. I hope she stays a long time."

"Yes, well, I need to tend to some paperwork here before we head out. Were you planning on coming with us?" He is hoping she says no, but part of him wants her to come along and help with the conversation.

"No. I'm a bit tired and don't feel like riding today. And I have my studies to catch up on."

"Very well, then, we'll see you around dinnertime."

She nods and heads back out the door, smiling to herself. Heading back to her room, she passes the guest room where Mira is. The door is shut, and she pauses for a moment, wanting to knock and go in to talk with her some more. As she stands there, she listens and hears what sounds like muffled sobs. "Is she crying?" She listens more intently, but the sound has stopped. "I must have been imagining it." She stands there a moment more, torn on what to do, but then decides to give Mira her privacy and check on her later.

She heads to her room and ponders her thoughts about Mira and Vespes. *He certainly seems taken with her, but I can't tell what she is feeling. I'll just try to get to know her more, and maybe she will confide in me.* Sighing, Trea pulls out her study book on geography to prepare for her next test. Her tutor told her it would be in a few days, so she had better get on it. Turning the pages, she pauses on a map of the Northern Territories.

Tracing with her finger, she follows the map from Silvenia, up past the Copper Hills, over the town of Brigon, to the River Glace. Past the river were forests and the Mountains of Palledor, and to the east of that, Icelandia, up in the far north.

"Such a far northern kingdom! I wonder if they even have a summer there." She stares at the map, trying to imagine what it must be like there. "Mira said they see white ice foxes and sometimes even snow leopards," she tells Mirabelle, who has her eyes closed and is purring contentedly. "It sounds like a fascinating place. But probably too cold for us."

She turns back to her current study chapter and begins to read about the topography of the western mountain region of Paredonia. "Ugh, Mirabelle, this is so boring! But I need to get a good grade on this test, so study I must. Let's go over the facts of this region again. The western mountain region is known for…"

While she studies, Mira is in her room, studying her mother's scroll. She wasn't planning on it; it seemed to draw her attention as soon as she entered the room. She lay on her bed for a little while, thinking about Arten, releasing a few fresh tears, wondering why he left her without a word, and then she reached for the scroll.

Pulling it out of her drawer (hidden inside the lining of one of her riding hats), she opens it once again. She sits on her bed, her eyes scanning over the instructions once more.

Win over the affections of the king and his royal family.

She closes her eyes and sees Trea smiling and talking, treating her like a sister already. She thinks of Vespes, his awkwardness around her, his gentleness. *But he is just like any other man. Luring me in so he can get what he wants. Selfish and cruel.* Her mind drifts quickly back to Arten. *He has broken my heart! I feel it shattered within me. Broken in a million pieces. Please come back for me! How can you be so cold?*

Another tear trickles down her face as she feels compelled to continue reading:

- *I must marry the king.*
- *Mother will come to take over the rule of this kingdom.*
- *I must poison the king. I must kill Vespes.*
- *I will have my own kingdom to rule over.*
- *To be a queen, I must pass the test.*

She sees her mother, the empress, standing before her. "I know you will not let me down."

"I must do this. I have no choice." She feels broken, overruled. "If I do this, I will have my own kingdom and any husband I want. Or perhaps Mother is right. Maybe there is no such thing as love."

"Seek power, not love, my daughter," she remembers her saying. "With great power you will rule. Love is a myth, and the price for it is a broken heart. Do not be deceived by your youthful heart."

Mira puts the scroll back inside the drawer. "I will do it. I will accomplish my task and become an empress like my mother. I will make Arten wish he had never left me!" She feels strangely empowered, and she stares at her fingertips smudged with more ink from the scroll. Her hand reaches up and marks stripes with it down her wet cheeks.

"I am powerful. I, Mira, will be queen. Everyone will fear me." She gets up and pulls out her bow and arrows. "Time for some target practice."

The Mysterious Picture

I look around the dimly lit pub. I am drinking down a concoction of warm apple cider ale, and there is a plate of baked fish set before me. Buddy is at my side, lying on the floor, and thankfully, no one has commented on that. As I sip my drink, I notice a picture on the wall. It looks strangely familiar. There is a door that is shut, and a man walking up to it. As I stare at the picture, it seems to come alive.

The man walks up to the door and stops. He raises his hand to knock. Suddenly, a server blocks my view and asks if I need anything.

"No, thank you, I'm fine."

I look back at the picture. It's not in motion now. Squinting, I try to put it in better focus but can't see it very well in the low light of the room. "Stay here, Buddy." I get up to take a closer look. Standing in front of the picture, I take it in.

There is a man facing toward the door, with his hand raised to knock. "Wait a minute, wasn't he walking up to the door when I first looked?" The picture is framed in wood painted with antique gold. I raise my hand to touch the edge of it. I take note of the man in the picture. He is dressed in a robe, with a brown cloak on his back. His hair is light brown and wavy, just grazing the top of his shoulders. I can't see his face.

"Miss, is everything all right?" The server approaches me as I stand staring at the image.

"Oh, yes, I was just admiring this picture. Can you tell me anything about it?"

He looks at it briefly. "I'm sorry. I don't know much about it. Would you like me to ask the owner?"

"No, that's okay," I say, not wanting to draw attention to myself. "I was just curious." I quickly sit back down next to Buddy, and he thumps his tail.

"Are you finished with your meal? Can I get you anything else?"

"Yes, I'm done eating. But I did want to see if there were any rooms available in the inn upstairs for tonight?"

"I'll check for you." He lifts up my plate and hurries off again.

As I wait, I look back at the picture. It doesn't move. "Wow, I must be really tired. My mind is playing tricks on me, boy," I say, patting his head below me.

Buddy pants and looks up at me with his dog smile. "Don't worry, I set aside some food for you. I'll give it to you once we get our room for the night."

The server returns and places a key down in front of me on the table. "Here you go, madame. It's for room 27, up the stairs and down the hall to your right."

"Thank you," I say, paying him for the dinner. "I appreciate it."

I don't bother to ask about the dog, mostly because I don't want to take no for an answer. Buddy and I quietly make our exit together toward the stairway. As we ascend, the room below darkens and the voices melt away. I walk down the hallway at the top of the stairs, slowly, as if in a dream. I touch my head, wondering if I had to much of that ale at dinner and now it's affecting me.

I pass a few other doorways, numbered 25, 26, and finally I come to room 27. It's a large wooden door on the right side of the hall. I put in the key and turn it. Stepping inside, I look around at our bedroom for the night. It has a small bed, with a little cupboard next to it, and a water pitcher on top. Buddy jumps up on top of the bed and looks at me, thumping his tail.

I suddenly feel very tired, and I lie down on the bed next to Buddy. Closing my eyes, I lie there for a moment. I don't know if I've fallen asleep or not, but the next moment, I shoot up from a knock on the door.

"Who is it?" I call out apprehensively. No answer. I look at Buddy, and he is asleep on the bed next to me. "I must have dreamed it," I reason to myself. Relaxing back into the bed, I lie awake for a while, staring at the ceiling. I realize sleep is elusive now, so I finally decide to get up and look at the map again over by the lamplight. I struggle to rise up but feel like I'm being pressed down. I can't move my arms. A sense of panic rises up in me, and I try to speak, but when I open my mouth, no words come out, only my breath.

Then, my chest feels so tight I feel like I can't take another breath. I close my eyes and hear my own scream inside my head. "Jesus!" I call out. It lifts. I can breathe again.

I sit up, gasping and rubbing my arms, which I can move easily now. Buddy jumps up, too, and licks my face. "I'm okay now, Buddy. I don't know what that was, though." I look around the room nervously. I should still be feeling fear, but I sense a presence in the room now that is full of peace.

I suddenly remember the Bible in my sack, and I reach over next to my bed and pull it out. Flipping it open, I scan through the pages, searching. There it is, Psalm 91. I begin to read through it: "He shall cover you with His feathers, and under His wings you shall take refuge. His truth shall be your shield and buckler. You shall not be afraid of the terror by night, Nor of the arrow that flies by day, Nor of the pestilence that walks in darkness, Nor of the destruction that lays waste at noonday" (Ps. 91:4–6 NKJV).

Terror by night. "I'd say that was definitely a terror by night. And I want no more of it. Jesus, be my shield. I rest in You." I pray a little while longer, feeling comforted and peaceful once again. Then I fall back into sleep.

As I sleep, light surrounds me in the darkness. I am not alone.

The next time I awaken, light is streaming in the only window, and I can hear the birds singing. Getting up, I open the shutters fully and look out. I am surprised by two birds that fly off my windowsill when I lean out to breathe in the morning air.

"Sorry, I didn't mean to frighten you!" I call out after them. I watch them alight on a tall tree next to the inn. Looking out on the town, I notice there are a few people walking about, and the sound of horse hooves clopping down the road. Buddy barks, and I look back at him. "Okay, I know, let's go down and get some breakfast." He jumps off the bed, tail wagging, and rubs against me. I pat his head.

Downstairs in the pub, I grab us both a biscuit and some water and then head for the front door to pay the host. I notice the picture again as we walk past it and pause again for a moment. It looks the same as last night, a man with his hand raised to knock on a wooden door.

"Do you think they will open the door?" says a man standing next to me. Startled, I look up at his voice and sees a tall man with blond hair and bright eyes. He is wearing a white shirt and brown pants. His eyes are bright and appear to look right into me.

"What did you say?" I stammer.

"I said, do you think they will open the door?"

"I…I don't know. I mean, it's just a picture. I don't know what to make of it."

"It's a picture of the king. He is knocking on the door. You must tell them to open it."

"Tell who?"

Just then, a man begins to yell, "Hey, who let that dog in here? No pets allowed!" I turn in the direction of the voice and see a large, burly man walking quickly toward us. I look back at the man who was just speaking, but he is not there. Looking around the room, I don't see him anywhere.

I face the burly man, who is now standing in front of me, frowning down at Buddy. "What's he doing in here? You're going to have to take him out."

"Yes, of course. I just need to pay my bill."

He holds out his hand. "You can pay me. I'm the owner. And if you want to stay another night, your dog will have to stay outside."

"I understand," I say. "I apologize. I will plan to stay somewhere else, then, tonight. How much do I owe you?"

"Fifteen gildens," he demands, still holding out his hand in front of me.

"Here you go," I say, handing him the coins.

"Very well. Now please take your pet outside, where he belongs."

I want more time to look around the room and search for the tall man, but the owner is standing there with his arms crossed, so I head outside, leading Buddy on his rope leash.

Outside, I look up and down the road, thinking maybe he just left the inn in a hurry. There is no one around except a small peddler making his way down the road with his mule and a cart full of vegetables. Sighing, I adjust my sack and cloak and look down again at Buddy. "I guess it's time to hit the road again, ready or not."

Walking on down the road, I try to remember the name of the other inn the merchant told me about. It escapes me. "Well, let's just keep heading down this road toward the castle and see where it takes us."

As we walk along, I think of the man in the pub by the picture. "That was odd," I say aloud to myself and Buddy. "In fact, everything surrounding that picture was strange." I remember the painting in my mind. I suddenly realize it reminds me of a picture of Jesus I saw when I was a child. Beneath the scene it said something. I search my memory, and it comes to me: "Behold, I stand at the door and knock" (Rev. 3:20 NKJV).

It is clear in my mind now, and I'm amazed at how this scripture verse just came to me. "God is trying to tell me something, Buddy." He looks up at me and stops, tail wagging in response. "Oh, right. Here's some more biscuit. I forgot about our breakfast, thinking about what that tall stranger said to me."

We share the last morsel of bread between us. "Let's explore this city a bit. Maybe we can find a more detailed map to Silvenia." We follow the main road as it circles widely around the castle. There are shops and barns, homes and cottages, both large and small. There are people all around us, walking to and fro, busy with their own lives.

Most of the stores in this city don't allow me to bring Buddy in, so I have to tie him outside. I find another bookstore and head in to see if there are any more maps available.

Inside, a clerk tells me they only have some historical books with maps in them but I am welcome to look at them. He points me in the direction of where they are located. I pull out a historical book entitled *Kings and Kingdoms: A Historical Record*. Flipping through it, I see many different references to places unknown to me. Finally, toward the back, I find a chapter on the kingdom of Silvenia.

I read a paragraph or two about a king who ruled there apparently many years ago, a King Rudgray. His wife was Queen Eleanor, and they had five children. I go on to read about their lives and what went on during their reign. It seems his reign was followed at his death by his son, who became King Jules, who also was married, and his wife was Queen Abigail. I follow on down the line of the genealogy, until I come to a familiar name of one of the descendants, Prince Rufus. "Could that be King Vespes's father that Dominic spoke of? The one that was injured and unable to rule?"

I ponder this as I glance out the window at Buddy. He is sitting patiently, tied to a post meant for horses outside the door. I flip through the pages, looking for a more detailed map of the kingdom, and find one with an old layout of the castle grounds and surrounding city. I study it briefly and then put it back on the shelf. It looks quite similar to Rondival, except that the palace seems larger there and it's more on the western side of the city instead of right in the center.

"Well, I can't be lugging around another big book with me while I'm traveling. I don't think I need to get this one," I reason to myself. Heading back out the door, I wave my thanks to the clerk. "Come on, Buddy, let's find that other inn and make sure it will welcome us both. Don't worry, we're in this together."

We continue on down the cobblestone road, with two diligent birds flying swiftly behind us.

The Bird

Julia looks down at her sleeping sister. She is breathing on her own, eyes closed, completely still.

"Can I have a few minutes with her by myself?" she says, looking at her mom and dad.

"Of course, dear. We'll be right out here in the hall." Josephine Alder grabs her husband's arm and pulls him gently toward the door. They walk out together and quietly close the door behind them. Julia looks around at all the humming monitors and tubes surrounding her sister. She has an IV, a catheter, and a heart monitor. She gently puts her hand on top of Kara's and squeezes it.

"Kara...Kara, it's me. Wake up, I need to talk to you." She touches her cheek. "Kara!"

No response.

"Come on, I need you to wake up and argue with me! How can you be in a coma when you were perfectly fine the last time I saw you?" She stares at her closed eyelids; they seem to flutter for a moment, then nothing. "Kara, I'm sorry. I'm sorry for how mean I've been to you. I'm sorry for pushing you away. I need you back, now. Please come back!"

The heart monitor pulses on the chart slowly and steadily. She watches a drop fall from the IV tube. Holding Kara's limp hand, she puts her head down on top of it. "I won't let you leave me!" The minute hand on the wall clock ticks slowly around, the only sound in the room as Julia waits, hoping for some sign of life from her only sister. She is still in this position when a nurse opens the door and comes in.

"I don't mean to disturb you, but I need to change her IV bag. It should only take a moment."

Julia sits up abruptly. "It's okay. I was just about to go out, anyway." She heads to the door and looks out into the hall.

"Are you all right?" her mother says, walking back up the hall to her.

"Yes, I'm fine. Where's Dad?"

"He went to find some coffee. Did you get enough time alone with her for now?"

"Yeah, I think I'll head down to the cafeteria, too, and find Dad."

"All right, I'm going to go in with her for a little while now."

"Okay." Julia hurries down the hall, not looking back at her mom. She doesn't want to cry, and she feels the pain bubbling up inside, threatening to spill out. Josephine turns and heads in to sit with her daughter.

Julia finds her dad standing in the cafeteria, looking out the window, with a cup of coffee steaming in his hands. She walks up to him. "Hey, Dad, what are you looking at?"

"Hmm? Oh, nothing in particular. I just got my coffee and was about to head back down the hall to see Kara." He pauses for a moment and looks at Julia. "It's just a little hard for me to see her like that. I guess it is for you too." He clears his throat. "Would you like something to drink? I can get you some coffee or something."

"No thanks. You can head back down there with Mom. I'm just going to sit here and wait for you in the cafeteria. Like you said, it's kind of hard to see her like that." He waits a moment, stirring his coffee. "And don't worry about me," she adds. "I'm fine. I just think I've had enough of hospital rooms for the moment."

"Okay, we won't be long." He turns and head back down the corridor toward Kara's room.

Julia sits at the little table by the window and pulls out her phone. She scrolls through Instagram for a few minutes and then puts her phone down on the table in frustration. Same old stuff, nothing of any importance. Drumming her fingers on the table, she looks outside to the parking lot.

The sun is beating down on the black pavement, and there are cars parked everywhere. To the right, there is a little sitting area with a bench and a few small bushes around it. She crosses her arms and rubs her sleeveless skin. *It's freezing in here!* she thinks to herself. *Maybe I will get some coffee just to warm up.* As she starts to get up, suddenly something rushes toward the window in front of her and bangs into the glass.

Julia jumps back, startled. "What was that?" She looks down and there is a bird, stunned, lying on the ground. "It flew straight into the window. Poor thing." She crouches down low to get a closer look. It's lying still, but she can tell it's breathing. Slowly it begins to move. She puts her hand to the glass. It jumps up on its feet again and shakes its head and wings, stretching them out.

It's a pretty bird, bluish-black, with a golden beak and white spots on its wings. It looks at her, cocking its head to one side, as if studying her. As she watches, it hops over to the bushes and picks up a leaf from off the ground and then hops back over to the window. It drops the leaf on the ground in front of the window and stands there, staring at her.

"What are you doing, little bird? You can't build a nest in here." She puts her finger up to the window, and he watches her hand curiously. "You're a funny little thing. I wonder if you're disoriented from your fall. I'll come out there to visit you." Julia gets up and heads to the nearest exit sign just outside the cafeteria. She pushes the door and heads out into the bright sunshine.

She notices the many cigarette butts on the ground leading up to the bench area. Slowly approaching the bushes, she looks down low for the bird. At the same time, a loud whirring noise disturbs the quiet. It's a maintenance man with a leaf blower, and he's heading straight toward the little grassy area close to Julia. He has earplugs in and sunglasses on and doesn't notice Julia until he turns fully toward her. Abruptly, he changes direction and heads away from her with a small wave.

She waves back, then turns back to look for the bird. It is gone. She looks all around but doesn't see it anywhere. "Well, I guess you weren't hurt. That's good." She walks up to the spot where he dropped the little leaf. That is gone too. There are a few scattered leaves on the ground, but none that look like the one he was holding.

She sits down on the little bench and slumps down, putting her hand in her pockets. She feels something in her left pocket. "Oh yeah, it's the leaf from Kara's room." She pulls it out and looks at it again. The colors are still vibrant and fresh. "I'll hang on to this for you, sis. I can see why you picked it up. It's very pretty. I will keep it with me as a way of keeping you close in my thoughts."

Sighing, she puts it back in her pocket and decides to sit outside and wait for her parents. They would see her through the window, anyway. Closing her eyes, she soaks in the warmth of the sun. The image of the brightly colored leaf hangs in her mind. She sees it on a large tree, then falling off, spinning in circles, until it reaches the ground. The ground is covered with these beautiful leaves. She hears birds singing and sees them flying around these trees, and every now and then, one swoops down and picks up a leaf and flies off. They look like the bird she just saw.

Opening her eyes, she looks around, past the bushes, into the parking lot. There are no birds to be seen now. Just a few people walking out to their cars. Julia feels empty and lost. "I feel like I need to do something, but what? How can I get you back, Kara? How can I fix things?" She feels like she needs a drink, to take the edge off; a couple of strong drinks would do the trick. "I just need to sleep. This is all too painful. I'm tired of feeling pain. At least you're not feeling pain, Kara, wherever you are. I need to find a way to get you to come back."

"Julia, are you okay out here?" She looks up and sees her dad and mom standing in front of her. She realizes she must have been mumbling to herself.

"Yes, I'm fine. Just feeling tired. Can we go home now?"

"Yes, of course. Let's go." The three of them head out to the car together, Ed with his arm around his wife, and Julia trailing along behind them.

When they arrive back home, Julia heads straight for the stairs. "I'm going to lie down for a little while."

"Okay, and remember, we're both here if you need anything."

"Thanks, Mom. I'm fine." Closing the door behind her, she waits a moment and then reaches up into her closet for one of her hidden stashes of alcohol. She opens a bottle of red wine and drinks a few gulps straight from the bottle. She feels the warmth ease down her throat and soothe her. "Just a few sips to calm me. I know how you bite back, and I definitely don't want to end up back in a hospital again."

Replacing the cap, she stuffs it under her bed and sits down. Looking at the floor, she sees a red wine stain that looks like it's been scrubbed—probably by her mother. The empty bottle that was there is gone. "At least she didn't say anything to me about it." She traces her feelings of guilt to anger, to bitterness. Rubbing her forehead, she lies back on the bed, stuffing the feelings down and away from her mind.

She tries to fall asleep but just lies there, staring at the ceiling. "A few more sips will help me sleep." She reaches under the bed again and pulls out the bottle again. As she does, something catches her eye. A flash of bluish-black at the window.

Julia drops the bottle and slowly gets up to go to the window. Incredibly, right there, sitting on the rooftop, just below her windowsill, is the bird she saw at the hospital. She is sure of it. She puts her fingers up to the glass, and the bird looks up at her and hops closer. "Did you follow me home?"

She studies it. It certainly looks like the same bird. Bluish-black feathers, gold beak, white spots on the wings. She remembers the leaf it had in its mouth. She pulls out Kara's leaf and holds it up to the glass. It hops forward, all the way up to the window. It cocks its head sideways and looks up at her.

"This is Kara's leaf. I can't give it to you. But I can tell you like it." She begins to open the window carefully, not wanting to scare him off, but curious to see what it will do. It hops back a few paces but doesn't fly away.

"Hi, little guy. Did you come to visit me?" She reaches her arm out the window toward it. He doesn't move; he is looking at the leaf in her other hand. "Sorry, I can't let you have that," she says, stuffing it back down into her pocket. It hops back a little more as she slowly climbs out the window onto the roof.

This is the kind of roof you can easily climb out on and sit for a while. It isn't steeply sloped beneath the window area, and when Julia and Kara were younger, they would sometimes sit out there for hours together, watching for falling stars. "I'll just sit right here with you, and we can get to know each other a little better," she says a few feet away from the bird.

It watches her with interest, and when she reaches out toward it this time, it flutters its wings and flies over her to the other side of the window. "What are you up to? Are you still interested in that leaf I showed you? Maybe you're hungry. I didn't think of that. Next time I'll have to bring you some bread or something." He watches her silently and hops a bit closer.

"Where did you come from? I don't think I've seen a bird like you before." They sit there together, watching each other for a few minutes. Julia tries to sit very still and waits to see if it will get any closer. "I feel like you're trying to tell me something."

Without warning, it flutters its wings and soars off the roof, dips low below Julia's line of sight, and disappears. "Wait, come back!" she calls out to her strange, new little friend. She sits there, waiting for a few minutes to see if he'll come back, but he doesn't. While he was there, she felt distracted from the pain, and oddly enough, this brought her a bit of encouragement and hope.

That is one thing she and Kara have in common. They both like animals and feel at ease around them. Their cat, Percy, has been missing for a while. He likes to wander, though, and had been gone for weeks at a time before but always seemed to find his way back home. Looking out below on the ground beneath her, she takes a moment to look for his fluffy gray fur, but there is no sign of him.

Climbing back in through the window, Julia picks up the wine bottle and stuffs it back up high in her closet. She paces the floor in her room for a few moments, thinking. Reaching her hand down in her pocket, she pulls out the leaf and places it on her dresser, inside her old jewelry box. She cranks the key, and the little ballerina inside twirls on its pedestal, the music box cranking out a melodic tune. Julia sits there, staring at it, wondering at the incident with the bird and thinking about Kara.

A Secret Room

Previously, in the forest of Elmwood...

Time is running short, and Lady Vallora realizes the importance of Kara reaching Silvenia in time. "She cannot be delayed any longer," she tells her sister, Sabine. "Something is wrong, out of place. I'm not sure what it is, but I think we need to send help."

"Why don't we send a starling back to her world to check on her family? I'm sure it is affecting their timeline as well. Maybe something from home is holding her back."

"My heart tells me we only have a few weeks left for her to accomplish her task. The evil coming from the north is getting stronger and needs to be pushed back. Do we know from the starlings if Dominic has reached her yet?"

"According to their last report, he is just a day away. Kara is staying in the kingdom of Rondival."

"Very well, let us pray that he reaches her by tomorrow. They cannot delay any longer than that. Send a starling to her home, as you said. Let me know as soon as you can what he finds out, if anything." Sabine nods and walks off toward the Sacred Forest, calling as she goes.

The starlings are in flight, circling above her head in the small clearing. "Flyn, where are you?"

A single bird descends and alights on her shoulder.

"Hello, fearless Flyn! I need you to go to the other world for me and check on Kara's home and family. Will you do that for me?" It chirps a quick response. "You know from Perk where she lives. I just need you to report back anything unusual. Look in the windows, follow where they go, and report back to me what you see."

It chirps a reply.

"No, you're not bringing any keys with you this time. This is just to check on her home and family and report back anything unusual that you may find. Go swiftly. I'll be waiting." She releases him up into the air, and he takes off, high into the sky, singing a clear note that echoes into the wind. He flies speedily, taken up by the currents of wind, to the portal in the sky.

It's been a few days now, and Sabine watches each day for Flyn's return. Perk and his flock have relayed to her that Kara has now left Rondival as of yesterday morning and is headed toward the Blain Bridge crossing with her dog. Perk and Blue stay close to her now, sending the others of their flock back and forth as messengers. Dominic has left Averton but has not found her yet—he has been asking questions around Rondival, at the inns and with a few contacts of his in the city. He's staying with one of his contacts at the moment, and they are searching throughout the city, working together. It is his old friend Morton, a shoemaker.

Morton knows all the places a newcomer in town might stay at, and they are asking everyone if they have seen a young woman with brown hair, light-blue eyes, and freckles, possibly wearing a red cloak, traveling alone. So far, no one remembers seeing someone like that. But they continue on diligently with their search, until there is just one more inn for him to check, the Gleaming Gables Inn.

"Excuse me," he says, walking into the pub, "my name is Dominic. May I speak with the owner or manager of this place?" Before him sits a large, stocky man at a little wooden table close to the entrance of the inn. He is focusing on counting some coins in a metal box before him on the table. The man ignores him for a moment, finishes calculating something in his head, lips moving silently, and then slams the box shut and looks up at him. Dominic takes a step back, recognizing that this man doesn't seem to be in a very hospitable mood at the moment.

With a furrowed brow, he states, "I am the owner. If you're looking for a room for tonight, we don't have any more rooms available. We are completely booked. You can check back tomorrow."

"Oh, no, sir. I just wanted to ask a simple question."

The man stares at him with a look of irritation on his face. "What is it? I'm quite busy at the moment."

"I'm looking for my friend, a young woman. She has brown hair and freckles, light-blue eyes, traveling alone. I thought maybe she might have stayed here per chance? She is not familiar with this city, and I think she might be lost."

"We get lots of people here that are traveling alone. And I don't remember seeing anyone like that. The only young woman I remember seeing here recently had a dog with her, and I wouldn't allow her to bring the dog in here, so she went somewhere else."

"A dog? What sort of dog? Do you remember? And do you recall if she was wearing a red cloak?"

"I don't know. It was a mangy-looking mutt, if you ask me. I have no idea what she was wearing. That was a couple of days ago. Now, if you don't mind, I need to get back to work."

"Of course. Thank you so much, sir." Dominic bows politely and steps out of his way. The owner brushes past him, with the metal box in his hand. Dominic looks around the pub for a moment, searching, but nothing catches his eye.

A dog? Could that have been Kara? I know she likes animals. Maybe she has found a new traveling companion. He ponders this as he goes back out onto the street. He is supposed to meet back up with Morton at his shop within the hour. "Maybe he's already found her," he says to himself hopefully, picking up the pace.

Morton is in his shop, inspecting the sole of a newly made boot, when Dominic arrives. Morton looks up and smiles. "How did it go? Anyone see her?"

"Not that I know of for sure. The owner of the Gleaming Gables mentioned seeing a woman traveling by herself with a dog a few days ago. That's my only lead. What about you?"

"Well, I just checked at the last inn on my list, Rafter Point. The owner wasn't there, but the lady in charge said there was a young woman there a few nights ago, with a dog, like you said. She only remembered her staying one night."

"Did she say anything else? Any other details?"

"Just that she was wearing a red cloak," he said, smiling.

Eagerly, Dominic grabs his newly found walking stick from the corner of the shop. "That's got to be her! Did she say anything else to the lady? Like, maybe where she was heading? Did she ask for directions?"

"No, not that she remembered. She did describe the dog in detail to me, though. She said that it was fluffy and had dark-brown fur with some white mixed in. She said it was a sweet dog and that they usually didn't allow pets to stay but it was very well behaved so she allowed it for that one night."

"Well, I better get going, then. She's got to be headed toward Silvenia by now. Even if she's still here in the city somewhere, you can keep a lookout for her and tell her to come and meet me there, at the Silver Palace. Do you have the map I left with you to give to her?"

"Yes, I've got it right here in my drawer," he says, patting the wooden cabinet beside him. He walks toward the back of his shop. "Here, take this sack of bread and cheese I purchased. You'll need it on the road."

"Thank you, my friend. I hope to see you again soon."

"Until then, safe travels to you!" They pat each other on the back, and Dominic heads out the door. Walking stick in hand, he heads back out onto the cobblestone road. He walks at a fast pace, feeling an urgency to make up for lost time. Before long, he finds himself at the southwest gate of the city, leaving Rondival behind. It is about ten miles or so to the Blain Bridge from there.

"On to Silvenia!" he says with determination.

*****

I stand at the entrance to the bridge. It's much broader than the other one and curves high above the river. Plenty of other people have been traveling along this road and passing on ahead of us with their horses and carts. "This is not like the other bridge," I tell Buddy. "I'm sure it's much safer. But maybe we should wait until someone else comes along before we cross it. What do you think, Bud?" He looks up at me, tail thumping.

"We've been walking for a long time. Why don't we sit down in the grass here for a moment and have a snack? Maybe someone else will come along and we can watch them cross over first." I sit down in the grass and pat the spot next to me. Buddy comes up alongside me and lies down, panting.

I pour him some water and then drink some myself. Then we share some bread and dried meat from my sack. Looking at the road, I say out loud, "I wonder how far it is to Silvenia after we cross over. We must have walked at least eight to ten miles already."

Looking down the road, I see two mules approaching, pulling a cart with a couple of people on board. "Yay! We are not alone!" I look down at Buddy, who is still chewing on a sausage stick. "Get ready, Buddy. We're going to follow them across."

As they pass, I see they are a family, a man and his wife, with three children in the back. They have baskets full of grain loaded all around them. I wave at them as they go by, and the children wave back. I let them get ahead a bit, and then we get up and begin to cross over the large bridge together.

The river is coursing swiftly below us, and it's a pretty sight, but I don't take time to linger. I remember all too well my last bridge experience. After we are safely across, I do take a moment to quickly peek under the bridge but see nothing except the river water and tall reeds of grass. "Come on, Buddy. Let's pick up the pace. The sooner we get to Silvenia, the better."

The sun is high in the sky now and beating down upon us. It's hot, and I am looking forward to being up among the shade of the forest trees that are visible just up ahead to the right. To my left, in the distance, there are not many trees; in fact, it looks like a desert, with sandy-looking mountains to the south. But up ahead, the road curves to the right and heads in a northerly direction, and there are many tall trees there and what looks like a thick forest. I remember from looking at the map that Silvenia is along the main route to the north, so we head in that direction. I look around for signs that point to the kingdom of Silvenia, but so far, I haven't seen any.

"I hope this is the right road, Buddy. We'll ask the next person we see along the road. Until then, we must press on." We are now on the outskirts of the forest, and there are many brightly colored birds flying around through the trees. I also notice some iridescent green and blue flowers along the side of the road that look very unusual. They shimmer in the sunlight and are dripping some kind of fragrant oil from their petals. I pick one up and get the oil all over my fingers. It smells fresh, like eucalyptus leaves, but also sweet like berries.

"These are amazing," I tell Buddy. "I wish Dominic were here, so he could tell me what these are." I hold my hands to my face and breathe it in. I feel my head clearing, with a sense of clarity and alertness. "Wow, this is better than coffee! I should bring some of this with me." I reach down and gather a small bunch and put it in my sack.

Since we left the bridge area, I have released Buddy from the leash, and now he is exploring deeper into the woods. "Buddy, don't go too far! I don't want you to get lost!" I can tell he is now on the trail of something, sniffing intensely and going farther in. The forest is getting thicker, but there is not as much underbrush as in the swamp area, and I can still see him.

He darts after something and then stops at the base of a large tree, barking. "What is it, Buddy? Come back over here!" He keeps on barking and looking up into the tree, one paw on the trunk. I look back at the road. "I can see plainly where the road is. I guess it can't hurt to go see what he's looking at." I walk forward deeper into the forest.

Sunlight comes down in shafts between the trees, and I soak in the beauty of the woodland scene around me. My feet crunch on the leaves below, and I look at all the different wildflowers around me. "Buddy!" I'm getting closer to the tree now, and I look up to see what he is barking at.

It's a large, wide-trunked tree with long piney branches hanging down. It looks very old. Squinting, I peer up into the thick branches but don't see anything at first. Then, suddenly, one of the knobs on the trunk opens like a window, and a bright little creature with wings flits out very quickly. Buddy goes crazy with barking and jumps around, trying to follow it. I try to follow it with my eyes, but it is very quick, flitting from tree to tree at a rapid pace. Then it comes back to the main tree where it came out from and settles on a branch high up above us. I can't make it out anymore.

Buddy sniffs at the base of the tree and scratches at it. "I think it's a vayaklos. We should leave it alone. Come on, Buddy. Let's get back to the road." And just as quickly as I've said this, a green vine on the ground suddenly moves and wraps itself around my leg at the ankle. It pulls me closer to the tree trunk.

"What in the world?" I gasp as it pulls me sharply and quickly to the tree. I reach down to undo it, and more of the vine shoots up and encircles my other leg as well. Buddy barks ferociously at the plant and tries to pull it away from me with his mouth. I remember my knife in the knapsack and reach inside quickly to find it.

Before I can locate it, the vine grabs onto my arms as well, and I am fastened to the tree. I look helplessly at Buddy, who is barking frantically. "Buddy, go get help!" He continues to bark and snap at the vine along the base of the tree.

Finally, he seems to recognize that it's not working, and he takes off, running back toward the road. "Good boy!" I call after him. "Go find someone to help us!" I watch him weave in and out of the trees as the vines pull me closer to the trunk. Then, just when it seems to have stopped, I hear a click, like a latch opening, and I am pulled into the tree itself.

The trunk becomes a door and opens into itself. The vines shift and release me as I'm thrust inside, and then quickly, the door closes, sealing me in. I find myself standing inside a dark, hollow room inside the trunk of the tree.

A small shaft of light is coming from above, and I look up toward it. It's coming from a high circular window, and there are a few others like it close by, but they are shut. I press on the walls of the tree surrounding me. "Where is the door handle? There's got to be a way to open this from the inside." Squinting in the dark, I can just make out the outline of the door, but there seems to be no doorknob or handle of any kind. "I need more light. What is this place?"

Slowly, my eyes begin to adjust to my surroundings. I appear to be in a small circular room. There is a little chair and table to the side and a wooden cabinet across from it. Looking at the walls around me, I notice there are assorted pictures in frames hanging all over the place.

There is one long rectangular frame up high, and I can see it has something written on it in large letters. I can't quite make it out. "I need more light!" I stand there for a moment, thinking what to do. Climbing on the table, I reach up to see if I can open another one of the small circular windows. "No, they're too high." Sighing, I climb back down and begin to sort through my knapsack to see if there is anything in there that may be a tool to help me get out of here.

As I rummage through my bag, I hear a small humming sound and look up. A tiny glowing light flies in the open circular window up high. I hold my breath for a moment and stare at it, not sure what to do. It moves quickly to the top of the rectangular frame and touches it. It lights up from within, like it has a light turned on behind it. Then, as I watch, the small flickering light begins to descend, touching each framed picture one by one, until every picture is lit up.

I am about to speak, but it quickly flies back up and out the window before I can even say, "Wait!" The room is now lit, and I can easily see my surroundings. I look up at the long rectangular frame and read the words "Room of Hope Deferred."

"How strange! I've heard that somewhere before. I think it's from the Bible." I begin to look at each picture, one by one. Just below this frame is a picture of a man with a crown on his head, a king. He is sitting on a throne. He looks young, possibly early twenties, and has dark-brown hair and a beard. He looks quite tense and serious. His crown is laid with jewels, and they look brilliant, sparkling even. I rub my eyes for a moment and take a closer look.

He blinks in the picture and turns to look at someone approaching him. The picture has come alive! "Just like the picture on the wall in the pub! What is happening?" I stare at the sight, unable to look away. Breathing in, I smell the scent of the flower oil on my face, and my vision gets clearer, sharper even. I can now see clearly into the room that is in the picture. "I must have rubbed that oil into my eyes," I say to myself, blinking in wonder as the scene begins to unfold before me.

In the picture, the king raises his hand to beckon someone forward. A young girl who looks about sixteen approaches him. She has long golden-brown hair and a sweet appearance about her. She goes up and takes him by the hand. They are having a conversation, but I cannot hear the words; I can only see them.

Then, he raises his other hand and beckons someone from his other side to approach. It is another young woman, with black hair, pale, and very beautiful as well. I can see she has something dark wrapped around her head, like a headband. As I look closer, I can see it move—the headband is alive! It is some sort of creature holding on to her with long furry fingers clasped around her head. It stays very still, but every time she gets close to the king, it reaches out toward his crown, as if to pull it off.

I shudder at the sight, blinking my eyes repeatedly. "What is this?"

The picture freezes, so I look beside it to the next one. It's a sinister-looking man, a puppeteer. He is holding marionette puppets on strings, and as I stare at it, they begin to move about. The main puppet in the center is a queen, with a tall spiky crown glittering with icy jewels. The puppet's skin is bluish white, with long golden tresses for the hair, and she is wearing a dark-blue queen's gown.

She has ahold of other smaller marionette puppets and is controlling them. She makes them move across the puppet stage, but all is controlled from above by the master puppeteer. I shift my focus to him. He has a dark, evil look about him, wearing a dark cloak. His eyes look cruel as he focuses on moving the puppets around. Then he speaks. I cannot hear what he says, but when he does, a flurry of horrid-looking creatures fly up and surround the puppets. The picture freezes.

In the next picture, I see another young man. My mind snaps to attention—it's Tom! He is sitting at a table in the kitchen of my home. I realize I am in the picture as well, seated next to him! My parents are there too. As I watch, the scene comes to life and he gets up, says goodbye, and then pushes his chair in and walks to the front door. It is a very strange feeling as I watch myself get up and follow him. He walks out without another word and shuts the door behind him, leaving me behind. My mom and dad come up behind me and put their hands on my shoulders. Then the motion stops. I feel the ache from the pain in my heart.

Forcing myself to keep going, I quickly look at the next picture frame and see a bird. It is dark blue, with a golden beak and white spots on the feathers. It is flying. As I watch, it goes into motion and lands on a rooftop. It hops up to a window, and I see the window opening. A girl climbs out onto the roof next to the bird and sits down. "It's Julia! Julia!" I call out to her.

Julia sits on the roof for a few minutes, watching the bird, talking to it. Then I see her hold something up in her hand. It's the leaf. "My leaf key!" I gasp. "Julia has it! Is she trying to find me? Julia!" I put my hand up to the glass on the frame, as if to reach into it. The picture freezes.

"Julia! I'm here! I can see you!" I stare at the picture of my sister sitting motionless now on the roof. "Julia," I say one more time, and all is quiet in the little room. I don't want to look away from the picture, not wanting to break the connection I feel, but it is gone. I do see something that I didn't notice before however. Looking past Julia toward the window, I see a reflection of light in the form of a person just behind my sister. "Is that an angel?" I cannot make it out, but I suppose it could be.

I realize I am crying now. "Julia!" I call out. "God, I want to go home! I want You to help my sister. Help us! Help me get home. Why am I stuck here? What is it You want me to do?" I look around the room, my eyes blurred with tears. I slump down and cry freely, feeling overwhelmed and full of emotion. "Jesus, help me!"

"I don't know who these other people are! How can I possibly help them?" I sit there silently for a moment, wiping away the tears. After a few minutes, I think about Buddy. And Dominic. "How is anyone going to find me in here? I need to keep looking at the pictures. Maybe it will show me the way out." I get up on the table again and look at the next picture.

It's an empty room with a suit of armor in it. I stand there, staring at it, but it doesn't move. Nothing happens. I look at the next picture. It's dark and blank, an empty frame. I climb back down, feeling weary and confused. I sit down on the small circular rug on the floor. Looking at the cabinet, I begin to open the drawers.

"Why didn't I think of this before? There could be some sort of key or map in here."

There are three drawers. I open the top one first. Inside, there is a candle and some flint and a tinder box behind it. I set it on the table and light it as quickly as I can because the light from the pictures are now growing dim. I can hardly see them now.

Opening the second drawer, I pull out a silky, dark-green scarf. Its edges are stitched in a V pattern of gold thread, and it has golden flowers embroidered on it. "This is beautiful!" I remark. I put it on the table next to the candle. Reaching back into the drawer, I feel around to see if there is anything else in there, but there is not. Finally, I open the bottom drawer, and it is filled with a blue-and-gold blanket folded neatly in a square.

I open it up and see the pattern on it is an interesting display of moons and stars with a dark-blue background. It is soft and warm, and I lie down on the rug with it and pull it over me. I let my thoughts drift away and fall quickly into sleep.

I have only been napping a short time when I hear a knocking sound that wakes me. *Rap, rap, rap.* It's on the outside of the trunk.

"Hello!" I call out, springing up from sleep. "I'm in here! I need help to get out!"

I listen intently but hear nothing else. "Please, is someone out there? Hello?"

"Open the door, Kara." I hear a man's voice, kind but commanding at the same time. I realize He knows my name, and I'm a bit startled.

"I don't know how to. There's no handle in here."

"Hold the candle low to the ground, and you will see a latch."

I grab the candle and quickly lower it down by my feet. "I don't see anything," I say, looking around the base of the room. "Wait, there's a small wooden part sticking out here."

"Push on that."

I push on the lever, and there is a click. The door begins to move in toward me, opening into the small room and filling it with light.

I blink at the bright light before me. There is a man standing there, and He is filled with light. Drops of what feels like liquid love flow through the light toward me. I am unable to speak and feel very weak.

He reaches toward me and offers His hand. I take ahold of it and am now able to stand up before Him. The light penetrates me, saturating my very being. The room is filled with energy, like electricity.

"I want to heal your heart, Kara. I need to take out the thorns. Will you let Me?"

"Yes," I manage to whisper, amazed and strangely calm.

He reaches into my heart and pulls something out. I feel a quick, sharp pain, and then it is gone. Holding it in His hand, He shows it to me. I see a long sharp thorn in the palm of His hand.

"There is one more," He says. "Be still."

This time He reaches up into my head and pulls out something. Again, I feel a sharp sting, and then instant relief. He shows this to me as well. This thorn is spiky, like a burr with sharp edges.

"What are…how did those get there?" I ask, struggling to comprehend.

"They are words from people that cut you, forming a wound, then the enemy placed his thorns in there to keep you from healing." He went on, "The thief does not come except to steal and kill and destroy; I have come that they may have life, and that they may have it more abundantly" (John 10:10 NKJV).

"Thank You! I feel so much better! I can't even describe how good I feel! Like I can climb a mountain right now!"

The light coming from Him is so bright I can hardly make out His face, but I know it is Jesus, and I can tell He is smiling at me. I feel perfectly at peace and complete. "Can I come with You?" I ask.

"Not yet. I still have an assignment you must complete for Me. And there are people who need your help. Will you do this for Me?"

I remember being told I had an assignment from the king, but I feel sad that I can't just leave it all behind right now and go with Him. I don't want to disappoint Him in any way. "Yes, I will go," I hear myself saying. "What is it you want me to do?"

"I need you to help me save the kingdom of Silvenia from the evil one. He is using his pawns to take over the land. He already has control of the north country, and many people have been killed. It must be stopped. I am giving you My power to enforce My kingdom instead of his."

"Who is the evil one?"

"In this place, he is called Mercurio. He is a thief and a liar. He has deceived many. This used to be a beautiful place, a paradise, but his influence has increased here, and he must be pushed back."

"What can I do? I am only a girl who is a stranger here. I cannot do this on my own!"

"I am giving you My power to represent me here. And you will not be alone. I am sending you help. This is their only hope. If you do not go, he will continue the takeover of this land until all is destroyed."

"But why me? I am nobody. I have no experience, no great strength, no skill in battles. I am out of my element here."

"That is why I have chosen you. You must totally rely on My ability working through you. But I must have your cooperation. I will not force this on you. Will you accept this task?"

I pause, thinking about my home, my family. I look at His face, and He already knows what I am thinking. "Your family is in My hands. Do not worry about them. Will you trust Me?"

"I will. I will do all that I can for you. Only show Me how to begin."

He walks past me into the tree and points at a picture, the one with the armor in it. It lights up again.

"First, put this on. It will protect you everywhere you go."

I watch in wonder as He pulls it out of the frame and places the helmet on me. There is also a large shield that looks lit by fire. He hands it to me, and when I grasp it, I feel strengthened. He then has me put on the shining breastplate, belt, and boots. Lastly, He hands me a gleaming sword with flames on it, which I also grasp and then hold to my side.

He spends the next half-hour instructing me how to use it, and my mind is filled with this knowledge, and I know it is in me. He tells me I won't forget it and that even if I do He will remind me of it. He then takes His finger and marks a spot on my forehead. "This is a gift. It's called discernment." He then touches my mouth. "You have power when you speak. Be careful to speak My words and never agree with the enemy." Then He touches my hands. "You have My power in you that heals. Use it freely." He tells me I have everything I need to complete my task and that He has help on the way right now.

He instructs me about the kingdom of Silvenia, the kingdom of Icelandia, and the surrounding areas. He tells me about King Vespes and the empress, Mira, Trea, Arten, and many others. He tells me my part, and it is so much information that it seems to take hours. He warns me about the devices of Mercurio and how to push his evil forces back. I am feeling overwhelmed at the enormity of it all.

"Kara, I have brought you here to the far side of the sea to help the people of Paredonia. They have stopped seeking Me and forgotten My Word. Mercurio has blinded them and seduced them with his deceptive schemes, the same as he does on your Earth. You are to remind them that I have saved them and they do not have to be taken over and ruled by the kingdom of darkness. Even here, I have not forgotten them."

"How am I going to remember all this? What if I fail?"

"I will be with you. You will not see Me, but you will remember all I have told you here. And you will have help. I have promised you this, and I cannot lie. You have been chosen for this task, so do not fear."

I nod silently, unable to think of anything else to say, although my mind is racing with all these thoughts. "Peace," He says to me, and I feel it, like a blanket, covering me. I close my eyes and let it envelop me completely. I feel that I have no cares, no worries, just His love, and it's all I could ever want or need.

I open my eyes again, and He is gone. I am on the floor, with the star blanket still over me. I sit up, looking around the little circular room. The green scarf is still on the table, and I pick it up and put it in my knapsack. The door of the room is closed, and I am still shut inside, but the panic is gone now. I know I have been chosen, and my heart is resolved to complete my task.

Back to Icelandia

Arten

Arten and his group arrive back at the empress's castle and have just unloaded the horses. Julius, Jude, and Kurt have already gone on to their domains. Vico and Arten are walking together up the stone path to the side entry door of the castle when he confronts Arten with a question.

"So what are you going to do about Mira?"

Arten stops. "What do you mean? I am going to do whatever the empress requires of me."

"Arten, it's me, Vico. I've known you all your life, since we were kids together in Roten Village. I know you care about her. So I repeat, what are you going to do? I am with you whatever you decide. I am not afraid of the empress."

Arten stares at his friend in silence. They are now standing in front of the archway entrance, and a guard is approaching them. "We will discuss this later," he affirms, walking ahead of Vico into the dark stone corridor. The guard recognizes them with a hand lifted in salute and then closes the large doors behind them, sealing it with a large metal bolt.

After a few moments, a tall thin man approaches them in the hallway. It is Hilio, Celia's head servant. "The empress awaits your report in her throne room. She requires you to go there at once."

Arten nods and looks at Vico. "We are ready to report." Then, with both of them following behind Hilio, Arten whispers to Vico, "Meet me just after midnight at the large oak tree by the stables where the target box is." Vico nods, and they walk on quietly down the hall to their meeting with the empress.

"Well, it's about time you returned. I was starting to have questions about your allegiance to me." She eyes them with coolness in her tone and taps her fingers on the arm of her throne.

"Our allegiance is to you, my empress. You have trained us to fight, and we fight for you alone. We have proven this in many battles won for you, and we are proud to serve as your faithful soldiers."

"So many words! Tell me, why is it you think I need so much convincing? Are you hiding something from me, Arten? Are you still to be trusted as chief commander of my powerful army?"

"Yes, my empress. I have returned as you have requested, and I am ready to report."

She narrows her eyes, her cold gaze fixed upon them. "Report, then."

"The princess is safe within the Silver Palace of Silvenia. She has the scroll and knows her assignment. She has already won over the affections of the king. All who live there have welcomed her, and it should not be long before we hear of their wedding plans."

"Very well. I will have you escort me there as soon as the wedding date is set. Ceyla is my loyal servant as well, and she will report to me any deceptions that arise. Is she close to Mira inside the palace?"

"Yes, in the very room next to her."

"That is good. Send Kurt back as my messenger to Silvenia with more gifts for the king. He can bring us word of their betrothal when it occurs, and then we will depart together for Silvenia." She looks up, shifting her focus to Vico for a moment. "You may go now."

They both bow and turn to leave the room. As they walk to the door, she calls out, "Wait! Arten, I have one more thing I need to discuss with you alone."

He halts and then turns back to the queen, glancing at Vico as he departs. "Yes, my empress."

"Your final test of loyalty may be here soon. If you pass this test, I will make you a ruler at my side. You will have great riches, your own people to command, your own land to possess. You will bow to no one other than to me."

He looks at her with a steady gaze. "And if I fail?"

She smiles at him coldly. "I do not accept failure. All who fail me are destroyed without delay. You know this."

He meets her eyes with a steady gaze. "What is this test?"

"If the princess betrays me, you will have to kill her as well." She pauses and looks at him inquisitively. "Is that a problem for you?"

"She is your only daughter! You want to destroy your heir?"

"Of course not. But if she chooses to betray me, I will have no other choice. I do not accept failure, and all traitors must be destroyed."

"She will not betray you. She is loyal to this kingdom, as am I."

"You have not answered my question to you. Or maybe your arguments are concealing your true response? To be chief commander of my army, you must obey me without question, without regard for your emotions. Or has she weakened your heart?"

"No! I will do as you say. My loyalty is to you and to this kingdom. I will pass your test if it comes to that."

"We shall see. You may go now. The cook has prepared food for you and the others in the dining hall. I'm sure you will be pleased to see your younger sister, Gaelyn, there. I have brought her in as a maidservant to help the cook, and she will be serving the food tonight." She pauses again and watches for his reaction. He opens his mouth, about to speak, and then restrains himself. She continues on, "Please, go and rest. Enjoy the food prepared for you. We will talk again tomorrow." She raises her hand to dismiss him, and he bows sharply and quickly departs from the room.

Later that night, Arten and Vico meet in the target area by the large oak. Arten grabs his bow and arrow and motions for Vico to do the same. They head toward the forest on foot. After they have walked a good distance from the castle, Arten addresses his friend.

"This is far enough," he says, keeping his voice low.

"Tell me."

"I have been given instructions to kill Mira if she betrays the empress. We know of her great cruelty. Truly, she has no heart and is willing to destroy even her own daughter."

"If we commit treason, we will be killed as well. Are you prepared to die for her?"

Arten looks fiercely back at the castle. "There is more. You saw Gaelyn serving as a maidservant in the dining hall tonight. While we were on the road, she took her from my parents' home and forced her to come here, to dangle her life in front of me as a threat. If I do not do all that she asks, my sister will die as well! She is only fifteen—she's never even been away from home." He rubs his hands through his hair, trembling with anger. "I could see the fear and plea for help in her eyes. She barely spoke to me. She only put her hand on my arm and squeezed it for a moment. I swear, I won't let any harm come to her!"

"Nor will I. We will find a way. I stand with you, brother, and there are others, too, that I know of who are weary of her cruelty and ready to take a stand."

"Who do you know? They do not speak to me."

"Of course they don't. You are the chief commander under the empress. But they speak to me. I am just a skilled hunter she uses from time to time. I am friends with many of the soldiers who come from our village, and know of their true allegiance, and it is not to her. We just need to form a plan, gather together, and come against her with united strength."

"How many of these men will join us? Her army has hundreds of soldiers, and within our company are many that have become cold-blooded killers just like her. You know how we are trained. Show no compassion, kill, destroy, and then sort through what's left for treasure. Comply or be thrown into Danere's pit. Their minds are controlled by the fear of her. Now, they look forward to the destruction of a village of people and have no pity for the innocent. How can we know who to trust? If our plan gets into the wrong ears, we and all those we care about will be destroyed."

"I understand it is a great risk, but what other choice do we have?"

"We can encourage Mira to carry out the empress's plan. Have her marry and then kill the king while we assist in the takeover. At least then I know that my sister will live." He pulls out an arrow and aims with it into the trees. "Then, once all is done, I can escape with Mira and return and rescue my family as well. We can go far away from here, where the empress will never find us."

"That is all well and good for you, but what about our people? And all the innocent people in Silvenia? Do you really want to have her kingdom spread and take over more lands? She will never be satisfied!"

Arten begins to pull out another arrow, and Vico grabs his arm. "Arten! She has to be stopped! If we don't stop her, who will?"

Vico

A Joyful Reunion

Buddy is back on the main road, trotting up and down it and barking at anyone that is passing by.

"Get back, mutt!" yells a man on horseback. "Get out of the way!" He trots quickly past the anxious dog. Buddy follows behind for a little bit, but the man kicks in his heels and canters off down the road.

No one pays him any attention, so he runs back to the tree and scratches at the base of the trunk. Whimpering when nothing happens, he lies down beside it and stays there for the next two hours, watching the road.

Then he hears a whistling sound. Snapping his head up, he looks through the trees and sees a man coming up the road. He is of short stature and carrying a long stick, humming and whistling a tune as he walks. Buddy jumps up and runs toward him, wagging his tail and barking. The man stops and looks.

"Here, boy! Well, look at you. Are you all by yourself?" Dominic looks around him, seeing no one else. "You fit the description of a dog I am looking for. Where is your friend?" He reaches down and pats him on the head. Buddy barks twice and wags his tail, then he begins to head for the forest again.

"Wait! Where are you going?" Dominic watches as the dog retreats back into the forest, barking as he goes. "Slow down, boy! I'm coming!"

A few moments later, they arrive at a large tree with a very wide trunk. Buddy begins pawing at it and barking. Then he hears a woman's voice. "Buddy! It's okay, I'm all right!" It came from inside the tree!

"Kara! Is that you? It's Dominic. I'm here too! Where are you?"

"Dominic! Is it really you?" I call out, hope rising within me.

"Yes, it's me! But where are you?"

"I'm inside the tree! There's a room in here."

"How did you get in there?"

"There were vines on the ground that latched on to me—be careful of them! Then a door opened, and I kind of fell in here."

"How do I open it? I don't see any kind of door."

"I don't know. I fell asleep in here and had a dream. In my dream I found a latch along the floor in here that will open it, but I can't find it now."

Dominic scratches his beard. "Perhaps if I feel along the trunk, I will find a latch here on the outside."

"That sounds like a good idea."

Dominic begins searching with his hands, pressing against the trunk.

"Oh, and I saw a vayaklos come in and out of the small circular window that's up high. It was glowing with light and came in and lit up the pictures in this room."

Dominic looks up and sees the window. "Oh, yes, I see it. How peculiar. This must be one of their trees."

"What do you mean?"

"They live in trees in the forests. That's where they hide during the day and also where they store their treasures."

"I don't see any treasure in here. Just a table and chair, a cabinet, and a bunch of pictures on the wall."

"It could be some kind of secret hiding place for someone, I suppose. Perhaps for someone on the run."

"On the run from who?"

"From Mercurio or one of his agents, perhaps. He has stolen away many to his underground world. He sends out trackers to hunt down those who escape."

"Do you know anyone who was stolen away?"

"Yes, a childhood friend of mine disappeared from our village when I was a small boy. The entire town searched for him, but he was never found."

"How do you know it was Mercurio that took him?"

"He preys on the young and innocent, and this lad was playing too close to the swamp—he'd been warned not to go there."

"The same swamp we walked through?"

"Yes, the very same. It is said that long ago, he was even able to capture a young wind child from up high in the mountain forests. Her name was Londine. This was before the alliance was made with the white wolves to help protect them there."

I am sitting on the floor of the circular rug, listening intently. "What happened to her?"

Dominic pauses, walking slowly around the tree, examining it from every angle, pushing and prodding on every bump on the bark. "Kara, I don't see any type of latch or opening out here, and it's beginning to get dark. Have you found anything yet on the inside?"

"No, not yet. I'll keep looking. I'm just so glad you're here! I'm so glad you're alive! I'm sorry I left you at the river. Will you please forgive me for running away and leaving you?"

"There is nothing to forgive. I told you to run! You did exactly what I wanted you to do!"

"Yes, I know, but I felt terrible about it. I thought the troll had killed you and that I was responsible for your death!"

"Kara, I know the dangers of this place and what I was taking on by serving as your guide. I am not afraid to die, but I didn't, so we don't need to dwell on that anymore. Let's put our focus now on getting you out of this tree!"

The sunlight has faded now into night, and Buddy is lying patiently by the tree, watching Dominic. Dominic is slumped down now, with his back leaning against the tree. Neither one of us could find an opening to the door after much effort, and now we are just sitting and talking. He is telling me of his journey through the underground and how he escaped. I am listening from within the tree, glad to hear the comfort of his voice and still feeling surrounded by the peace that was given to me.

After Dominic finishes telling of his escape, I catch him up and then relay to him what was revealed to me in the pictures. I don't speak about my visit with Jesus, as I feel that is too sacred and for me alone. I tell him of the people I saw in the pictures, describing the king and the two young women, the puppeteer and his strings controlling the people, especially the queen. I describe how the pictures were lit up by the vayaklos and then, as I looked at each one, they came to life, showing me a glimpse of each person's story.

"And I saw Julia, my sister, back at home. She had my leaf key in her hand, and there was a starling by her. I think she's trying to get to me. Can she use my leaf key to come here too?"

"No, it will only work for the person it's assigned to. But that's interesting that she was holding on to it. You say there was a starling there too?"

"Yes, it definitely looked like a starling bird from this place."

"It could be she feels some kind of nostalgic connection with you by keeping ahold of your leaf key."

"But why was she revealed in the pictures here? It must mean something."

"I don't know, Kara. I'm sure time will tell."

I bunch my knees up under me and sit quietly for a moment. "Tell me what happened to the wind girl that was captured by Mercurio."

"Oh, yes, that is a sad story. Her name was Londine. She was taken from the forest of Elmwood, up in the mountains of Shazir, where the windfolk live. It is a sacred land, and it was unheard of that one of Mercurio's agents would travel that far into their domain. Their world is pure and good, and his world is purely evil. His spells don't even work in their land, but at that time their borders were not well protected. An evil agent of his, Danere, called the son of Mercurio, found her in the woods and captured her. She was young and beautiful, around the age of fifteen, I think. He stole her away, and she was forced to marry him and live in the underground world, surrounded by darkness."

"Was she never found? Did no one try to rescue her?"

"Many tried. There was a great battle between the windfolk and Mercurio's army. During this time, she was found in the underground and had begun her escape with two other windfolk and a guide. This guide was actually one of my ancestors, Ansel. He was my great-uncle on my father's side. Anyhow, they reached the surface and were escaping on foot through the forest when Danere came out from behind a rock and shot her with an arrow. She was holding her baby girl, only two years old at that time, which he snatched up and escaped back down a tunnel into the underground. Londine died there, on the forest floor, with Ansel and her windfolk kin by her side. The arrow had shot her through the heart."

"That's terrible! What about the baby? What happened to her?"

"One of the windfolk—I think his name was Elkensor—went after Danere through the tunnel. My uncle and the other windfolk man tried to follow him as well, after they saw Londine was gone. But the tunnel had already closed back up. They returned another time as well, on a rescue mission to try to retrieve them, but barely escaped with their lives. They could not find Elkensor or the baby. Many windfolk died in those battles, and the fighting then ceased for a time. They set up stronger borders with the animals' help to protect their sacred forest, mainly the white wolves, but there are also bears and other animals that help them as well. Their land has not been invaded since."

"What was the name of Londine's baby girl?"

"Celia."

"You don't mean the empress Celia? The one I saw in the picture in here?"

"We believe she is one and the same."

"She is evil! I saw the things she was doing in the picture. She was killing people, having them thrown into a dark pit with beastly creatures in it! I also saw her in a dark room, making some kind of black poison from a book of spells. She uses it as ink and then writes on a scroll. Then she is somehow able to control the ones she gives it to. I saw her hand one to her own daughter. She is plotting right now to kill the king and take over Silvenia. That is why I am here, Dominic. I am supposed to help stop her!"

Dominic sits there attentively, taking all this in. "Was this information revealed to you in these pictures? If that is so, truly falling into this tree was no accident. The Great One has arranged this place for you to find out your assignment."

"Yes, I agree with you. I was also shown that we do not have much time. A few weeks at most. I've got to find a way out of here!"

Dominic looks up at the tree, thinking. "I could drop my food and water flask in the window to you and then go on ahead to Silvenia and find Vale. He is the high commander under King Vespes and the one who commissioned me to find you and bring you to Silvenia. He is very wise and will know what to do."

"How far is it to Silvenia from here? I don't want to be stuck in here for days!"

"It would only be for one day more at the most. Hmmm, let me think how to get this pack up through that high window."

While he paced back and forth, thinking, the forest began to light up with lights of the vayaklos blinking all around them in the dark. He was staring at the open portal in the tree when one of them flew up and into it again, descending down the trunk tunnel toward Kara.

"Kara! Do you see it?"

"What? Oh! Yes! Hello, there, please, don't leave! Can you show me how to get out of here?"

There is no reply. The flitting light glides down toward the pictures again. It hovers over one in particular and touches it. It is lit up from behind the glass, and I slowly climb up on the table again to take a closer look. I move slowly, not wanting to scare it away.

It hovers over the picture, and just as I am about eye level with the frame, it quickly flies up and out of the tree. I am able to catch a glimpse of a tiny fairy-looking creature, beautiful, with long white hair and iridescent wings.

"Oh, they are lovely! I saw it up close—the vayaklos, I mean," I tell Dominic.

"Yes, I just saw it fly back out. Did it show you anything?"

"It lit up another picture in here. I'm looking at it now."

"What is it?"

"It's a picture of this room. It's not moving or coming to life like the others—wait! Something's happening. It's showing a crack in the wall. Here it is, beside me." I run my finger down the groove in the wall that I didn't see before. "It's lighting up now in the picture, and the light is moving down the crease in the wall to the floor." I climb down from the table and follow the line down to the floor. "There it is! The lever, I see it now!"

Quickly I push on it and hear a click. The door of the trunk opens inwardly toward me, and I step out into the open air, greeting Buddy and Dominic with joyful hugs.

The Proposal

There has been no word from Arten and his group since they departed Silvenia over three weeks ago. Mira paces her bedroom floor, resigned with anger and sorrow at the thought of him. *How could he leave me like this? I trusted him! I love him and despise him at the same time. No! I must resolve to only hate him! Men are beasts! They steal your heart away when you offer it freely and then crush it and hand it back to you in a million shattered pieces.*

Her head feels foggy again, and she sits down on the bed. *Why is it when I want to hide in sleep, you come find me in my dreams? It's not fair. Even my thoughts won't let me escape you!* She rubs her head with both hands and then rises to her feet when she hears a knock on her door.

"Milady, it's Ceyla. I'm sorry to bother you, but one of the men from Icelandia has arrived back at the palace. I thought you'd want to know."

Mira runs to the door and opens it. "Is it Arten? Where is he? I need to speak with him."

"I don't know. I was just heading out to breakfast when I heard them announce a guest arriving from Icelandia."

Mira pauses for a moment. "I was just about to head down for breakfast myself. Why don't we walk down together?"

"Yes, milady."

They head down the curved staircase together. As they enter the dining room, she hears men's voices. Her heart is beating rapidly, and she is unsure what to do or say if Arten is truly back.

"Princess, good morning!" King Vespes bows and smiles at her.

"Greetings, Princess Mira," says Kurt, bowing before her.

"Kurt! You've returned. Where are the others?"

"Only I have been sent back at this time, with another gift from the empress to the king."

"Oh, I see. Well, it's good to see you again. Excuse me, I'm going to get some tea." She quickly heads over to the table and sits down.

"May I pour you some tea, milady?" asks Ceyla.

"Yes, please." Mira pushes her cup toward the steaming pot Ceyla is holding and tries to hide her emotions once again. Ceyla sits down beside her as another servant comes in to bring them both some breakfast.

"Are you not hungry this morning?" Ceyla remarks, watching as Mira pushes the eggs around her plate.

"Not very."

King Vespes finishes talking with Kurt and walks over to the table to sit across from Mira. Kurt leaves the room, and it is just the three of them.

Mira looks up at Vespes and forces a smile. "Where's Trea? Isn't she usually the early riser around here?"

Vespes laughs. "She's not really much of a morning person, to be honest. I think she has just been excited to have you here as a guest. Maybe the excitement has caught up with her and she's sleeping in this morning."

"Can we bring you something else to eat this morning?" he asks, noticing she hasn't touched her plate of food.

"Oh, no, I'm fine. Just not terribly hungry right now." Mira forces herself to take a small bite.

"I was thinking, maybe, if you'd like to go riding today, we could go exploring up in the Copper Hills, just north of here."

Looking up at his face, eager and smiling, she almost feels sorry for him. But then she remembers that men are beasts and cannot be trusted. She remembers her assignment.

"I'd love to," she replies.

Trea walks in the room, a sleepy grin on her face. "Good morning! I must have slept in. Did I miss anything interesting?"

Mira turns to her. "Vespes and I are going riding out in the Copper Hills today."

"Oh, that's exciting! It's a beautiful place to go riding."

"Would you like to come with us?"

"Oh, that's all right. I don't want to intrude."

"You're not intruding," exclaims Mira. "Please, I'd love it if you would come too."

"Ceyla, you can come too if you would like—the more, the merrier."

"No, thank you, milady. I prefer to stay put right here, if that's all right with you. I'm not as skilled a rider as you are."

"Very well, then, it's just the three of us. Perhaps we could invite Kurt as well," says Vespes, remembering his other guest. "Erol, please go check with him. I believe he went back to his room for a bit."

Bowing, Erol quickly leaves the room.

"I'll go get changed into my riding outfit," Mira says, rising to her feet.

"I'll walk with you, milady," says Ceyla, pushing her chair back as well.

Back in her room, Mira pulls her riding garment out of the closet. She gets out her riding hat and feels for the hidden scroll tucked inside. Holding it in her hand, she feels compelled to open it and read over the words once again. Like poison, the words sink into her mind. She then pushes it under another garment in the drawer and finishes dressing.

She feels her heart resisting, wanting to rebel against her mother. "You must follow my instructions. You must pass the test." She feels weak and fragile, anxiety pressing down on her. *I cannot do this! She wants me to trick him, to kill him! She wants me to become like her.*

Sighing heavily, she pulls on her boots, feeling the effects of the poison ink, in her skin, in her mind. "I have no other choice. Arten has left me. I am on my own. I must obey her and accept my fate. I will have my own kingdom then, where I can make my own choices. Then I will be free."

She meets them down in the stables. "Where is Kurt? Isn't he coming along?"

"He was too tired from his journey back here. He said another time, perhaps."

"All right, then. Let's go exploring!" says Trea with a grin.

Mira and Vespes grab their bow and arrows while Trea climbs up on her horse. "Do you want to bring yours too, Trea?" he asks.

"No, I won't need it. I just like to ride."

"Very good. Let's be off, then."

They ride out the city gates a little while later and head toward the northern hills.

"You see those amber-colored peaks in the distance?" he asks Mira. "Those are the Copper Hills. Just over the highest peak, you can see the Great Sea."

"Yes, we rode close to there on our way here. But we didn't go up high. We stayed on the low path, the main road leading to Silvenia."

"Yes, of course. I think you will enjoy seeing the view from up high today."

"Vespes, shouldn't you warn her about the snakes?"

Mira looks at Vespes as he trots along on his horse beside her. "What about snakes?"

"My father was injured up here when a snake spooked his horse over a year ago. The Copper Hills aren't known to have many snakes, but there was one out there in his path that day."

"Your father, is he still alive?"

Trea goes on with the story. "Yes, he is. But he stays in his bedroom, up in the South Tower. He has been ill, not able to join us even for meals anymore. He has lost his memory and much of his strength."

"I'm so sorry to hear that. Is there anything I can do to help?" She says this with some degree of sincerity, knowing what it is like to be without a father.

"No, but thank you," says Vespes. "He has nurses and attendants around the clock to assist him. We visit with him as well, but sadly, he does not remember us anymore."

"We have another sister too," says Trea. "Her name is Delvana. But she is now married to King Greffen and lives with him in the kingdom of Volkenland."

"I've never heard of Volkenland. Where is that?"

"It is far south of here, past the desert of Cardonne."

"I see. And your mother, where is she?"

"She died shortly after I was born," Trea responds. "I never knew her, but her name was Adele."

"That's a lovely name. I am sorry for your loss. My father also died when I was a baby. He died in battle."

"I am sorry to hear that as well. What was his name?"

"Bernard, Bernard Tremonde III, actually."

They ride on in silence for a while. Finally, they come to the highest peak of the Copper Hills, and a broad view of the ocean spreads out before them.

"Beautiful!" says Mira. They climb off their horses, one by one, and walk along the top of the hillside while the horses graze on the dry grass baked brown from the sun.

Mira walks close to the steep ridge that leads down to the valley far below them.

"Be careful, Princess. There are a lot of loose rocks along the ridge."

"Look!" says Trea, climbing up on a large rock. "It's a cliff eagle, there on that tree down close to the bottom."

They step up closer to her, looking down below. "I don't see it," says Vespes. "Where?"

"It's there," says Mira, taking a step farther down and pointing. "On that large extended branch of that tall pine tree."

Suddenly, the rock she is standing on shifts. In a split second, it comes loose and she tumbles down with it a few yards down the rocky hillside. Gravity pulls at her, and she finds herself sliding, grasping at the ground, trying to stop herself.

"Mira!" Vespes bolts after her and begins to slide himself, stopping himself by grabbing onto a large boulder sticking out.

"Mira! Vespes! I'm coming to help you!" Trea says as she begins to gingerly step down toward them.

"No! Stay there, Trea. I've got a grip now, and I can climb down to get her. You stay there at the top!"

"But I can help!"

"I need you to stay there in case someone needs to ride to get us help. Listen to what I say!"

"All right. Just be careful!"

Vespes slowly makes his way down the ridge toward Mira as small rocks and pebbles crumble under his feet. "Mira, are you okay?" he calls out.

"Yes, I think so. But I may have injured my ankle. It hurts when I put pressure on it to try to stand up."

"Don't move. I'm coming to get you."

Slowly he makes his way toward her as Trea watches from above. Finally, he reaches her spot and takes a look at her ankle. "It looks a bit swollen. Don't try to put pressure on it. Just wrap your arms around my shoulders and I'll lift you up."

She obeys him without a word. He manages to lift her up, and they make their way back up the rocky hill, very slowly, with rocks scuttling away from his steps. Finally, they reach the top and Trea pulls them both to safety with outstretched arms. "You made it! Mira, are you hurt?"

"She has twisted her ankle. We need to take it easy with the horses and head back to the palace to get it wrapped up. Can you ride on your horse, Mira?"

"Yes, I think so."

Vespes lifts her up onto her saddle, and she winces. "I just can't press with my one leg to guide him."

"It's okay, I'll lead you," he says, grabbing ahold of her horse's reins. "We'll just take it slow, and he can follow along with my horse."

"All right," she says, getting a good grip with her hands on the saddle.

They head slowly back to the castle, taking care over the many hills and bumps. Arriving back, Vespes quickly dismounts his horse and lifts her off carefully. He gives instructions to the servants and carries her up to her room. Placing her down gently on her bed, he grabs a pillow and props it up behind her. "Are you in much pain? I have instructed the nurse to come up and wrap your ankle. Is there anything else I can do for you?"

She looks into his eyes. "You are very kind. I will be fine. It's only a twisted ankle. I just need to rest it."

"If anything had happened to you, I would never forgive myself. I should never have taken you up there."

"No! I loved it! It wasn't your fault. It was only an accident. Please don't be so hard on yourself."

He crouches down beside her. "Mira, I care about you. I think I am in love with you. I don't want us to be apart. Stay here with me in Silvenia. Marry me!"

She stares at him. This is what she's been waiting for; she just didn't think it would happen so fast.

"I know this is sudden. I've been having these feelings for you ever since you arrived. I can't explain it. I just know I want you to be my wife."

She looks into his eyes and feels no love for him except for that of a brother. *He is kind and gentle,* she thinks to herself. *Why does he have to be so kind? Why does he have to make this so difficult for me?*

"I am sorry," he says, rising to his feet. "I have spoken too quickly. I cannot expect you to return my feelings so soon. I was just hoping that…never mind, I will let you rest now. Please forgive my haste." He turns and heads quickly toward the door.

"Wait, yes! My answer is yes." She hears the words escape her own lips as if they were separate from her somehow. "I will marry you."

The Silver Palace

Dominic and I walk steadily up the road together, with Buddy at my side. We can see the Silver Palace towers now up ahead in the distance. The wind has been blowing steadily from the north, and the sky is partially covered with billowy gray clouds.

"We might get rained on before we reach the gates," remarks Dominic.

I look up at the clouds. "Yes, and it's quite breezy too. I hope we don't get soaked."

We go over our plan again for when we reach the palace gates. Dominic will ask to speak with Vale, the leader of King Vespes's army, and say that we have been summoned by him to the castle. Vale can then inform us of the current situation with the king and how we can be of service. I will explain to him my revelation of the evil plans of Empress Celia and Mercurio against King Vespes and the kingdom of Silvenia. Then we can devise a good plan together of how to proceed.

"We must be sure that we can speak with him in private, before anyone else. He is the only one who knows of your coming here to help. He is the one who commissioned me to be your guide and bring you to Silvenia."

I look at him, thinking. "I still don't fully know my part to play in all this. Much was revealed to me at the tree, but I wasn't shown everything. How will I know what to do?"

"That is why we all need one another. There are many pieces to this puzzle. You are here on divine assignment from the Great One Himself. He will make known to you what you must do at the proper time."

"But what if I miss it? What if I do the wrong thing? I have this incredible assignment to complete, and I want to be brave and wise.

But I'm also just Kara Alder, twenty-four years old, from Nesterley, New Jersey. I've never done anything amazing or outstanding. I just wish I had more confidence in myself!"

"Maybe that's why you have been chosen. You must rely completely on Him to guide you and accomplish this task. He is the one who created you. He knows everything about you, and He must have given you everything you need to do your part. It's on the inside of you and just hasn't had a chance to come to light yet. Challenges have a way of bringing out the best and the worst in us. Trust what He has placed in your heart, Kara."

I place my hand over my heart, remembering the thorns He removed. I feel for the pain and realize it is gone. My memories of the past are still there, but the pain and hurt are gone. Peace rises up within me once again, and I smile with the freedom of it.

"You seem different since your experience in the tree, Kara. Something has changed."

"Yes, I feel different, more peaceful, perhaps braver. You are right, Dominic. I must have faith that He will show us the way." As I am speaking, the clouds suddenly open up and rain begins to fall on us in big, watery drops. Laughing, we begin to run toward the tall city gates just in front of us down the road. Buddy speeds up and runs ahead of us, then circles back around, barking with excitement and spurring us on.

"I think he's herding us," I say with a laugh as we quicken our pace.

We pass through the city gates and run the rest of the way to the palace. At the palace gate, two armed guards greet us. Dominic informs them that we are expected by Commander Vale and are scheduled to meet with him. We are ushered into a covered waiting area just inside the gate. The rain is steadily falling now, and I look up at the large silver tower in front of us.

"It's so big!" I say to Dominic. "Much bigger than the castle in Rondival."

"Yes, Silvenia is a much larger, more established kingdom. I think you will like it here. It is a beautiful place with lovely scenery on all sides. I know it's hard to tell right now with all this rain, but you will have to take a tour later and look around."

"Yes, I hope we get to do that."

Buddy huddles close to me, every now and then shaking his fur vigorously to dry himself off. After a few moments, one of the guards returns. "You are to follow me. As you said, Commander Vale is expecting you, and I am to bring you to the commons area. Right this way." He looks down at the dog for a moment but then says nothing else.

We follow him up a pathway to a side entrance. It opens to a hallway that leads to a large meeting room with high ornamental ceilings. There is a man seated at a table inside. He has wavy brown hair and a short beard. It seems impossible to guess his age—he looks youthful and strong—but there is a wisdom that comes with age in his eyes, and he also has a few silver streaks in his hair. *I can't tell if he's twenty or fifty!* I think to myself as I get closer. When he stands to greet us, I realize he is quite tall as well.

"Welcome! My name is Vale. Commander Vale of King Vespes's army, to be exact. I am so glad you have come." He crosses the room and holds out his hand and clasps our hands in greeting. "I was expecting you sooner, though. Were there difficulties in your journey?"

Dominic and I glance at each other, and then I reply, "Yes. There was a troll at one of the bridges, and we got separated for a while trying to get away from it."

"Yes," Dominic adds, "and then it took us a while to find each other again."

Vale nods solemnly. "I am sorry to hear about your trouble. I expected some resistance to your coming here, but we did our best to maintain the highest secrecy for the safety of you both. I am glad you are here now. There is much I need to tell you about the current state of affairs here in Silvenia."

I interject, "If you don't mind my asking, how did it come about that you sent for me to come here?"

Vale smiles warmly at her. "Yes, of course. It was through Lady Vallora of the windfolk. She sent me word that there would be help coming to our kingdom in the form of a young woman from another land. She even knew your name, Kara—is that correct?"

"Yes, and what did she say about me?"

"She said that you would come at a time of dire need. I'm afraid that time is now."

I glance at Dominic, who is focused on Vale and listening intently. "Please tell us what is happening," he urges.

"King Vespes has gone against the wisdom of the royal council and betrothed himself in marriage to Princess Mira of Icelandia. Her mother is the empress Celia Tremonde, known for her wickedness in the Northern Territories for some time now. She has long sought to take over our land, even before the king was born, but he refuses to listen to us." He pauses for a moment, walking back over to the table and pulling out some chairs for them to sit down. "Please, sit and make yourself comfortable while I tell you the rest. I am having a hot supper prepared for you as we speak, and your rooms are being made ready as well."

"Thank you." Dominic nods, and they both sit down in the large cushioned chairs at the table. A servant appears at the door and waits. Looking up, Vale motions him forward. "These are some warm, dry blankets to help you dry off from the rain. You may go now, Marcus."

The servant nods and departs quickly, shutting the door behind him.

"Now, where was I?"

"You were telling us of the king's betrothal to Princess Mira and about the empress," says Dominic, resting his arms on the table in front of him and leaning in to listen.

"Right, and along with this news, now the king has become quite ill. He only gets up for meals and then retreats back to his room immediately, hardly eating or drinking anything. We have tried to get him to at least postpone the wedding plans until he is feeling better, but he refuses. He seems bent on getting married as soon as possible. He will listen to no one, not even his sister, Princess Trea."

"What does Princess Trea think about all this?"

"She is unaware of our history with the empress and is happy about the upcoming marriage. She approves of Princess Mira but also is concerned about her brother's health and wants him to wait until he is feeling better. He refuses to listen to her. In fact, the only person he wants around him now that he will listen to is Princess Mira. She spends a lot of time with him, talking with him, reading to him. He is obsessed, unable to focus on anything else but her."

"But isn't that just a symptom of being in love?" I ask.

"I would say yes, on his part. But with her I suspect treason. She is not the empress herself, but as her daughter, they are probably working together. I have no proof of this, but I have been warned in a dream. About a year ago, I had a dream of this kingdom being taken over by the empress, with her killing whoever stood in her way, burning and destroying our peaceful land. It was so vivid and real to me that I went to see Lady Vallora of the windfolk up in the mountains of Shazir. We have been friends for many years, and she is very insightful and wise. She told me what I had dreamed before I could even speak it. We realized that this vision was a very real threat. The empress comes from the underground and has ties to Mercurio, the evil one. If she is allowed to take over Silvenia, it would be just the beginning. We have to stop this evil from spreading."

I nod, affirming, "Yes, I was shown a picture of Mercurio, and in it he was controlling the empress and her actions. I could hardly look at it—his image was so dark and evil it radiated out from him and repulsed me. I could also see that she has power over her daughter as well. She uses a poison that she makes and places it on a scroll. She was giving her daughter a scroll in the picture, and I could see that when she took ahold of it, her mind was clouded and she was greatly weakened."

"A scroll, you say. What did it look like?"

"It was a rolled-up piece of pale-yellow parchment, and it had black ink on it. She tied it closed with a thin black ribbon."

"She sent some type of scroll to the king as well. Perhaps you could take a look at it and tell me if it looks the same. She could be attempting to control him as well."

"Yes, of course." I nod.

Vale rises and pulls on a cord by the wall to summon Marcus. After a few moments, he appears back at the door. "You may enter," says Vale.

"Yes, Commander."

"Marcus, I need you to check and see if King Vespes is in his room. If he is there, do not disturb him, simply come back and tell me. If he is not there, I need you to check on his desk for the scroll from the empress Celia of Icelandia. Do this very discreetly, as you must not be seen. It is for the king's protection. Once you find it, bring it directly to me. Do you understand?"

"Yes, Commander."

"You may go."

The servant bows and leaves with haste. Vale looks back at Kara and Dominic. "Fear not, Marcus is my most trustworthy servant. He has been with me for a long time, and you can be sure he is on our side. If the scroll is there, he will find it," he says. "We can talk more later, after we secure the scroll. I'm sure you are hungry and tired from all your traveling. Please, let me escort you to the dining room."

"Thank you," I say. "But what are you going to tell the king and his family about me? Who will you say that I am? And is it all right for me to keep my dog with me here?" I reach down and pat Buddy on the head, looking up at him hopefully.

"You are Lady Kara Cortere, cousin of King Greffen of Volkenland, who is married to Princess Delvana, the king's other sister. We will say that you have heard of the upcoming wedding and was sent ahead of Princess Delvana to offer congratulations and to see if you can be of any assistance to Princess Mira with the wedding preparations." He looks down at Buddy and, with a smile, reaches down to pet him. "I can see he is a valiant and special dog. He is most welcome here. The king has no pets of his own in the castle, just the horses, which he loves to ride, and Princess Trea has a cat. We will have to introduce them to each other. King Vespes loves dogs. He has always wanted to have one, but his father did not permit it. I do not think he will object to…what is his name?"

"Buddy, his name is Buddy," I say with a sigh of relief.

As we make our way to the dining room, Vale gives instructions to one of the servants we pass to inform King Vespes and Princess Trea of our arrival and that he is escorting us to the dining hall. The servant nods and heads up the stairs with this news.

As we walk to the dining room, I look around in wonder at the magnificence of the palace. Every room we pass is adorned with beautiful paintings and chandeliers that glisten with colors of light dancing on the walls. The furnishings are luxurious, with vibrant colors everywhere. I blink with amazement at the sight, taking it all in. Finally, we enter the dining room. There is a long table with roses at the center of it, and two candelabras on each end. Servants bow and greet us as we walk in, and we are invited to sit at the table.

As we approach the table, a pretty young woman enters the room from the other entrance, dressed in a regal gown. She looks to be about sixteen and has a warm, friendly look about her. Commander Vale bows to her, and Dominic and I follow suit.

"Welcome! I am Princess Trea. The king would like to welcome you also, but he is not feeling well at the moment. I am so glad to meet a new cousin!" She looks then at Dominic. "And are you family as well?"

Before Dominic can respond, Vale speaks up. "Princess Trea, let me introduce to you Dominic of Oakendale. He is traveling along with your cousin Lady Kara Cortere of Volkenland as her friend and guide. They have just arrived from a long journey, and I was seeing to their comfort. Lady Kara has also brought along another traveling companion, as you can see, her dog, Buddy. I was hoping that we could introduce Mirabelle and Buddy so they could become friends as well."

Trea has already crouched down to pay close attention to her new canine guest. Buddy responds by licking her hands and wagging his tail profusely. "Of course, I am so glad you brought him! It looks like he may need a proper bath after being in the mud and rain out there." She glances at their clothing and the blankets that are still wrapped around them. "Would you like to change first before you eat? I can have the servants reheat the food for you if you would like to go make yourselves more comfortable first."

Dominic looks at me knowingly and responds, "I think we can do that after. It's been a while since we've eaten, and we're both quite hungry."

"Very well, then. Please have a seat here with me here at the table. I will have the servants prepare a dish for Buddy in the kitchen area. We can introduce him to Mirabelle later. She's catnapping up in my room at the moment," she says with a smile.

"Thank you so much," I say, thinking that I already like this new pretend relative of mine.

During dinner, Dominic helps to steer the conversation away from me and my life in Volkenland, my contact with Delvana, and so on so that I will not accidentally say the wrong thing and give myself away. I nod and say a few general words of agreement to his stories of my supposed life there. Then I ask about King Vespes and his upcoming marriage plans and how I can be of assistance.

"Well, Vespes wants to be married as soon as possible," she says to them. "I've been trying to get him to wait a little while since he has suddenly become ill. He thinks I'm just agreeing with our royal advisers, who don't want him to marry her, but he's wrong. I like Princess Mira. I don't know why they object so much, but I do think that he should rest right now until he is better before continuing with the plans and preparations."

"Is the king resting now?" asks Dominic.

"Yes, he is lying down, and Princess Mira is up there, reading to him and helping him with his obligations to the kingdom. Usually, Erol, his butler, would be doing that, but he's made it clear he only wants Mira with him right now." Sighing, she continues, "I guess I'm just not used to having to share my brother's attention so much. It's been just me and him as a family for so long."

"That must be difficult for you. Do you and the princess get along well?"

"Oh, yes, she's very sweet. I thought we'd be able to spend more time getting to know each other with preparing the wedding and all, but since Vespes has been sick, she hasn't wanted to leave his side. And he doesn't seem to have tolerance for anyone else but her right now. It's a bit strange to me, because Vespes always makes time for me, especially since our father's accident." She looks saddened for a moment and then continues, "But I have to adjust to this. I'm sure things will improve after he is feeling better. And besides, I'm not losing a brother, I'm gaining a new sister and friend!"

"When do you think we will get to meet them?" I ask.

"Well, he has been coming down for most meals, except for tonight, of course. I would think probably by breakfast tomorrow morning we can make the introductions. Would you like me to show you to your rooms now? I'm sure you must be tired from your journey here."

"Yes, that would be nice. Thank you!"

"Of course. Come with me this way," she says, leading us to the stairway in the grand hall. After we get to the second floor, she leads us down another hall to another hidden stairwell behind a dark-green door. It is a circular stairway up to the third floor, where there is another hall leading to many more splendidly ornate rooms. She opens an ivory door painted with small flowers on it for me. "I hope you will be comfortable here. This is one of my favorite guest rooms on this floor."

Inside, I look around at the delicate flowers painted on the wardrobe and on the chest in front of the canopied bed. "It's lovely." I smile.

"There's a bath area to the left behind those curtains. Just pull on this cord if you need Marta. She'll be your maidservant while you're here with us, and she can get you anything you might need."

"Thank you so much."

Trea smiles and starts to go back out with Dominic to show him to his room. Turning back for a moment, she says to me, "Dominic will be in the room down the hall with the blue door. As of right now, you are my only guests on this floor. Marta will be in the room across from you, and George, who will assist Dominic, is down the hall as well in the room next to him. Please make yourselves at home. Breakfast is served at nine o'clock, so I will look forward to seeing you then. And once again, welcome to Silvenia!"

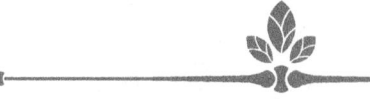

Jonathan

Julia heads down the corridor away from Kara's room. For the past month, she has been visiting with her sister daily, reading to her, talking to her, and just sitting with her in silence. There has been no change. In fact, the doctor told her parents yesterday that if there is no improvement soon, they will have to move her out of the hospital to hospice care. Julia knows this is bad news. Hospices are for people who are dying, for people with no hope for recovery.

But Julia still has hope. It feels like a tiny burning ember deep inside her, but she is determined to keep it alive. She carries Kara's leaf with her everywhere and whispers prayers under her breath to a God she doesn't really know. The news from the doctor yesterday has clouded her thoughts again, and she walks along aimlessly back toward the cafeteria, not sure what she is doing or where she is going.

"Chapel," says the sign above the door to her right. *I haven't noticed this room before,* she thinks to herself. Before she can talk herself out of it, she pushes open the door. Inside is a small windowless room with a stained glass image of a cross at the front. There is a light behind it, and it glows with colors of brown and purple and red. She feels drawn in and takes a few steps toward it.

Sitting down in one of the little wooden pews, she looks around curiously. There is soft music playing from a speaker on the floor. It sounds like hymns from an old church. Like the one her grandmother used to go to. She closes her eyes and listens for a moment. "God, are You here?" She hears the whisper of her own voice and nothing else.

The room is empty and quiet. She slumps down in the pew and stares at the image of the cross. "I know I haven't spoken to You in a while. I'm sorry," she whispers. She feels a tear brim up in the corner of her eye. "Are You here? Do You see me?"

Suddenly, the door pushes open, and she quickly wipes away the tear and glances up at the intruder. It's a young boy, probably about seven or eight. He walks in by himself, carrying a notebook with him. He sits down in the pew behind her. He is talking quietly to himself and seems oblivious to her.

Who is this kid? And where are his parents? she thinks to herself, slightly annoyed by the intrusion. She closes her eyes and listens to his conversation with himself. She can't quite make it out. He's talking quietly and rapidly, something about bugs, different kinds of bugs.

"Did you know there are seven different types of crickets?"

"What did you say?" says Julia, turning around and looking at him.

"There are seven different types of crickets and fifteen different types of grasshoppers," he says, lifting up his notebook to show her his drawings of them. "This is a common field grasshopper, and this is a meadow grasshopper."

"Oh, that's interesting. Did you draw all those by—"

He interrupts her excitedly in midsentence. "The scientific name for the meadow grasshopper is actually *Chorthippus parallelus*," he says, glancing up at her for a moment, blinking and then staring back down at his notebook again. He goes on to tell her about the other species he had drawn, barely pausing to take a breath. Julia sits watching him, listening quietly, fascinated by his rapid recitation of facts and information.

He stops for a moment and looks up. Then he pulls a pencil out of his pocket, lays his tablet down on the pew, and begins to draw. She watches him, focused for a moment on this young stranger. He is distracting her from her pain for a moment, and for that she is grateful. "What are you drawing now?" she asks.

"An *Omocestus viridulus*, which is actually a common green grasshopper. They like to live in tall grass and prefer a wet climate."

"My sister is in a coma," she says to the back of his head as he leans over his paper, focused on his drawing. He makes no motion that he hears her.

"Desert locusts can swarm in the billions," he says, not looking up. "But they mostly live in Europe, Asia, and Africa."

"I see. May I see your drawing when you're done?"

"Yes," he says matter-of-factly.

Julia leans back in the pew again and closes her eyes. The boy continues drawing and talking to himself quietly.

"Crickets like to eat carrots and lettuce and leaves of plants. Crickets are omnivores, and grasshoppers are herbivores. Here is my picture of a grasshopper eating a leaf." He lifts up his tablet to her.

Julia turns and looks. "Oh, wow, that's really good. You're quite an artist." The picture triggers her memory, and she pulls out Kara's leaf from her pocket. "Do you know what kind of leaf this is?" she asks him.

He reaches out to grasp it, and she hesitates for a moment and then hands it to him. "Be careful with it," she says, gingerly handing it over.

He stares at it for a moment. "It looks like a mixture of an elm and a maple leaf. I've never seen a leaf like this one before. Where did you get it?"

"My sister found it."

"I don't know as much about plants as I do about insects. Did you know that praying mantises are carnivores? They eat other insects instead of plants like grasshoppers do."

Suddenly, the door to the chapel pushes open and a woman rushes in when she sees the boy. "Jonathan! I told you to wait in the hall for me, not to go into another room. I've been looking for you for ten minutes!" She looks up at Julia, apologizing, "I hope he didn't disturb you. He likes to talk to people."

"Oh, not at all. I can tell he is very smart. He was telling me about insects."

"Yes, he loves to talk about them. Come along, Jonathan. Your father is waiting for us down the hall."

He gathers his notebook and pencil and walks toward the door with his mother.

"Bye, Jonathan." Julia waves. "It was nice meeting you."

"It's a key," he says softly, walking out the door.

"Wait, what did you say?" she calls after him.

"The leaf," he says. "It's a key."

Julia rises up and starts to walk after him.

"Come on, Jonathan. Don't bother the nice young lady. It's time to go." His mother hurries him along the corridor, and Julia watches them walk away together down the hall.

"Did he say the leaf is a key? What does that mean?" She walks up to the cross picture and puts her hand on it. "What did he mean? Was that supposed to mean something to me or was that just random words from a boy dealing with some type of autism?" She pulls the leaf out again and looks at it.

The leaf is a key. His words echo in her head the rest of the day. She lies in bed restlessly that night, thinking of Kara, the boy, and the bird that followed her home. Finally falling asleep, she slips in and out of dreams, of castles, birds, and large colorful trees with leaves falling all around.

Marta

I feel the warmth of the sunlight streaming in through the window. Opening my eyes, I see it casting rays of colors onto my bed in shifting patterns of red and gold. The wind is blowing softly, and the sheer curtains of the window drift up and down. Looking around this elegant guest room, I think of my bedroom at home. I think of my mom and dad and Julia, missing their familiar faces.

I sit up and see my Bible on the bedside table. I had been reading it late last night before I fell asleep. Putting my hand on it, I pull it over and begin to read where I left off: "Wait on the Lord: Be of good courage, And He shall strengthen your heart; Wait, I say, on the Lord" (Ps. 27:14 NKJV).

Closing my eyes, I search to see Him again. "Jesus, help me. I need You to guide my steps. I don't know what I'm doing here. I know You have a plan, and I'm depending on You." I wait quietly for a while, listening expectantly. I hear nothing but feels peace inside that I am here now, somehow in the right place at the right time.

I hear bells ringing and decide I had better get up to be ready in time for breakfast. I am just finishing getting dressed when I hear a knock on my door. "Coming!" I call out.

I open my door, and a young girl is standing there. "Pardon me, Ms. Kara. I am Marta. Is there anything you need this morning before you go down to breakfast? I am here to assist you."

"Oh, I'm just fine, thank you. Is it time to head down for breakfast now?"

"Yes, madame. Would you like me to show you the way?"

"Actually, I think I would like to wait for my friend Dominic. Have you seen him yet this morning?"

"Yes, I think I see him coming down the hall now."

I look up and see him approaching. "Good morning! Shall we head down to breakfast together?" he asks.

"Yes, let's."

"I'm just going to tidy up your room a bit while you're out, Ms. Kara."

"Thank you, Marta."

She does a small curtsy and heads into the room. Dominic and I head toward the stairwell together.

"Did you sleep well?" he asks.

"Yes, very well. Did you?"

"Yes, very well indeed."

"I'm glad you're here with me, Dominic."

"Yes, I'm very glad of it too!" He extends his elbow, and we descend together, arm in arm. "Don't worry about what to say to the king. Just be yourself and follow my lead."

As we enter the dining room, a servant hurries to pull out my chair. Trea is there, talking with another beautiful-looking woman at the table. The king is nowhere in sight. As we approach, Trea looks up and smiles at us. "Good morning! Please, come sit down and join us. Mira, these are the guests I was telling you about, Lady Kara of Volkenland, and her friend and guide, Sir Dominic."

"Please just call me Dominic," he says with a little bow in her direction.

"And call me Kara."

"Let me introduce to you my new, soon-to-be sister-in-law, Princess Mira."

"Hello, it's so nice to meet you," she says graciously.

I attempt an awkward little curtsy before sitting down next to Dominic. "We are so glad to meet you, Princess."

"Please just call me Mira."

Before they can ask, Trea explains, "The king was planning on joining us for breakfast, but I'm afraid he is still feeling poorly. Perhaps later today there will be an opportunity to visit with him. I really am getting quite concerned. I should call for the doctor to come out again today and check on him."

"I think he is just very tired, and his body is trying to recover its strength," says Mira. "I'm sure he will be better soon. I really should go back up to him now and try to get him to eat something. He asked me to bring him some juice and toast."

"Of course," says Trea. "Talia, would you please get some toast and juice ready for Mira to bring up to the king?"

"Yes, Princess Trea."

I look over at Mira, trying to get a read on her. Then I glance at Dominic, and he nods encouragingly. "Congratulations on your upcoming marriage," I say. "I will be happy to be of assistance to you in any way I can."

"Thank you, Kara. Trea has already been so helpful. Vespes and I just want to be married as soon as possible. We are so excited to spend the rest of our lives together!" She says this with a little too much forced energy, and the words sound false and empty to me, but Trea doesn't seem to notice this.

"Yes, we have the servants working on the details of getting the dress ready and procuring the flowers and the decorations."

"We don't want a big wedding. Just a small ceremony here with close friends and family. We are so glad you are here to join us." Mira smiles at me and Dominic.

"We are glad to be here," says Dominic. "Have you set a date for the ceremony?"

"Yes, Vespes wants us to be wed on the next Sunday, in the chapel right here in the castle."

Trea's eyes fly open wide. "That's in less than a week! Will your mother even be able to get here in time?"

Mira looks down for a moment, her countenance fading. "I'm sure she will be here. Anyway, you mustn't trouble yourselves. We don't want a grand event, just an intimate gathering. That's what Vespes wants."

"Oh my goodness, we still have so much to do! I must go speak with Cora at once! Please excuse me." Trea rises and heads with urgent steps toward the kitchen.

Mira also rises up as Talia hands over the king's breakfast tray to her. "I'll go check on Vespes. He's probably hungry by now.

Please excuse me as well," she says to us and heads back toward the stairway.

Dominic and I find that we are the only two left in the dining hall now. I look over at him as he finishes up his toast with jam. "What now?" I ask.

"Well, there's not much time until the wedding, that's for sure."

"I do hope we get to meet with the king today. I think we really need to speak with him before we know how to proceed."

"I would agree with that. But I don't know if that will be possible, seeing that he only wants Mira attending to him." He looks over at me, pulling at his beard thoughtfully. "Perhaps I can be a distraction." He lowers his voice considerably, coming closer to me. "I could ask to visit with both of the princesses for a tour of the gardens. I could say you are tired and went for a nap, and they will feel obliged to be hospitable to me as their guest and show me around. Then I can ask Vale to take you to see the king while he is alone, and he can stand guard and prevent any interruptions while you are there."

I feel a bit nervous at this suggestion. "But he hasn't wanted to see anyone other than Mira. Not even his own sister! What if he's in a bad mood and decides to have me beheaded or something!"

Dominic laughs. "He is known to have a bit of a temper, but I don't think he has had anyone beheaded yet. No, my dear, but on a serious note, you do need to meet with him and, if it seems right at that time, warn him of what you were shown."

"But he doesn't know me at all. Why would he listen to a complete stranger?"

He looks at me with understanding. "Just go see him. The time is short, and if we hesitate too long, we may fail in our attempt to save this kingdom. Kara, the king has been ill, but has it occurred to you that if this is the work of some type of poison, it could be killing him?"

"You think Mira is trying to kill him?" I whisper back.

"It's certainly possible. We must do everything we can to protect the king and preserve the kingdom of Silvenia. I think that is our highest priority."

I close my eyes for a moment and search my heart. "All right," I agree. "I'll go. I'll be in my room, waiting for Vale to bring me to the king."

Dominic nods in agreement, rising from his chair. "I'd better get busy, then!" He heads out and leaves me sitting there, lost in my thoughts.

Meanwhile, Marta pulls up the flowery quilt to the top of the bed and then adjusts the pillows on top. As she leans over the bed, her metal hair clip falls out and falls behind the back of the bed. She hears it land on the wooden floor. Crouching down low, she tries to reach it with her arm, but it has fallen too far under. Her hair is undone and falling in her eyes now as she tries to get to it. *Maybe I can reach it with my leg,* she thinks, glancing back at the door to see if anyone is watching. No one is in the hall that she can see. *Still, I better get up and shut the door so no one will wonder what I am doing sprawled out on the floor underneath the guest bed.*

With the door now shut, Marta walks back over to the bed and sits down low on the floor, facing the bed. She takes off her shoe so she can feel the metal clasp with her foot and pull it toward her. Reaching with her leg, she scans the area up close to the wall at the head of the bed. She feels something metal and tries to grab it, scrunching her foot over it. It doesn't budge. *Hmmm, maybe it's stuck in the floorboard.* She tries again, using more force, and ends up scraping the bottom of her foot over it.

Wincing, she pulls out her leg. "What have I done?" There is bright-red blood dripping from the sole of her foot now. She can see a jagged gash about an inch long, and her foot throbs with pain. Reaching up, she tries to grab one of her cleaning rags to stop the flow of blood. She scoots over to the bedside table and manages to grab one.

"Drat!" she says out loud, pressing the cloth to her bleeding foot. After a few moments, she peels back the fabric, and more blood comes gushing out again, spilling onto the floor. She quickly presses it back on. Sitting there for a moment, she remembers back to a time when she was about five years old. She was running outside with her sister, playing tag, when she suddenly fell forward onto the gravel and scraped up her knee. Blood was pouring down her leg, and she cried out with pain and fear. Her mother was there quickly, running over and crouching down to see her wounded knee. With a kiss on the head, she picked up her daughter and carried her inside, applying an ointment and binding up her wound. She remembers the love and comfort she felt that day as her mother then picked her up and held her, rocking her in a big rocking chair, telling her that she would be just fine.

Her mom is gone now; she died three years ago, when Marta was twelve, of pneumonia. "I mustn't think of her now. That won't help anything," she says to herself, wiping away a tear. "I just need to get downstairs to Cora. She will know how to help me." She wraps the cloth around her foot tightly and tries to stuff her foot back in her shoe. Finally, she gets it all in there and, wincing, pushes herself up to a standing position.

She hobbles over to the door, and right as she's about to open it, it opens on its own and I stand there with a surprised look on my face. "Oh! Sorry, I forgot you were in here, Marta. I almost knocked you over!"

"It's all right. I just hurt my foot, and I need to go downstairs to see Cora. I will finish cleaning your room when I get back."

I look at the young girl and can see the distress on her face. "Oh my goodness, please sit down for a moment. Let me help you." I gesture toward the peach velvet chair right beside her.

"Oh no, I couldn't. I already got blood on the floor beside your bed. I'm so sorry."

"Marta, please, I'm happy to help." I help her ease into the chair and crouch down to look at her foot.

"How did this happen?"

"Well, I was making your bed when my hair clasp fell out and dropped under the bed. I couldn't reach it with my arm, so I was using my foot to try to grab it. It must have gotten stuck in a floorboard or something, because it scraped the bottom of my foot."

I look under the bed. "Oh, I see it. But it's over by the wall. I think what you scraped your foot on was that nail that's sticking up under the bed." I head back over to Marta. "May I take a look at it?"

Marta nods and gingerly pulls her foot out from her shoe again. I carefully unravel the cloth and look at the jagged gash. "It's still bleeding. But I think with proper help and a good bandage, you'll be right as rain!" I quickly wrap it back up, and as I do so, I remember Jesus's words to me: "You have My power in you that heals. Use it freely."

I pause for a moment and then speak to Marta. "I will get you the bandages and ointment you need, but first, may I pray for your foot?"

"Yes," she answers in a quiet voice.

I place my hand over the injured area softly. "In the name of Jesus, I command this foot to be healed! Amen." That's all I can think of to say, and then I look up at Marta. She is crying.

"What's wrong? Did I hurt you?"

"No, no. It's just been a long time since someone has stopped to be concerned about me. You remind me of my mother. I was just thinking about her. She died when I was twelve." The tears continue to pour down her face.

I feel compassion rise up in me and I reach out to hug her. I hear a soft voice inside: *Tell her I love her and want to be her Savior. Tell her she has a heavenly Father who watches over her all the time.* I tell her this as quickly as I hear it, and she cries harder.

"Marta, do you know who Jesus is?"

"I've heard of Him from my mother. She would sing us songs about Him."

"He's real. He wants you to know He loves you. He has saved you from your sins. Will you ask Him into your heart?"

"Yes, please! I want to know Him."

I pray a quick prayer with her. "Just repeat after me. Jesus, You died and rose to life again to save me from my sins. Please come into my heart now and be my Savior. Amen." Marta repeats the words and then looks up at me, beaming. "Does He have my mom with Him? In heaven?"

"Yes, and now that you know Him as your Savior, too, you will join her there one day."

Marta smiles. "I feel so good! Like I'm not alone anymore."

"You're not. He will always be with you. His Holy Spirit lives inside of you now, and His Word says He will never leave you or forsake you. You must begin to read His Word every day now so you can grow in Him and get to know Him."

"Where do I find His Word?"

"It's in the Bible. Do you have a Bible?"

"No. But I think I saw one in the large library downstairs when I was cleaning in there. Do you think they would let me read that one?"

"I'll ask for you," I reply, smiling back at her. "Now, you just rest there a moment and let me get you a proper bandage! I'll be right back." I rise and head back out into the hall. Marta smiles and lets out a little sigh as she leans back into the padded chair. She feels like she's wrapped in a blanket of peace, and she doesn't want to move or change anything in this moment.

After a few minutes, I return along with Cora, who is carrying a basket full of bandages and ointments. "Marta, my dear girl, let me take a look at your foot and get you all fixed up."

Marta extends her foot to her, and Cora gently unwraps the cloth, which is now soaked with red blood. She tosses the soiled cloth to the side and looks at the wound. It has stopped bleeding now, and the underside of her foot is crusted with dried blood. She takes a wet cloth and gently washes it clean, then she examines the cut.

I am next to Cora, looking at it too, and I let out a little gasp.

"What's wrong?" asks Cora.

"Nothing. It's just that…I mean, when I left here a few minutes ago, there was a large gash that was bleeding an awful lot. Now it's closed up and doesn't look bad at all!"

"Yes, I agree, it doesn't look bad at all, just a little scrape that's already closed up and should heal just fine. But I can see it did bleed a lot by the look of this cloth. How odd!"

"What? Let me see!" Marta pulls up her foot and looks at it again in wonder. "Oh my gosh! It's totally better! How could that be?" Marta can hardly believe it. "It doesn't even hurt anymore. Cora, Kara prayed for my foot, and now it's all better. She asked Jesus to heal my foot, and He did!"

"Well, good for you! I'm glad you're okay. I was worried there for a minute when Kara was describing it to me on the way up here.

I don't think you even need a bandage now, by looking at it. Do you want me to put one on, anyway?"

Marta looks at her foot again and sees it is completely sealed up with healthy-looking pink skin all around it. "No, I don't need it. I'm fine!"

"All right, then. I'm heading back down to the kitchen. It's a very busy time for me!" Cora rises up and quickly heads back out of the room, carrying her basket.

"And don't worry about cleaning the rest of this room right now," I say. "I've got to get ready for something and need a bit of privacy."

"Of course, Ms. Kara. And you won't forget about getting the Bible for me, right?"

"I will make that a priority." I smile at her and give her a quick hug before she leaves the room.

Closing the door, I turn and begin to pray quietly. I thank God for Marta's miraculous healing and then pray for the right words to speak to the king. I pray fervently, my words coming out rapidly, and suddenly, I realize I am praying in another language. "I'm praying in tongues! I forgot that I can do this!"

I remember that I had prayed to receive the baptism in the Holy Spirit as a young girl in a church camp meeting. I had been able to speak in tongues then and was very excited about it at first. Time had gone by, and I had gotten busy with school and friends and forgot all about this wonderful gift from God that I had received.

Listening to myself, I am amazed at the syllables that flow out of me without effort. I let it flow, remembering that this is the Holy Spirit praying through me, God's will, His perfect plan! "Lord, let Your kingdom come, let Your will be done in this place!" I say in English, extending my hands out around me as I pace the room, praying.

I feel the presence of the Lord in the room. Realizing this, I kneel down in front of the bed and close my eyes. I feel a weighty presence around me and stop speaking. Raising my hands up to heaven, I wait in silence.

Rap, rap! came the knock on my door. Vale has arrived to bring me before the king. It is time to go.

Gaelyn

Gaelyn is in the kitchen, drying dishes and putting them away. She hears men outside, making noise in the courtyard, and looks out the small circular window. She sees a group of men talking and others just milling about. Some of them are carrying sacks and loading them on the back of a cart. She watches them quietly for a moment, and then she sees him. *There he is! That's the young man who was kind to me when they took me from my home in Roten. He said his name to me. What was it?* She searches her memory for a moment. *Friedrich! That's what he said.*

She watches him with curiosity as he carries a sack past her to the cart. He doesn't see her watching. He's a bit on the short side, small but strong-looking, with brown hair and a gentle manner. She remembers how he pushed the other soldier away from her who was making lewd comments and manhandling her. She remembers how frightened she felt that night and that he tried to comfort her, telling her that he wouldn't let anyone harm her.

And now she is here, working in the empress's castle in Northern Icelandia, far from home. She remembers her mother crying and her father being restrained as they took her away from them. At least she knew Arten was here. *Where is he now?* She looks out among the soldiers, searching for his familiar face. Finally she spots him; he is up by the stable area, talking to Vico—Gaelyn remembers Vico from their hometown as well. Arten and Vico had grown up together in Roten and had always been close friends.

"Gaelyn, once you finish with that, I need you to bring me some potatoes from the food cellar below. We will need that for the supper tonight," says Berta, the head cook.

"Yes, ma'am," Gaelyn responds. Berta eyes her with a knowing look. "Keep your eyes in here and out of trouble. It's best to keep a low profile in this place. Especially for a young girl like you."

"Yes, ma'am. I was just looking for my brother," she responds, her cheeks reddening a bit as she dries the last bowl. "I'll head down to the cellar now for those potatoes." She hurries out of the room, away from Berta's watchful eye.

Descending down the cool, dark stairwell, she blinks to help her eyes adjust to the diminished light in the cellar. There is a small window at the top of the cellar toward the ceiling, and she can see the men's boots as they pass by on the turf above her. It's cold and dark in this room, and though she is glad to be free for a moment, she doesn't plan on staying down here for too long. She looks around the shelves for the potatoes.

There are vegetables all over the place, in sacks and baskets. She hears a scuttling sound, and looking to her left, she sees a rat run under a large sack in the corner. With a shudder, she makes a mental note to steer clear of that side of the room.

On a long narrow table over by the window area, she spies the potato sacks. As she walks over to it, an idea begins to form in her mind. *If I just pull that table over under the window and put another chair on top of it, I could reach that high window and possibly climb out through it to escape!* She plays this image out in her thoughts for a moment.

But it's so cold outside at night, and home is a very long journey from here. I probably would get lost trying to find my way back. And even if I did get home, what's to stop them from retrieving me and bringing me right back? She paces back and forth in the dark cellar. *Think, Gaelyn, think. You're not helpless, you are brave, like Arten,* she encourages herself. *I could still find my way to a road and just get out of here! Find a town or small village where I can lie low and be safe, and then return home later, after the empress has forgotten all about me.*

She looks around her, the plan growing in her mind. *There's plenty of food here that I could pack up in a sack and bring with me. And I'll wear layers of clothing to protect from the cold. Arten taught me how to build a proper fire, though I'll probably have to wait a few days before I can do that, so they don't track me down.*

She begins to grab an assortment of vegetables and hide them in batches on the right side of the room to retrieve later. Suddenly, she hears footsteps approaching the stairs above her. The door opens abruptly, and she hears boots clomping down the wooden stairs. She looks up to see who it is.

It's him! The young man who was kind to me the other night. She looks at his face, and he looks back at her and pauses, a bit startled in the moment.

"Oh, hello," he says, smiling at her. "I was sent down here to retrieve some more grain sacks for the soldiers."

"And I was just getting some potatoes for the supper tonight." She smiles back at him. "I think those are the grain sacks over there." She points to a low shelf full of large brown cloth bags.

He begins to walk toward them. "How are you doing? I've been thinking about you and hoping you were doing all right here in the castle."

"I'm fine. I just miss my home and family."

"I know how that feels. I was taken from my home, too, when I was twelve."

She looks at him, intrigued. "Have you been able to see your family since then?"

"No," he says, grabbing two large bags of grain. "But I hope to see them soon." He eyes her, contemplating how much he can say.

"What is it?" she asks, urging him on. "Please, speak freely."

Looking up the stairs, he pauses for a moment. The door at the top is shut, and they are alone in the cellar. Finally, he blurts out, "I am planning to escape and eventually return to my family home. But first, I must get away from here." He watches her eyes, hoping he can trust her. "You must not speak of this to anyone. Can I trust you?"

"Yes!" she answers quickly. "But I have one request."

"What is it?"

"Take me with you!"

He looks at her with surprise and amazement on his face. "You want to come with me?"

"Yes! I was just down here, thinking of how to escape on my own, but with the both of us together, we could help each other. Look, I was just storing some food to retrieve later and bring with me. I think we can climb up to this window—"

"Gaelyn!" yells Berta from upstairs. She hears her steps approaching the stairwell. "What is taking you so long? What are you doing down there?" She opens the door to the stairs and looks down.

"We'll speak later!" she whispers urgently to Friedrich, touching his arm as she hurries back up the stairs, leaving him there. He watches her ascend, new feelings of hope rising within him.

Berta scolds Gaelyn for daydreaming and not doing her work as she lifts the potato sacks out of her arms.

"I'm sorry, ma'am. I had a little trouble finding them at first."

"Never mind. Just go outside to that little wooden table and get to work peeling those. I'll need two large bowlfuls for tonight."

"Yes, ma'am." Gaelyn grabs a peeling knife and two large bowls and heads outside to get started. She has just started her work when Friedrich comes back outside, carrying sacks of grain on his shoulders, and he passes by in front of her. On his second trip back with more sacks, he pretends to trip and drops a sack close to her on the ground.

As he kneels to pick it up, he whispers, "Meet me in the cellar tonight, at midnight."

She nods at him and continues peeling, acting focused on her task, stuffing down her feelings of fear and hopeful excitement.

"Hey, boy! Hurry up with those sacks and leave the pretty lady alone. Can't you see she's trying to work?" yells a rough-looking soldier walking toward her with two others.

Friedrich quickly picks up the grain and walks in front of them toward the cart.

"Go on!" One of the other soldiers pushes him out of the way, and they continue walking toward Gaelyn. She doesn't look up.

"Hello, miss," says the first one. "You just let me know if anyone is bothering you out here, and I'll be sure to take care of them for you." He crouches down in front of her, and she is forced to look up at him.

"I'm fine, thank you. No one is bothering me." She lifts her knife for a moment in front of her face and holds it there, glaring at him with defiance.

"She's a fierce little beauty, isn't she?" The other one laughs, ribbing him in the side.

"That's the way I like them." He grins widely, showing a wide gap in his smile from a missing tooth.

"What's going on over here?" barks Arten, approaching from behind with Vico.

"Nothing, Captain. Just making sure no one is bothering this young lady while she works."

Arten walks up to him confrontationally, with Vico at his side. "Leave her alone. She is my sister, and if anyone even looks at her sideways, I will deal with him swiftly." He pulls out his long knife strapped to his side. Vico grabs his as well and stands beside him.

The three men back up, hands in the air. "Yessir, Captain. We don't want no trouble."

"Now, get back to loading. We have to be ready to leave here by dawn."

Gaelyn looks up at Arten, questioning, "Where are you going?"

"We have to return to Silvenia. We are bringing the empress there for her daughter's wedding."

The gears in her mind begin turning. *This will make it easier to escape!* she thinks to herself. "How long will she—I mean all of you—be gone?"

"For a while, my dear girl," comes the empress's voice from a balcony high above them.

Startled, Gaelyn looks up and sees her dark profile up high on the circular stone deck.

"But don't worry, you will be coming along as my personal maidservant. Aren't you glad? You'll be there for all the festivities along with your brother." She speaks in a cool, commanding tone, her back stiff and straight as she looks out over her army.

"Yes, Empress," she replies weakly, alarmed at this turn of events. *What about Friedrich?* she wonders. *Is he thinking we can try to escape tonight? This might be our only chance!* She goes back to peeling the potatoes, her mind racing with thoughts of what to do. The empress lingers, peering out over her balcony, and Gaelyn feels that menacing presence above her, watching everything.

Friedrich

Secrets

I open the door, and Vale is standing there. "May I come in for a moment, Ms. Kara?"

"Yes, of course," I reply, closing the door behind him quietly.

"We have obtained the original scroll that the empress sent to King Vespes. Just looking at it, I cannot tell anything sinister, but I would like you to examine it later this evening, perhaps after dinner."

"I will be happy to."

"Very good. The king is alone at this moment, but he is not well. He may not give you the warmest of welcomes, but this is the best opportunity to catch him alone, since Mira and Trea are both out walking with Dominic in the garden."

"I am ready to go see him."

We proceed out into the hall and head down the stairs to the king's bedroom. "I will be right outside the door if you need me and to make sure your conversation is kept private. If Mira returns unexpectedly and I see her downstairs, I will knock on the door with three knocks to prepare you, and you can make a quick exit before she comes up."

"All right." I feel myself tremble as I stand before his bedroom door.

Vale knocks on the king's door. "Enter!" We hear from inside.

Vale opens the door and says to the king, "Your Highness, may I present Lady Kara, your cousin from Volkenland. She has an urgent matter that she needs to speak with you about." Before he can object, Vale gently pushes me inside, and I stand there awkwardly in front of the king.

Vale retreats with a quick bow while the king coughs and pushes himself up in his bed to a semisitting posture. "Commander Vale! This is quite irregular! What is the meaning of this?"

"I beg your pardon, my king, but I trust you will see this is quite urgent."

The king coughs again, glancing up at me. "Very well, but make this quick. I am not myself at the moment, and I need to rest." He eyes me warily.

I study his face and see a young man with handsome features, brown hair, and a short beard. His hair is tousled and sticking up on the side, and he has dark circles under his eyes. Despite his unkempt appearance, he has a noble-looking face, and his eyes appear gentle yet dark and intense, as if he is troubled by something. I feel strangely drawn to him.

"I apologize for my absence and disheveled appearance, my cousin," he says. "I have not been well. What is this matter that could not wait?"

My words tumble out. "I apologize for the intrusion as well, Your Majesty. I come before you with concern for your well-being and the well-being of your beautiful kingdom. I have been sent from the Great One to pray for you so that you can be made well, and to let you know that your kingdom is in great danger."

"The Great One? Do you mean God? Are you telling me you've been sent from God? I thought you were just my cousin from Volkenland, here to attend my wedding." He attempts a laugh but instead coughs again and winces, grabbing his side.

"Please, I can see you're hurting. Will you let me pray for you?"

"Yes, go ahead," he whispers, his face contorted with pain.

I step forward and gently place my hand over his. "In the name of Jesus, I command this pain to leave!" I watch his face and see it gradually relax. He looks up at me, and I take a step back.

"Who are you? How did you do that?"

"It wasn't me. It was the power of God. It was Jesus."

He rubs his forehead. "Well, I do feel a little better now. What is that you were saying about my kingdom being in danger?"

Rap, rap, rap! comes a knock on the door.

"Enter!"

"I beg your pardon again, Your Highness. Are you ready for your lunch to be brought up?"

"Yes, and you can bring up some food for my cousin as well."

"Oh, I realize I need to go right now. Please, may we continue our discussion later?"

"What? I thought you had urgent news for me that couldn't wait!"

"I wanted to pray for you—that was part of it. The rest, I will have to tell you later. I must go see to something first. You do feel a bit better now, don't you?"

"Yes, the pain in my side is gone." He pauses, looking at me curiously. "Be sure to come back later so we can finish this talk."

"Yes, Your Majesty." I curtsy and hurry out the door. Vale walks with me down the hall, and we pass Mira walking toward us with the king's lunch tray.

"Hello, Mira," I say as we cross paths. "I finally got to meet the king, and I said a little prayer for him to get better," I say with a warm smile.

"Oh, that's nice," she says with a surprised look on her face.

"I'll see you at dinner!" I state, walking down the stairs with Vale at my side. Mira stands outside the king's bedroom door with the tray for a moment, watching us descend.

What was that about? she wonders. *Is that girl up to something? Or am I just being paranoid?* She heads into the doorway and sees Vespes sitting up in bed, looking more alert than usual. "Vespes, my darling. Are you feeling better?"

"Yes, the pain in my side is finally gone, but I still feel tired. You just missed my cousin Kara. She came to see me."

"Yes, I saw her in the hall. She just came to visit with you?"

"She said she had something urgent to speak with me about, and then she said a prayer for me. I have to admit, I do feel a lot better now."

"Well, then, are you hungry now? I brought you up some lunch. It's chicken soup and toast."

"I think I could probably eat something now. Will you bring your lunch up here as well and join me? We can sit at that little table over there by the window."

"Okay," she says, laying his tray down. "I'll just go back down and get some for me too."

"Don't trouble yourself. I can just call on Erol to bring it." He reaches for the cord at his bedside.

"No, that's all right. I need the exercise. I don't mind getting it myself." She quickly heads over to the door before he can object.

"Okay, I'll wait for you." He smiles at her, and she smiles back, but her smile quickly fades into a frown as she turns back out into the hall.

Something has changed, Mira thinks to herself. *He should be weaker, but now he looks like he has more energy.* She feels for the vial of poison in the folds of her skirt pocket. It is still there. She feels the cold glass against her palm and holds it tightly for a moment. *I will make sure he drinks all his tea today. Maybe I should put an extra drop in there just to be sure.*

She then puts her hand to her chest, feeling for her secret scroll. Inside her bodice, neatly tucked inside, it stays well hidden. The poison ink on it feels addicting to her, and it penetrates her mind. Her thoughts are dark now, and she feels hatred for Kara, for her interference. *Who does she think she is? She is no match for me. She will have no influence on the king—I will see to it!*

*****

Vale and I enter into a small private room adjoined to the commons area, where Dominic and I first met with him. Dominic is waiting there for us, along with Marcus, Vales's trusted aide. He pulls out a chair for me, and we all sit around a table together.

"This is a very private room with thick walls," he says. "No one can hear us, and we should not be disturbed in here. Please, Kara, tell us how it went with the king, and then we can show you the scroll the empress sent to him."

"I apologize," I begin. "I really didn't have much time with him. All I got to do was say a quick prayer for him before Mira returned. I didn't tell him anything yet about our suspicions regarding Princess Mira."

"How did he seem to you?" asks Dominic.

"He was coughing quite a bit and looked like he was in pain when I first observed him. After I prayed for him, he said the pain in his side was gone, and he looked much better. He even asked me to come back to continue our discussion later."

"That is good," Vale remarks. "I'm sorry you didn't have much time, but maybe it's better that way. Now you can look at the scroll and tell us what you think about it." He nods at Marcus, and Marcus pulls out a key and unlocks a small chest behind him. He pulls out the scroll. It's tied with a thin black ribbon, and the parchment paper is a pale-yellow color. He opens and unfurls it before them. Inside it shows a black-inked letter written with an elegant style. "Take a close look at it, Kara. Do you notice anything?"

I read over the letter to the king. It simply looks like a formal letter, signed with the empress's signature at the bottom. "It looks like the scroll I saw before, at the tree. The empress uses a poisonous black ink. It weakens and controls the recipient. Whatever you do, don't touch it!"

"This scroll was removed from his room yesterday. Perhaps we will see the king strengthen and begin to get well now that he is not so close to it."

"Perhaps," says Dominic. "But there is still the question about Princess Mira. Is she on the empress's side? Is she against the king, trying to kill him and take over the kingdom as well? Maybe she has some poison of her own and that is why she is keeping so close to him."

"That is possible," agrees Vale. "But how can we find out for sure?"

"There is only one way," Dominic states. "She must be watched closely, when she thinks no one else is around."

"And how are we to do this?"

I speak up. "While I was in his room, I noticed there is a tall cedar chest on the floor in his closet. It has an open slot on the front side where you can open it, and there are boxes piled on top of it. Vale, if you could arrange for the king to come down to breakfast, since he is feeling a little better now, perhaps I could fit inside the chest and watch from that small opening. When Mira brings him his afternoon tea, I could see if she is doing anything out of the ordinary when they are alone in his room together. I don't particularly like this idea of spying on them, but I don't see any other way to catch her if she is doing something harmful to him."

"That sounds like a good plan to me," he responds. "You will need help, though. I will find a way to get Mira and the king to come down in the morning and then have Marcus go up to help you clean out anything in the chest. He can help you climb in there and then pile the boxes back on top. Can you handle being in there for a few hours? I can create some sort of diversion to get them both out of there after the lunch hour is over, and then Marcus can come back to help you out."

"What if Mira or Princess Trea asks where I am? What will you say?"

"We could simply say that you weren't feeling well and went to your room for a nap."

"Yes, and I will keep them busy with engaging conversation as well," says Dominic.

"What if you can't get him to go down to breakfast tomorrow? He has missed a few days of meals in there already."

"I will do my best to convince him. I'll say the servants heard he was feeling a bit better and Cora prepared a special breakfast for him. I will tell him it would encourage everyone to see that he is doing better and they would be all the more eager to assist with his wedding plans coming up this Sunday." Vale looks around at them, continuing, "If I can't get him to come down, then I think we can wait one more day and try again."

"It's worth a try," says Dominic. They all nod in agreement.

"Very well," says Vale, rising up from his chair. "Until tomorrow, then. If anything new or unforeseen comes up before then, let's meet back here to discuss our plans. Is everyone in agreement?"

"Yes," they all say together, pushing back their chairs from the table.

"I think it's time to get some lunch," says Dominic to me as we head back down the hall together.

"Sounds like a good plan to me," I say, and we walk back to the dining hall. As we enter into the room, we almost bump into Cora.

"Oh! Are you ready for lunch? I can have the servants bring out some chicken salad and croissants that I just prepared."

"That would be lovely," I respond. "Thank you."

Cora heads back into the kitchen and instructs Talia, "Take that food I prepared out to Ms. Kara and Sir Dominic right away. They are in there now."

"Yes, ma'am," she replies, grabbing a silver tray.

As Talia heads out with the food, Cora rubs her ankle. She twisted it a bit when she quickly turned into the dining room ahead of Kara and Dominic. She takes a seat on the wooden stool, thinking, *What were they doing down the hall in Vale's private study? Who are they, really? Isn't it strange that King Greffen's cousin would come so promptly for the wedding, even before his own sister Delvana? What was it they said? Oh yes, that they were sent ahead to help with the wedding preparations.* She looks out into the dining room and sees them there talking and eating. She watches them closely, trying to make out what they are saying.

"What is it, Cora?" asks Talia, coming back into the kitchen.

"Oh, nothing. I was just thinking about Delvana. I hope she and King Greffen will make it here in time for the wedding."

"I'm sure she wouldn't miss it. I look forward to seeing her too."

"Yes, well, let's get busy cleaning up these dishes. It's just a few hours until dinnertime, you know!"

"Yes, ma'am," Talia responds. She begins gathering up the dirty bowls and plates, watching Cora's face. Cora gets up, and Talia notices she is limping. "Ms. Cora! Are you all right? It looks like you are limping!"

"Yes, I'm fine," she responds, straightening a bit. "Just old age catching up with me. I think I will head up to my room for a bit before it's time to get the dinner ready. Make sure to put all those plates away, Talia."

"Yes, ma'am, I will." She watches Cora leave the room, still limping slightly, and continues washing the dishes by herself.

Hidden

Julia continues to visit Kara daily, talking to her, reading to her, and just sitting in the silence with her. She talks about everything she can think of. "I've been reading up on comas," she says to her. "There are studies that show people come out of them quicker if they keep hearing familiar voices speaking to them. So here I am, your familiar voice. I'm just going to keep at this until you wake up, sis."

She looks at her sister's face. Her eyes are closed, and there is no change, at least nothing Julia can detect. A nurse comes in to check vital signs. "I'll just be a moment," she says, smiling at Julia.

"That's fine," Julia responds, rising out of her chair. "I think I'll take a bathroom break."

Nodding, the nurse pulls her machine forward and begins to wrap Kara's arm in a cuff. Julia heads out into the hall and begins walking. Soon, she finds herself standing in front of the chapel room again. Pushing open the door, she peeks inside. She realizes she is looking for the boy she met in there, Jonathan.

Ever since that day of their meeting, she keeps wondering at his words: the leaf is a key. *What did he mean by that?* She keeps hoping he will wander in there again and she can ask him more about it. She walks in and sits down for a moment, sighing. She stares at the cross before her. Reaching into her pocket, she pulls out the leaf again. Its colors are still vibrant—such a resilient leaf!

"God, are You here? Please heal my sister! I'm sorry for everything. I've stopped drinking. Well, except for that one time last week when I was really down." The room is still and quiet. "God, please help me. I'm trying! Please bring my sister back. I don't know what I will do without her."

She closes her eyes and slumps down in her seat. Suddenly, she feels a presence in the room, but she doesn't open her eyes. She hears a soft voice: "I am here. I *see* you, and I *love* you." Startled, she opens her eyes and looks around. No one is there. But she knows what she heard.

"God, was that You?" She closes her eyes again, straining to hear. The room is quiet, and a sense of peace washes over her. It's unexplainable. Nothing has changed, but she begins to feel hope. She walks up to the front of the room. In front of the cross, there is an open Bible. She looks down onto the page. It is open to Genesis 16. She begins to read this chapter, and then her fingers stop on verse 13. It reads, "You are the God who sees me" (Gen. 16:13 NLT).

Tears form in her eyes as she slowly comprehends the truth. "You see me! You love me! I believe—I am still Yours! You haven't forgotten me or cast me aside. Thank You, God!" Covering her face, she lets the tears flow freely. After a few moments, she whispers, "I know You have Kara in Your hands. I know You've heard my prayers. Help me to trust You."

She hears the door opening and looks up. An older woman comes into the room and quietly sits down in a back pew. Julia wipes her face and leaves the room, a new feeling of hope rising up in her heart. She heads back to Kara's room and spends the rest of the afternoon with her, reading to her from one of their favorite books from childhood, *The Magician's Nephew* by C. S. Lewis.

As she reads, every once in a while she glances up at Kara's face, watching for any change. At five o'clock, she stops, closing the book. Rising up, she stretches her arms and yawns. "I'll be back tomorrow to continue the story, Kara. Love you." She bends down to kiss her sister on the top of her head before she leaves the room.

She hears a soft moan.

"Kara! Are you trying to say something, Kara?" She leans over her, listening and watching. Nothing. She remembers reading that sometimes people in comas do make noises, such as moaning sounds. She waits a few more minutes, putting her hand over Kara's and watching, but sees no other change.

"Okay, I'll see you tomorrow," she says, heading back out. As Julia shuts the door, Kara's limp hand reaches up in the air for a moment and then drops to the bed. Julia walks down the corridor toward the exit but stops at the nurses' station for a moment. The head nurse is sitting there, talking with another nurse. "Yes, why don't you go check on her?" She nods to her. Then looking up at Julia, she says, "Ms. Alder! How are you today?"

"I'm fine. I just wanted to let you know that I heard my sister, Kara, make a noise while I was in there with her. It sounded like a moan. Do you think that could mean anything?"

"We were just talking about her. The nurse noticed her pulse was a little high a few moments ago and went to check on her. I'm sure she's fine. Many patients in a coma make sounds while in that state. It's not uncommon."

"Did you say her pulse was high? What could that mean?"

"It's probably nothing unusual. If it continues to stay up, then we will examine her further. Here comes her nurse back down the hall now," she says, looking up at the approaching nurse. "Doreen, how is Ms. Kara doing?"

"She's fine. I checked her vitals again, and they are back to normal."

Julia nods and looks back at the head nurse. "Don't worry, Julia," she says. "We will keep a close watch over your sister. Now, why don't you go home now and get some rest yourself?"

"Yes, I will. Please let us know right away if there's any change."

"We will, dear. Have a good night."

"You too," Julia responds, walking slowly to the exit.

Back in the Silver Palace, Kara is lying in her bed, asleep and dreaming. It is one o'clock in the morning. Mira is in Kara's room, hovering over her with a brass candlestick in her hand. She is watching Kara sleep. She doesn't know why she came in here except that she felt driven to.

She will turn the king against you. Strike her now! comes a voice inside her head. She grips the candlestick tightly, considering. *She is dangerous! Take her out. Strike her!* it comes again. Kara stirs for a moment, turning her head to the side, her breathing slow and steady.

Mira takes a step back and comes to her senses for a moment. *What am I doing in here? I've got to get back to my room!*

She turns and heads out the door quickly. In the hall, she stands there for a moment, trembling. Her head aches. "What is wrong with me?" she says to herself. "I need to go lie down." She returns to her bed and lies there awake for a while, thinking.

Why do I feel so much anger toward Kara? I don't even know her. Where are all these suspicions coming from? She's just the king's cousin. She's here for the wedding. The wedding! It's in just a few days. Can I really go through with this? She feels ill at the thought of taking her vows and then killing her husband. She feels for the scroll but then remembers she takes it off at night. *There it is, on my bedside table, sticking out from under my robe.* She reaches for it and then stops herself. *I'll look at it again in the morning.* Turning over, she allows her troubled mind to rest, and soon sleep catches up with her.

When morning comes, Mira sits up in her bed and looks at the candlestick beside her on the table. She vaguely remembers going to Kara's room during the night, but it seems like a dream. *Did I really go there last night?* She dresses and gets ready to head down for breakfast, the scroll fastened back into her bodice again. It's three days until the wedding, and she's got to be ready to follow through with the plan. Her mother will be arriving anytime now. Just thinking of this fills her heart with a cold feeling of dread. She realizes there is no turning back now.

As the scroll presses against her skin inside her garment, she feels her resolve returning. "I must be sure he drinks all his tea today. I will put an extra drop in as well. Mother will be pleased with me, and I will be on my way to freedom with my own kingdom, away from her, to rule as I please." She feels another headache coming on. "I didn't sleep well. I just need some coffee, and then I will feel better and my thoughts will be clearer," she says to herself, rubbing her forehead. She steps out into the hall to go get some.

She notices Commander Vale is waiting at the top of the stairs. "Good morning, Princess Mira. The king has come down for breakfast this morning. He seems to be doing much better. He asked me to escort you down so you can join him." He offers his arm to her.

Unsettled, she compliantly takes his arm, and they walk down the stairs together. She realizes she mustn't let her feelings of alarm show. "And how are you this morning, Commander?"

"Very well, Princess. Thank you for asking. Did you sleep well last night?"

"Not as well as I should have. I just keep thinking of details about the wedding plans. I do hope my dress will be ready today. I am looking forward to trying it on."

"I'm sure you will look lovely in it. I know the servants have been keeping very busy to make sure everything is ready in time for Sunday."

"Yes, and I am so grateful for everyone's help." She smiles at him as they enter the dining room, and Vespes rises from his chair to greet them.

"Thank you, Commander Vale. Good morning, my love. Please, won't the both of you be seated here by me? Cora has prepared a wonderful breakfast this morning."

Mira and Vale take their seats at the table alongside Dominic and Princess Trea. "Where is my cousin Kara? I was looking forward to seeing her as well," says the king.

Dominic speaks up. "She told me to apologize for her absence this morning. She didn't sleep well last night and decided to stay in her room and nap for a while until she felt better."

"I see. Well, we won't disturb her, then. Trea, would you mind checking on her later today to see how she is doing? I enjoyed getting to meet her yesterday and was looking forward to finishing our talk."

Mira looks at Vespes and chimes in, "Yes, I would also like to get to know her better. Since she is my soon-to-be cousin, I was thinking we should have her fitted for a bridesmaid gown as well."

Trea looks up from her breakfast and joins in the conversation. "I have sent word to Delvana, and she and King Greffen should be arriving soon as well." She turns to Mira. "Should I have them prepare three bridesmaid dresses, then? One for each of us?" Looking then at Vespes, she continues, "And I know King Greffen will be the groomsman for Della, but what about me and Kara? Who will escort us?"

Vespes smiles at his sister. "Commander Vale can escort you, and perhaps our other fine guest, Sir Dominic, can escort Kara?" He looks over at Dominic, who is distracted, rubbing his hand over his bald head, wishing he had worn his hat to breakfast because it is so cold. "Sir Dominic?"

"What? I'm sorry, what did you say?"

"Princess Mira would like to have Kara be a bridesmaid in the ceremony. Would you be a groomsman for me and escort her down the aisle?"

"Yes, of course! I'd be happy to."

"And, Vale, would you do me the honor and escort my sister Princess Trea?"

"It would be an honor to do so," he responds.

Trea finishes up her plate quickly. "There's still so much to do to get ready. I will make sure the other large guest room is ready for Della and King Greffen today. And I will check on the flowers too. Please excuse me," she says, rising up from the table.

As they are finishing up their food downstairs, Marcus and I are up in the king's bedroom, working at a frantic pace to get me inside the closet chest before the king and Mira return. Finally, I am safely hidden, and he piles all the boxes on top and moves the other items they've pulled out of the chest to the back of the closet. "I'll be back to help you get out in a few hours, Ms. Kara. Are you all right in there?"

"Yes, I'm fine. There's plenty of room in here, and I have a good view of the room from here. Can you see me at all?"

He looks at the chest tucked away in the darkness of the closet. "No, I can only see your eyes if I crouch down low and close to the closet. No one will know you are there. I should go now before someone comes down this hall. Tea is served at 11:00 a.m., and lunch shortly after that. I will be back after lunchtime to retrieve you, once Commander Vale gets them both out of the room again. Be safe!"

"Thank you, Marcus! I will be fine. You better go before someone sees you in here."

"Goodbye for now," he says, looking out the door and into the hall before he ventures out. No one is there, and he quickly heads out of the room and back down the stairs to the dining hall. As he passes by the open doorway, Vale looks up at him and he nods, knowing all is in place. Their plan is in motion, and he must find a way to get both the king and Mira back out of that room at lunchtime to free Kara.

Vale glances over at Dominic. Dominic pulls up his small stature in the chair and speaks up. "King Vespes, would you be up to meeting with me and Commander Vale in the chapel before or after the lunch hour, to talk about the ceremony details? We only have two days to prepare, and I want to help in any way I can."

Vale joins in. "Yes, this would be very helpful from a security standpoint as well. I know you want everything to go smoothly."

Vespes listens and nods. "I suppose we should do that. I am feeling a bit better. Perhaps this would be a good time now."

"I just have to speak with Marcus and clear up a few details with my men on duty this morning before we can meet," Vale replies. "Can we meet around noon, after your teatime? It would give you a little more time to rest as well."

"Fine, we will plan to meet at noon in the chapel," says the king. "Until then, my friends." He rises from the table and extends his arm to Mira. She links her arm in his, and they begin to leave the room.

As they are walking out, Trea and Cora come back in the room, and Vespes looks at his sister. "Trea, why don't you and Mira also come to the chapel at noon so you can be in on the ceremony plans as well? And Kara, too, if she's feeling up to it by then."

"I'll be there! And I'll check on Kara in a little while too."

Dominic speaks up. "Actually, she told me to check in on her at teatime so I can let her know."

"Oh, okay, then. I do hope she will be able to join us. I will need to get her measurements for the dressmaker too."

"I will let her know. She will be so excited."

Trea smiles and goes back to talking with Cora about the menu plans for the wedding. Cora walks beside her and is taking down all the instructions. She ponders Kara's absence from the breakfast table. *Perhaps I will do my own checking on her as well,* the cook thinks to herself, nodding at Trea as she goes on talking about the intricate details for the wedding cake.

Journey to the Palace

Gaelyn quietly slips on her shoes and grabs her sack stuffed with her clothes. It's just before midnight, and she is preparing to head down to the cellar to meet Friedrich. "It's now or never," she whispers to herself, opening her door into the hallway as quietly as she can.

The castle is quiet, and she makes her steps as quiet as a mouse. She only gets about three steps down the hall when she hears a man's voice. "Halt! Where are you going?" It's one of Celia's guards, waiting just outside her door.

Gaelyn turns around slowly, trying to speak casually. "I was just going to the privy."

"I will escort you," he promptly responds.

"That's really not necessary," she begins to protest.

"By orders of the empress, I am here to watch over you and make sure you are prepared to leave with her first thing in the morning. Why are you carrying a bag?"

"What? Oh, this? It just has some personal items in it so I can freshen up before bed. Not that it's any of your business." She starts walking down the hall. He follows her and stops outside the door to the privy, crossing his arms.

"I'll be waiting for you." He smiles at her, leaning against the stone wall.

Inside, Gaelyn tries to think of what to do. *There's nothing I can do—he's watching my every move! I should have known she'd be watching me, especially after her remarks to me yesterday in the courtyard. Why did I think it would be easy to escape?* She sighs, closing her eyes for a moment. *I'm sorry, Friedrich. It doesn't look like I'll be meeting you tonight.*

The guard follows her back down the hall to her room and takes his place outside her door. "Good night, miss. I'll be right here if you should need anything." He grins at her as she shuts the door on him.

In the cellar, Friedrich waits patiently in the dark. He hears the rats scuttle along the floor. *Where is she? It must be well past midnight by now. Did she change her mind?* He knows if they don't leave together tonight, then he will be expected to ride along with the empress's army on the journey back to Silvenia. He remembers other cities where they have attacked as her army. *I will not kill for her anymore! The empress must be overthrown! But what about Gaelyn? I need to speak with her and tell her what I know. Maybe something happened, maybe someone caught her leaving her room to come down and meet with me.* He decides to wait a while longer. Leaning against a grain sack, he feels sleep begin to overtake him. He shakes his head and his arms, trying to stay awake.

Suddenly, he hears a clomping sound. Someone is coming down the steps! He jumps up and looks around him, blinking. Sunlight is streaming in from the little window above, and he realizes it is morning. He must have fallen asleep.

"What are you doing down here?" comes a woman's voice. It's Berta, standing at the bottom of the stairs, hands on her hips.

"I…uh, I'm just getting one more sack of grain for the cart. Excuse me." He grabs a sack and hurries past her up the stairs.

She watches him suspiciously, muttering to herself. "You better hurry up. The men are all ready to go out in the front!"

"Yes, ma'am!" He runs down the hall to the front corridor and sees servants and men hurrying in every direction.

"Let's go, soldier! Grab your gear and head to the front!" Kurt passes by him, shouting orders as he walks by.

"Yes, sir!" He feels for his knife on his belt and heads to the front with the other men. Blending in as best as he can. He searches up the line of people for Gaelyn. Up at the very front of their entourage, he sees the empress on her black horse, and right next to her is Gaelyn, on a small chestnut mare. She is too far ahead and doesn't see him.

"I won't leave you," he whispers in her direction. "I will look out for you."

"Onward, let's go!" Arten calls out, and the whole company moves forward. Vico and Kurt are out in the front with Arten, close to the empress and Gaelyn. Friedrich is in the center of the empress's army, in full battle gear, with the other soldiers. He is on a small but sturdy horse and keeps pace with the others.

On another road, in the far south, comes another company of people from the kingdom of Volkenland. King Greffen and Queen Delvana travel in a carriage, accompanied with their royal guards and a few servants as well. Unknown to her family in Silvenia, Delvana is carrying her first child, and she is eight months now into her pregnancy. They are traveling slow, for her comfort, as she had shown a few signs of premature labor last month.

Delvana insisted that she would not miss her brother's wedding, and their doctor finally agreed she was past the danger and well enough to go, provided they take it slow and bring along her personal nurse for the journey. King Greffen has turned out to be a good man and is kind and affectionate with Delvana, and she is growing to love him, much to her surprise. He is older than her, but he treats her with kindness and respect, even when they were first married and she refused to be with him. He waited patiently and never forced anything on her.

As time went by, she began to see him in a new light, and a strong attraction began to develop in her for him. He loved her unconditionally. She saw this, and a trust between them grew. Now they are expecting their first child together, and she is very excited. She can't wait to surprise Trea and Vespes with the news. *Won't they be surprised and happy when they see me!* She smiles to herself in the carriage as they ride along.

"What are you thinking of?" asks the king.

"I was just thinking about the looks on my brother's and sister's faces when they see us. It will be such a glad reunion!"

"I am glad you are so happy. You are beautiful, my love."

Delvana smiles as he reaches for her hand and kisses it. "I am happy, and I can't wait to get there. How much farther is it?"

"We should be there by nightfall." She smiles and rests her head on his shoulder as the carriage moves along steadily to the north.

The road is rocky, and Delvana is bumped around repeatedly in the carriage despite their slow pace. "Are you all right, my dear?" asks King Greffen with a look of concern on his face.

"I'm fine," she replies quickly, though she has felt a few uncomfortable twinges in her abdomen with all the jostling about.

He is not convinced. "Would you like us to stop for a little while? We can spread out some of the food you brought and have us a picnic, and you could rest a bit without being bumped around."

"All right," she responds. "But just for a little while."

"Fritz! Stop the carriage. We're going to rest for a bit."

"Whoa, horses, whoa!" They hear from the front of the carriage as it comes to a stop. Delvana takes King Greffen's hand as he helps her down, wincing at another slight twinge as she descends the steps. She takes a deep breath and pauses.

"Maybe we should just turn around and go back," says the king, looking at her face.

"No!" she quickly responds. "I'm fine, Greffen. Really, you worry too much."

"All right, but promise you'll tell me if you begin to feel anything out of the ordinary."

"I promise. Come on, let's have some lunch. I put sandwiches in that red-and-white sack there."

He pulls it down and spreads out a blanket for them to sit on. Delvana gives him a reassuring smile, and he sits down beside her, feeling concern for his very pregnant wife. He realizes how much he loves her and wants to protect her and his unseen child that is soon to be born into this world. She is his first and only love, and he has waited a long time to find her. King Greffen is determined not to let anything bad happen to his wife or their baby.

"You look deep in thought," she remarks. "What is on your mind?"

"Nothing," he responds. "Just enjoying our lunch." He smiles back at her and then glances over at Nancy, her nurse. He is glad they brought her along, and it puts him back at ease for the moment. Even if she did go into labor early, they have Nancy to help them. Plus, in just a few more hours, they will be safely in the kingdom of Silvenia. There is nothing to fear.

Treachery

I watch from my hidden place in the darkness of the closet chest as Mira and the king enter into the room. Mira walks him over to his bed and pulls back the quilt for him as he climbs in. He looks tired again, but the look of pain on his face from the other day is gone. "You should rest now, my love. We have a busy afternoon planned for us now, so try to get some sleep. I will bring you some tea to help you wake up again in a little while."

The king smiles at her. "All right, but give me a kiss before you go."

She pulls the covers up to his chin and goes to give him a kiss on his forehead. He pulls her to him and kisses her on the mouth. She feels herself clench for a moment and then kisses him back. "All right now," she says backing away. "You need to sleep. I'm going to go freshen up a bit. I'll see you in a little while."

He releases her and turns over on his side as she steps back out of the room. I move slowly and quietly to position myself so my leg doesn't fall asleep, and I watch him drift off. He opens his eyes for a moment, looking around the room, and I hold my breath, afraid to make a sound. Then he closes his eyes again, and soon his breathing is quiet and steady and I know he is truly asleep.

Time passes by slowly in my cramped hiding place, and I try to think of happy thoughts instead of how uncomfortable I feel. I let my thoughts drift back to a Christmas morning at home when I was a child. How happy Julia and I were climbing out of bed and running to the living room to see all the presents under the tree. I remember singing Christmas carols and waking up our parents early in the morning—how happy we were together that day! I focus on these images in my mind. I remember staring at the nativity scene on our mantel and wishing Jesus a happy birthday. I hear a quiet voice on the inside, "I was with you then, and I am with you now."

My heart bursts with love for Him. *I love You, Jesus! Thank You that You're with me! I need Your help so much. Protect me!* I feel peace wash over me there in the hiding place. The fear leaves, and I quietly continue waiting in secret.

After about an hour, I hear footsteps approaching. The door opens, and I can see Mira entering with a tray in her hand. The king is fast asleep, and she sets the tray down quietly on the little table by the window. I watch Mira glance over at the king and then pull something from her skirt pocket. It's a little vial, and she opens it with her back to him and pours a few drops into his tea. Then she quickly seals it back up and stuffs it inside her skirt pocket.

Approaching his bed, she gently touches him on the shoulder to wake him. "Vespes, it's time to wake up. I have your tea."

He stirs and looks up at her, smiling sleepily. He props up in the bed and starts to get up. "I can bring it to you," she offers, grabbing his cup.

"That's all right. I need to get up, anyway. I'll come sit at the table with you." He steps into his slippers and walks over to the little table. She pours herself a cup and sits down with him there.

I watch as he slowly sips his tea. I feel an urge to jump out and stop him but restrain myself. I know that I can only wait and watch for now. I listen as they talk about the wedding ceremony plans together.

"I hope your other sister, Delvana, arrives soon. I can't wait to meet her."

"Yes, I am looking forward to seeing her too. She should be here soon." The king gets up for a moment and walks toward the closet. I freeze in place and try to breathe very quietly.

"What are you doing, love?" Mira asks.

"I need to get some clothes out for the rehearsal practice. I can't stay in my pajamas all day."

"I can get it for you. Please sit down and rest and finish your tea." She moves toward him and gently pulls him back to the table.

His mind begins to feel cloudy again, and he stumbles for a moment, and Mira grabs his arm. "See, you're not as strong as you think yet. Take it slow, darling." She helps him sit back down and hands him his cup. "Drink. You need lots of fluids, the doctor said."

"Yes, ma'am!" He laughs at her commanding tone and drinks the rest of it down.

"Now, let's see what you have to wear here that would be appropriate." She gets up and begins to sort through some of the garments hanging in the closet above the chest. "This is a nice shirt." She pulls one out and shows it to him. "What do you think?" She turns to look at him.

"That's fine," he says. "My gray pants would go well with that, the ones hanging there to the left."

"What's in this chest here?" she asks. I sit frozen still, praying silently not to be discovered.

"Oh, nothing. Just some old winter clothes that I don't wear very often."

Mira pulls down the gray pants and shirt and lays them out across his bed. Suddenly, Vespes begins coughing a lot and doubles over in his chair. "Vespes! Are you all right?"

He continues coughing and tries to get up but falls over onto the floor. "Vespes! Let me help you back into bed, and I'll go get your cough medicine for you." She reaches down to help him get up, and they manage to get over to the bed together.

"I don't know what happened. I was feeling fine all morning." He falls back into bed and begins coughing again.

"I'll go get your medicine," Mira says, heading out of the room.

I watch from my spot, sure now that the king is being poisoned by Mira. I look at Vespes. He is grabbing his side again, as if in pain, and I feel compassion for him. *I need to get out of here and put a stop to this!* I think to myself. *But how is Vale going to get me out of here now?* I realize I might be stuck in the closet for a while longer, and that alarms me immensely.

Vale has been lingering in the hall downstairs, watching for Mira and the king to come out so he can send Marcus to get Kara out of the bedroom. First, Ceyla, Mira's handmaid, comes down the stairs and goes into the kitchen with Cora. "Kara's not in her room," she reports to the head cook. "I knocked on her door, as you requested, and even peeked inside, and she is definitely not there. I don't know where she could be."

Cora nods. "Very good. Thank you, Ceyla. I will look for her myself. Please let me know if you do see her."

"Of course," she replies.

Mira also comes down the stairs and heads toward the kitchen as well. Vale crosses over to her. "Princess Mira, is it time for us to head toward the chapel now? Is the king on his way?"

She glances at him. "No, he's not feeling well again. I don't think we will be able to do that this afternoon. I'm going to get his cough medicine."

"Oh, I see. I'll let Dominic and Kara know as well." He bows politely and heads back down the hall.

In Vale's private room, Dominic is waiting there along with Marcus.

"Are they headed to the chapel now?" asks Dominic.

"No. The king is not feeling well again, and now I don't know how we can get both him and Mira out of that room so we can rescue Kara. Any suggestions?"

"We can tell them the doctor needs to see him," suggests Dominic.

"No, the doctor can just go up to his room."

"Right."

They sit and think for a few minutes, and finally Marcus looks up. "I have an idea. It's not great, but it's the only thing I can think of that will get them out of there quickly."

"What is it?"

"We will start a fire in the next room. We can contain it in the large bowl for the pitcher. They will smell the smoke, and we can rush in and say we need to get them downstairs for safety until the fire is put out. Then I can get Kara out." He looks around at them. "What do you think?"

"Let's do it. Dominic, why don't you be the one to start the fire in there, and Marcus and I will be ready to escort Mira and the king out of the bedroom?"

"Should I bring another servant, too, to go with Dominic and help safely get the fire out? Who can we trust?"

"How about Victor?"

"Yes," agrees Vale and, turning to Dominic, says, "Victor is Marcus's younger brother. He can be trusted as well and will do what we ask without question."

"Dominic, you head up the stairs to the room next to the king and we will meet you up there shortly."

Dominic nods and heads back out down the hall. Soon, he and Victor are in the room next to the king's bedroom and Vale and Marcus linger down the hall, waiting for their signal to alert the king. Victor strikes the flint and sparks the fire in the bowl filled with scraps of paper and old rags. Smoke begins to fill the room, and Dominic opens the door a crack and holds the bowl close to it, letting some smoke filter out the door.

Vale looks at Marcus. "Let's go. We have to make this convincing!" Heading over to the king's door, he pounds on it.

"Enter!" says the king in a raspy tone, and Mira jumps up out of her chair. "What is it?" she asks.

"There's a fire in the room next to you. We have to get you both downstairs immediately!" He walks over to the king's side and begins to help him up.

"What? How did this happen?" Vespes rises up with concern on his face but quickly doubles over with pain again.

"We can fill you in once we get you and the princess safely downstairs. Please, put your arm around me now and let me help you."

The king complies with Vale, and Marcus helps lead Mira out of the room as well. She looks back down the hall as they head for the stairs and sees the smoke in the air.

Once they are downstairs, they help the king get comfortable on the soft couch in a large sitting room. Looking at his pale demeanor, Vale notices with alarm how much the king has changed since breakfast. He looks at Marcus and nods, giving him the signal to go back upstairs and help Kara get out of her hiding place.

"Erol!" calls Vale to the approaching butler. "Watch over the king and the princess for a moment while I make sure they are getting that fire out upstairs. I'll be back as soon as I can, Your Majesty."

The king begins another coughing fit, and Mira reaches for his water. Erol helps the king get positioned more comfortably, grabbing an extra pillow from a nearby chair. Vale rushes into the room next to the king's bedroom and sees Victor pouring water on a smoldering pillow in the bowl. He looks up at Vale. "We can say the candle in here was left burning overnight and was too close to this pillow."

"Good," responds Vale. "Where is Dominic?"

"He's checking on Kara. Marcus got her safely back to her room and is straightening up the king's closet now." Vale nods and quickly goes back out to the king's room. Marcus is just exiting the doorway. "The chest is back in order," he says quietly. "No one will know she was there."

"Let's go back down and report to the king that the fire is safely out. Then, while I stay and chat with the king, let Dominic and Kara know to meet us in my private room downstairs in about an hour."

"Yes, sir," responds Marcus, and they head back downstairs together to speak with the king.

Within the hour, everyone is settled down and they are able to escort the king back to his bedroom. Mira agrees to stay by his side and read to him while they wait for the doctor to come and check on him. Vale sends for the doctor as soon as he comes back downstairs, alarmed at how ill the king appears now.

Vale returns now to his private room to meet with the others. He opens the door, and sees me, Dominic, and Marcus seated around the table. I look up at Vale as he pulls out a chair and sits down to hear my report. Urgently, I speak out. "She is poisoning him, Vale. She is trying to kill the king!"

"It is just as I suspected! We must go arrest her now!"

"Wait!" I say. "Jesus gave me instructions to always pray and check with Him first. Let's pray together now and see how He wants us to proceed." I look around at them. "Please!"

Dominic smiles at me and pulls his little Bible out of his inside coat pocket. "Thank you for reminding us, Kara."

I reach out, and we join hands to pray. They all look at me, so I begin, "Father in heaven, You know the king is in danger and that Mira is poisoning him. How should we proceed?"

We all get quiet and sit there, waiting. After a few minutes, Vale looks up at me. "I confess that I haven't prayed in a long time. Not since I was a boy. I had forgotten." I smile at him. "How long do we wait?" he asks. "Is anyone hearing anything?"

"I think I heard Him say, 'Go and speak with her,'" I say.

"That could be dangerous for you to go alone. She has plans to harm the king, and she could easily try to harm you too."

Dominic speaks up. "I am reminded of a scripture." He opens up his Bible and begins to thumb through it. "Here it is." Then he proceeds, "Behold, I give you the authority to trample on serpents and scorpions, and over all the power of the enemy, and nothing shall by any means hurt you" (Luke 10:19 NKJV).

"Yes, I believe that," I say. "I think I am supposed to go to her alone. You can all be close by, and if you hear me call for help, please come! And while you are waiting for me, please pray!"

"We will do as you ask," responds Vale.

Confessions

It is evening now in the Silver Palace, and the doctor has come and gone, telling the king to continue with rest, fluids, and the cough medicine he has prepared for him. He assures Princess Trea he will be back again tomorrow and will keep a close watch on her brother.

Vespes has finally stopped coughing and fallen asleep, while Mira was reading to him. Looking up at his face now, she decides this will be a good time to retreat back to her own room for the night. She is feeling tired herself and is getting to the point where she just wants all this nightmare to be over and done with. She has given the king three drops of the poison today since he seemed to be recovering. Now she realizes how strong it is. He looks much worse than before, and his breathing is raspy and labored.

She tries not to think of how kind he has been to her. *That doesn't matter. He is a fool to love me. All men are fools!* She thinks of Arten again and feels her heart ache with sorrow. Then she shifts that thought to the back of her mind, feeling overwhelmed with weariness. *Mother will be here soon. I must complete this task, and then things will get better for me.* She instinctively feels for the scroll hidden inside her vest. It releases a tremor of fear through her frame. *I cannot fail her.*

She walks into her room, shutting the door, and then almost jumps out of her skin when she sees me sitting there in the chair by her closet. "What are you doing in my room?" she demands.

"I need to speak with you," I say, rising up out of the chair.

"Can't this wait until morning? I'm very tired now."

"No, it cannot. It's about the king. I know what you are doing to him."

"What are you talking about? I am helping to take care of him!"

"Show me what is in your pocket, then," I say boldly, looking Mira in the eyes.

"There is nothing in my pocket. How dare you bring your accusations against me! I demand you leave my room this instant. I am calling for the guard." She begins to head to the door.

"Go ahead. Then you can show them as well. We know you are trying to kill the king."

I watch Mira's face, and her eyes suddenly turn dark. She lunges at me and knocks me to the floor, grabbing me around the throat. "You cannot stop me," she hisses at me. "I will kill you first!"

I struggle beneath her, marveling at Mira's strength. In a flash, I remember the picture in the tree. Mira approaching the king with an evil-looking creature wrapped around her head. It was reaching for his crown. Before I can even think, I blurt out, "You evil spirit, I bind you and cast you out in the name of Jesus!"

"No!" shrieks Mira. "You can't make me leave!"

"Yes, I can," I say, feeling a strange, new boldness as I work to pry off Mira's hands from my throat. "And stop attacking now, in Jesus's name!" I gasp.

Mira's hands release me instantly, but she still looks dark and angry. She sits still on the floor in front of me. "Release her now!" I demand. "In Jesus's name!"

"Stop saying that name," it pleads, sounding like a whining child using Mira's voice.

"I will continue to say it until you release her and go," I state, getting bolder. "Jesus…Jesus!"

"I don't have to go. She has the scroll. She wants me here."

I pause and look at Mira. "Mira, what scroll? Do you have a scroll?"

Mira stays silent, her eyes dark and cloudy.

"In the name of Jesus, reveal the scroll," I command.

"It's in her vest," Mira says in a weak voice, and then she slowly pulls it out and shows it to me.

I am careful not to touch it. "Mira, what is on this scroll? Can you open it for me?"

"No," she whispers.

"Jesus," I say.

Mira grimaces and slowly unfurls the scroll and shows it to me. I quickly scan through it, reading over all the empress's wicked instructions.

I look at her. "Mira, do you want to kill the king?"

"Yes," she whispers, then begins to shake her head no repeatedly. I can see she is struggling to be free.

"Mira, do you want to be free of this?"

She doesn't answer but nods, and a tear slips down her face. "Mira, take the scroll and tear it up. Say, 'I turn away from this evil in Jesus's name. Please forgive me, Jesus, and save me now. Be my Lord and Savior.'"

Mira repeats the words and slowly begins to tear up the scroll, her hands shaking. Suddenly, her hands clench and she can't continue. "I can't! It won't let me!" she cries.

"In Jesus's name, release her now and go from this place! I take authority over you, evil spirit, and break your power! She now belongs to King Jesus. Go!"

"Ahhh!" she cries out and collapses on the floor. She lies still there for a moment and then slowly rises back up to a sitting position. The darkness has left her eyes, and they are filled with tears now. "It's gone!" she gasps. "I am free!"

I reach out and take her hand. Mira looks at me with sorrow in her eyes. "I'm sorry, Kara. I'm sorry I tried to hurt you and the king. I'm sorry for everything!" Her tears stream down her face. "You can call the guards to arrest me now. I will go with them willingly. But..." She suddenly looks afraid again. "My mother, the empress... she will kill me when she sees I have failed. Even if the king locks me away in a cell, she will come find me and kill me. You don't know what she is capable of."

"We won't let that happen. The same God who delivered you right now from that evil spirit will deliver you from her power too. King Jesus has defeated every evil power of the enemy, and now that you have prayed and received Him as your Savior, He will protect you as His own."

"But how? She is on her way here right now, and I am supposed to wed the king the day after tomorrow. She will have her army with her and has never been defeated in all the cities she has attacked. If she finds out the wedding is off, she will begin her attack on Silvenia without delay."

"Let us meet with Commander Vale and the king and reveal all this to them. God will help us come up with a strategy to defeat her."

Mira looks stricken for a moment. "I have to confess my cruelty to Vespes. He deserves so much better. I do feel love for him, but as a brother only. My heart belongs to someone else."

I look at her, seeing brokenness in her unguarded face. "Who is it?"

"Arten, the commander of my mother's army. But he has left me. He does not feel the same."

"I am sorry," I reply. "I have known the pain of a broken heart too."

"And now we have to go break another heart. Let's go and get this over with. I will accept whatever fate the king decides for me."

"I will go with you and speak up for you. He needs to understand that you were being controlled by her evil powers. He will be upset at first, but I think he will understand once we explain everything."

Mira nods with a look of resignation on her face. "I am ready to face him."

We rise up together and head for the door. I turn to Mira. "Let me inform Commander Vale of our plans to speak with the king. He is waiting in the hall for us." Mira agrees, and we step out together.

Commander Vale approaches us. "Ladies, how can I be of assistance?" he says, looking expressly at me.

"Princess Mira has agreed to confess her true intentions to the king, and I am going with her. She is willingly doing this and agrees to cooperate with his ruling on this matter."

He looks at her with surprise and nods in agreement. "I will escort you over," he replies.

The three of us walk to the king's bedroom together, and Vale knocks on his door.

"Enter!" he calls out from inside.

Vale opens the door and presents us. "I apologize for disturbing you at this hour. They have need to speak with you, my king."

"Of course," he says, coughing a bit and rising to a sitting position in bed. "Please come in, both of you. Commander Vale, would you pull over those two chairs for them?"

Vale does as he asks and then departs the room. King Vespes looks at the two of us with curiosity. "What is so urgent? Is this about the wedding plans?" Then he looks more closely at Mira's face. "What is it, Mira?"

"Vespes, I…I have to confess something to you."

He looks at her and then at me. "What is this about?"

Mira looks down at the floor. "I don't know how to do this except to tell you straight out. I was sent here by my mother, the empress, with specific plans to seduce you, marry you, and then kill you so she could take over the kingdom of Silvenia."

"What are you talking about?" he balks. "We love each other. We're about to be married!" He looks at her incredulously, clenching his fists.

"No, Vespes. I do not love you like that. I love you like a brother, and I'm so sorry for what I've been doing to you. You've been nothing but kind to me."

"What do you mean? What have you been doing to me except spending all your time with me, caring for me, reading to me? I don't understand."

She looks down again, unable to meet his gaze. "I've been poisoning you with a vial my mother gave me. That is why you have been sick. I'm so sorry! I know I have no right to ask for your forgiveness, but—"

"You've been poisoning me? You wanted to kill me!" He begins to tremble with both anger and sorrow, and his demeanor changes. "I trusted you, Mira! This is unreal. This is treason!"

"Please, Your Majesty," I interject. "She was under a spell concocted by the empress Celia. It was controlling her and causing her to do things she did not want to do. The empress is the true villain here. She is the one who wants to kill you and take over your kingdom, not Mira."

"Please believe me," says Mira. "My mother, the empress, is secretly a witch who works for Mercurio, the ruler of darkness. I have seen the evil she can do. We have to stop her before she takes over this kingdom. She has already taken over most of the cities of the North."

The king pauses, silent for a few moments. Then, as he sits up taller in bed, his face hardens. "Commander Vale!" he calls out.

The door opens, and Vale steps into the room. "Yes, Your Majesty?"

"Arrest Princess Mira and take her to a cell in the tower. She has confessed to treason, and I want her out of my sight."

My mouth falls open, and I put my hand on Mira's arm. Vale hesitates for a moment, looking at Mira, and then steps forward to take ahold of her other arm.

"Take her away!" Vespes shouts.

Vale quickly leads her out of the room, and she does not resist.

"You may go as well," he says roughly to me.

"Please, Your Majesty," I object. "May I remind you the empress will be here by Sunday morning with her army in tow. Let me help you stop her!"

"You, how can you possibly help me stop her?"

"I have been sent here by King Jesus to help you. He showed me Mercurio's plan to use the empress as his pawn to defeat you. He wants to take over all of Paredonia for his evil kingdom. Silvenia is just the beginning! He has caused the people here to forget about God, to forget the Bible and the truth that He sent His own Son, Jesus, to save them. But He has not forgotten them. He wants to save this land and all the people in it."

"But how can God help us do this?"

"He is more powerful than Mercurio. We need to pray and ask Him for a strategy to defeat him and the empress. He will show us what to do."

He looks her in the eyes. "Why would He want to help me? I haven't prayed to Him since I was a little boy, and He didn't answer my prayers then. He let my mother die!"

I respond, "I am sorry that happened to you. But God did not kill your mother. Jesus says in His Word, 'The thief does not come except to steal, and to kill, and to destroy. I have come that they may have life, and that they may have it more abundantly' (John 10:10)."

I go on, "Jesus brought me to you to save your life and the lives of the people in your kingdom. You need to put your trust in Him and allow Him to help us!"

He looks at me. "Who are you really? Where did you come from? Are you an angel sent from God to help us?"

"No, I am not. I am Kara Alder. I'm from another land, far from here. But that is not important. What is important is that God brought me here for this purpose. For you and all of Silvenia to come back to Him. To read His Word again. He has made you king of this land and has positioned you for this time in history. Will you give Him your heart and make Him your Lord? He is knocking on the door of your heart, even now. Will you let Him in?"

He closes his eyes for moment, and a memory that has been locked away in his mind comes to light: He sees himself as a little boy lying in his bed. He is talking to God, asking Him why he took his mother away to heaven. "I feel so alone now, God. I miss her! Why don't You care?" He sees tears form in his eyes, and they spill over onto the pillow. He remembers the ceiling above him change in a flash, and suddenly, through his little boy's eyes, he sees a beautiful meadow with a man in it who is walking toward him. He is lit up and has gentle eyes full of love. He speaks to him, saying, "I am with you always. I will never leave you or forsake you." Then he sees a woman come walking toward the shining man, and she is smiling and waving at Vespes. He realizes it is his mother, and he reaches for the ceiling, calling out to her. She blows him a kiss, and he waves back at her, saying, "I love you, Mom!" Then, just as quick, the image is gone from his sight.

"Yes, I remember Him now." He pauses. "He said He would always be with me."

I smile at him. "Why don't we ask Him what He is saying to you right now?"

"All right," he responds, grabbing her outstretched hand and closing his eyes again.

I begin, "King Jesus, please speak to Vespes and tell him what You want him to know. We need Your wisdom, Lord."

We both get quiet for a moment and wait. Vespes squeezes my hand, and a tear falls from his face. I look up at him. "What is He saying to you?"

"That He loves me and is still with me. And He is on my side." He pauses for a moment. "And He wants me to forgive Mira."

"Are you willing to do that?" I ask.

"Yes," he says quietly, his voice catching. "I love her, Kara. Even though she was trying to kill me. But she doesn't love me, not in the way I need her to. But I won't keep her a prisoner here. I will let her go."

"Truly, she was being controlled by the empress. And the empress was attempting to control you as well. Do you remember the scroll she sent you?"

"Yes. What about it?"

"The empress writes with a poisonous ink that has a spell on it. It clouds sound judgment and puts the person who reads it under her control. King Jesus showed me this. And Mira had one as well. It was controlling her. We destroyed it, and now she is free from that control."

"Yes, I remember that scroll she sent me. Where is it? I had it here in my room, and I remember feeling ill after I read it, but I wanted to keep it near me for some reason."

"When we suspected foul play on the part of the empress, we had it secretly removed from your room for your protection. We planned to inform you as soon as we knew for sure, but we didn't know if Mira was in on it too. Now that the truth has been revealed, we need to come together and pray for the strategy to take out the empress. You need your army ready to defend Silvenia."

He sits up straighter in his bed. "Call Commander Vale back in here. The empress and her army could be arriving any moment now. We have no time to waste!"

I jump up and run to open the door to call for Vale. I look down the winding stairway and see him leading Mira off down the hall. "Commander Vale! Come back!" I call out.

He stops, looking up to me. "The king wants us to come back?"

"Yes, please, come back," I say with a smile on my face.

Vale and Mira return to the king's bedroom. Vale is still holding Mira by the arm, waiting for the king's instructions. "Yes, my king? Has there been a change?"

"Yes," he responds, still not looking at Mira. "I need you and our army council to meet with me here in half an hour, along with Kara and whoever else you deem necessary. We are going to come up with a plan to defeat the empress and arrest her for my attempted murder. Right now, I need to speak with Princess Mira alone."

"Yes, my king," he says with a bow. Then he and I leave the room together.

Twenty minutes later, Mira leaves his room. Her eyes are red and swollen from crying, but she has a look of peace on her face. The king has offered her mercy and forgiveness, and she is overwhelmed at this. It is so unlike anything she is used to. He isn't even going to lock her in a cell; he is releasing her. She is free! What kind of man is this? She truly regrets all the pain she has caused him.

She knows she still has to face her mother, who will be arriving soon. Will his army be able to defeat her? Is Arten going to lead the fight against Vespes with the empress's army? These and many other questions pop up in her head as she walks slowly back to her room.

Closing the door inside her room, she shuts her eyes and whispers a prayer to the God who saved her. Perhaps He will show His mercy to the kingdom of Silvenia and rescue them from this evil enemy attack. She prays for courage. "Help me be brave, Lord Jesus. Protect us here!"

Will

Julia takes a seat in the cafeteria with her lunch tray. She has just finished spending the last two hours with Kara, reading to her again. The physical therapist arrived to manually exercise Kara's limbs and check on her responses. Her vital signs were stable, but there had been no real improvement. Julia still shows up every day, spending time with her sister, and then time in the chapel alone, talking with God. Her faith is growing, day by day. Julia can see how hard it is on her parents, and the toll it is taking on them, especially her mother.

Amazingly, Julia has found that she is the one now encouraging people to have faith that God is going to bring Kara back. Maybe it is because she wants it so much and refuses to consider anything else. Her father now only comes to visit once a week, but her mother still comes with Julia in the mornings and stays for about an hour. Kara's friend Sonia also comes by at least once a week. Julia stays for hours each day, refusing to quit. She has totally stopped drinking now, and her mind is clearer. She has begun reading the Bible every morning before she comes, and sometimes she reads it to Kara in her hospital room. And she prays, a lot.

This afternoon, as she sits eating a tuna fish sandwich, a good-looking young guy wearing scrubs takes a seat across from her with his own lunch tray. Startled, she looks up at him.

"Hello," he says with a friendly smile. "Do you mind if I sit with you here?"

"Um, no," she says, slightly annoyed at his boldness. "That's fine."

"My name is Will. I work here in the hospital."

"Oh, that's nice. What do you do?"

"I'm training in the radiology department," he says, continuing, "I notice you come here a lot. Like, every day. Are you visiting someone, or do you work here too?"

"I'm visiting my sister. She is in a coma," she says in a bit of a challenging tone, thinking she is not in the mood to be flirted with.

"Oh, I'm sorry. I didn't know." Then he goes on, "If you don't mind my asking, what happened to her?"

"She had a brain aneurysm," she says, looking down at her coffee and stirring it a bit. "I visit her every day and read to her." She hesitates for a moment and can see what looks like pity showing in his eyes. "She's going to wake up," she says defiantly. "I have faith in God, and He is going to wake her up!"

"I believe in God too," he responds gently. "With Him all things are possible."

Her defenses dropping, she smiles at his response, seeing him in a new light. They continue their conversation through the lunch hour, and Julia finds him easy to talk to. Suddenly, he glances at his watch. "I've got to go now. I only get thirty minutes for lunch. Do you want to meet for lunch again tomorrow? I really enjoy talking with you."

"Sure," she says quickly before she can talk herself out of it. "I'd like that."

He gets up and begins to head toward the exit. "See you tomorrow, then!" He gives a quick wave and is gone. Julia smiles to herself, feeling warm on the inside. *I guess I have a new friend!*

In the days to follow, they meet every day for lunch, and Julia realizes how good it is to have someone to confide in. She comes to trust him, and they begin to spend time together on the weekends too. But what means the most to her is the time they spend together in the chapel at the hospital, talking about Kara and even praying for her together. She feels a new sense of hope and comfort. It's obvious they are attracted to each other, but she can tell he is being sensitive and taking it slow, helping her work through things in their conversations.

Once, while they are in the chapel alone together, Julia tells Will about the boy Jonathan and what he said about Kara's leaf. "He said it was a key. A leaf key. Do you think that could mean anything?"

"I don't know. Can you show it to me?"

She pulls the leaf out of her pocket. It is still vibrant in color, and she holds it before him in the palm of her hand. "It's very pretty," he says, studying it. "But I don't know why he would say that. Maybe he was just making things up that came into his head, or maybe he is some kind of genius who knows things we don't. Didn't you say you thought he was autistic?"

"Yes, I think so. He knew a lot about insects. He went on and on about them and had a spiral notebook with drawings of them and their scientific names." She pauses, remembering. "Also, there was this bird…oh, never mind. It seems silly now that I'm saying it out loud."

"What? Tell me. I won't think you're silly."

She looks at him gratefully. "Okay, well, there was this bird I saw when I was in the cafeteria. It crashed into the window, and I thought it might be injured. But then it hopped closer to the window and looked up at me. It had a leaf in its mouth that he dropped on the ground, and then he cocked his head to the side, watching me. I went outside to find him, but he was gone. Then later, when I got home, there was a bird at my window. It was the same one! And he was interested in Kara's leaf. I was holding it, and I showed it to him. He hopped closer to see it. I even climbed out on the roof to sit with him, and he didn't fly off right away until I put it back in my pocket. Then he took off, and I haven't seen him since."

"How do you know it was the same bird?"

"I could just tell. He was a bluish-black color with white spots on his wings. And he was watching me through the window, just like at the hospital. Later, I looked up what type of bird it could be. I think it's called a starling."

"That's amazing. It you do see it again, try to take a picture of it. Maybe God's trying to tell you something."

A Windfolk Spy

On the night before leaving Icelandia, Vico spoke with the soldiers he knew and trusted from his hometown of Roten. He was able to gain the support of about one-fourth of the empress's army, and they met together with Arten in the woods late that night to form a plan.

Friedrich was not from Roten, but he caught wind of what was happening from his friend Korin. Korin had been taken from Roten shortly before Friedrich was taken from the nearby village of Dale. They had become friends during battle training, and Korin had once saved Friedrich from being struck with a spear by holding his shield up in front of him during one of their battles. They continued to look out for each other, and when Korin was invited by Vico to join in the secret plot against the empress, he asked if Friedrich could come too. He assured Vico that Friedrich was not loyal to the empress and that he would help them to fight against her.

This group of villagers-turned-soldiers had no love for the cruel empress and were prepared to do whatever it took to overthrow her. They were tired of being forced to carry out her wicked plans against the villages in the North. Their hatred of what she had done to their people outweighed their fear of her. So they pledged their allegiance to Arten and Vico at this night meeting in the forest. They pledged to fight against Celia in her attack on Silvenia. Arten would meet with Commander Vale, the leader of King Vespes's army, privately when they arrived. He would advise him of their group's secret plan to help protect the king and overthrow the empress.

Arten figured they would be arriving the evening before the wedding, and that would give them time to plan out the strategy with Commander Vale. He also needed time to speak with Mira. The empress would want her killed, and she expected him to do it!

He had to find a way to get her safely out of there before the battle began. He realized he loved her and would die protecting her if it came to that.

And then there was Gaelyn. His younger sister was being carefully watched by the empress and would be targeted by her if he stepped out of line. He had been discussing this problem with Vico when one of the younger soldiers walked up to him. "Excuse me, Commander Arten. My name is Friedrich. I know you are Gaelyn's older brother."

This caught Arten's attention. "Yes, what about it?"

"I know you are concerned for her safety. Gaelyn and I...well, what I mean to say is, we have become friends since she has been here. If there is anything I can do to help protect her, I offer you my sword as well." He held up his small sword, looking Arten in the eye with earnestness on his face.

Arten looked at him skeptically, sizing him up. "I will keep that in mind. Thank you, soldier."

"Yes, Captain." And he walked back to the group of men waiting by the trees.

Arten looked back at Vico. Vico shrugged his shoulders. "I don't know him, but he's a close friend of Korin."

"He's kind of small," remarked Arten, "but he has a brave look about him. We may find a use for him."

Vico nodded. "What will be our signal to begin the fight?"

"Let's speak with Commander Vale first," he said, glancing back over at Friedrich and Korin.

The men continued talking and planning for another hour and then, in small groups, quietly headed back to their quarters to sleep for a few hours before dawn. Friedrich headed back with Korin, and he was excited at this turn of events. He was a bit frightened, too, because he had heard what the empress did to the soldiers who failed or betrayed her. He had heard of Danere's pit to the underground world and the people she had thrown in there, never to be seen or heard of again. He would wait now for Gaelyn in the cellar to tell her of this new plan against the empress. He knew she just wanted to escape, and he did too, but maybe this would be a better plan for them both.

He shook off fearful thoughts, determined to only think of victory. He turned to Korin. "I can't wait to see her defeated, her wicked rule overturned. It will bring freedom to all the people in the North!"

"Yes," Korin agreed. "And we will be part of this marker in history. Our families, our children, will live free!" He smiled at Friedrich and slapped him on the back. "Now, we should go get some sleep. Dawn will be here before we know it."

It is now well into their journey, and very soon they will be arriving in Silvenia. They have passed over the Copper Hills, with the Great Sea behind them now. The sun is getting low in the sky, and they will be there before it sets.

Up at the front of their entourage, a soldier holds Icelandia's blue-and-white flag, an emblem of an icy star, blowing in the wind. Gaelyn rides beside the empress, silent under her cold gaze, speaking only when spoken to. She is comforted that Arten is close by, however, and earlier in the day, she had spotted Friedrich in the group of soldiers following along behind them. He caught her eye and smiled. She was glad to see him there.

Back inside the Silver Palace, Delvana and King Greffen have just arrived and are enjoying a happy reunion with Princess Trea and King Vespes. Delvana notices that despite her brother being happy to see her and sharing his joy with her regarding the new baby on the way, he also seems preoccupied. He excuses himself after about fifteen minutes of visiting with them, saying he has an important meeting that cannot wait. He assures them he will see them again at dinner.

So Princess Trea continues visiting with them, and all is going well until she mentions Kara. "Lady Kara has been here for a few days now, and we have been enjoying our time with her, and Sir Dominic too."

Delvana looks at her blankly. "Lady Kara? Who is that?"

"You know, Lady Kara, King Greffen's cousin. She said you sent her on ahead of you to help with wedding preparations. Don't you remember?"

Delvana and Greffen look at each other in confusion. He finally speaks up. "I don't have a cousin named Kara."

Cora is standing just inside the kitchen doorway, putting away some cups and listening to every word. "I knew it!" she whispers to herself. "She's a windfolk spy!" She files this away to herself and determines to keep a closer watch on this impostor named Kara.

"There must be some mistake," says Delvana.

Trea rises up from her seat with alarm. "Let me go speak with Vespes and find Kara. We need to find out what's going on. I'll be right back!"

Trea hurries out of the room to go speak with her brother while conflicting thoughts begin to fill her mind. *Why did Kara lie and say she was King Greffen's cousin? Who is she really?* Soon she is at Vespes's door and knocks urgently.

"Enter!" he calls out.

She opens the door and finds Vespes sitting up at his breakfast table with Commander Vale, Kara, and Dominic. The color has returned to his face, and he looks much improved. "Vespes! You are feeling better?"

"Yes, I am. But we are in the middle of an important meeting at the moment. Can this wait, my sister?"

She looks at Kara and then back at the king. "No, it cannot. I need to speak with you privately for a moment. Please!"

"All right," he sighs, looking at Kara and the others. "Would you all please step out for a moment while I speak with Princess Trea?"

"Yes, of course," replies Commander Vale. They all rise together and exit the room. Kara notices Trea is looking at her strangely as she heads out the door.

When the door is shut, Trea speaks without hesitation, "Vespes! Kara is not King Greffen's cousin! She is some kind of impostor. Delvana and Greffen both told me just now that they don't know who she is!"

He looks at her patiently, letting her express her concern, and then responds, "I know. She is from another land, far away from here. She has been sent here to help us. It was necessary to keep her true identity secret for a time. You must trust me in this. I will inform Della and Greffen as well after our meeting."

"Sent by who? For what purpose? I don't understand."

"Sent by God, Trea." She looks at him wide-eyed. "It's kind of a long story, which I don't have much time to explain right now, but here is what you need to know." He goes on to explain to her about how Lady Vallora and the windfolk were part of helping Kara get to Silvenia. He explains about the evil intent of the empress and how she had been controlling Mira to deceive them. "Now we are formulating a plan to arrest the empress and stop her wicked plot. She wants to take over Silvenia, but we are one step ahead of her now. But all this must remain a secret among us. The empress will be arriving at any moment, and we have to be ready for her."

Trea listens with amazement. "So Mira has been deceiving us too? Are you still going to marry her?"

"No, I am not. She doesn't love me," he says with some sadness in his voice. "It was all part of the plan to take over Silvenia. But she has revealed the empress's plans to me, and I have forgiven her." He decides not to mention Mira's part in poisoning him, thinking his sister has enough to process at the moment. "We are still going forward with the wedding ceremony tomorrow to throw off the empress. She must think nothing has changed. We are planning to have her arrested in the chapel area during the ceremony. That is what Commander Vale and I were just discussing."

"You're going to have Mira's mother arrested?"

"Yes, Trea. Mira herself has told us that she is evil, just like my advisers have been trying to tell me. She wants me dead, and the kingdom of Silvenia for herself."

Trea blinks in recognition. "I see. What can I do to help?"

"You can bring Della and Greffen to come speak with me regarding this situation after I finish speaking with Vale and Kara. I need us all to be on the same page."

"All right," she agrees, getting up to leave.

"And, Trea," he adds, "The empress will arrive with her army in tow. Don't be afraid. God is on our side, and He will protect us."

She nods at him, surprised to hear him talk about God in this way. She leaves the room feeling charged up by all this new information, and glad to see her older brother looking stronger and braver than she has seen him in a long time.

Princess Trea

Arrival of the Empress

Friedrich's horse reaches the top of the last hill, taking it slow over rocks and muddy areas to the grassy flat area near the ridge. Looking down, he can see the towers of the Silver Palace in the distance. They make their descent much quicker, with gravity assisting them.

Soon they are entering in through the front gate of the kingdom of Silvenia. He hears a trumpet blast announcing their arrival. Villagers watch from alongside the road as their horses march past. The empress's army gathers in the courtyard of the palace, under a large tented area.

Mira hears the horn blast from inside her room and watches them approach, her eyes searching for Arten. "There he is!" she whispers to herself, watching him dismount his horse and assist the empress down from hers. She feels a cold wave of fear when she sees her mother. She will have to face her very soon.

Vespes and Commander Vale have just finished talking with her about the plan to proceed with the ceremony in the morning. "We will have the empress in the small space of the chapel, without all her military support around her. It will be the best time to arrest her," said Vespes. "Commander Vale will have our soldiers ready for this confrontation. We will expose her treachery, arrest her, and take her to the stone cell in the tower to await trial for her plot to murder me and take over Silvenia. Our army will be ready to push back her soldiers should they put up any resistance."

Mira reminded them of her dark powers as a witch. "You must be prepared for anything. She is sly and cunning. And she has never been defeated in any of the towns of the North."

"Our kingdom is large, and our army is powerful too. She will have no choice but to surrender," the king had responded.

And so the plan was set. Vespes would act as if his health was still failing, even though he was rapidly improving now without the daily dose of poison in his tea. The family would attend the small ceremony in the chapel, with plenty of armed guards close by, ready for action. Commander Vale would sit close to where the king would be standing, with Delvana, Greffen, Trea, and Kara in a nearby pew close to an exit door, in order to make a quick escape to the safe room. There were underground tunnels that led to this safe room and also to a guest cottage on the other side of the stable grounds.

King Vespes was very concerned for Delvana; he didn't even want her in there in her fragile state, but it would look too suspicious to the empress if his own sister did not attend the wedding. According to their plan, the king and his sisters, along with Kara and Mira, were to leave the room quickly as soon as Commander Vale gave the signal to the king's guards to arrest the empress. The king wanted to stay and fight if necessary, but Commander Vale and Dominic reminded him that if anything happened to him, Silvenia would be without a king, and also, he was still recovering his strength. So taking their advice, he agreed to allow Marcus to lead them to the secret room until the empress was contained, and her army subdued. They would be safe there until Commander Vale came to retrieve them.

Mira continues watching out her window, keeping just out of sight. She doesn't want to be spotted by her mother. She watches as Commander Vale escorts the empress up to the front entrance—he is explaining to her that the king is recovering from an illness and won't be down to greet her until dinner is served. Her mother looks tall and commanding, fierce and beautiful, but Mira is well aware of the evil that lurks in her heart, simmering just below the surface.

She remembers one time as a child, she was playing with her dolls in her mother's throne room. One of the soldiers approached the empress and was giving her a report. Suddenly, as the empress raised her hand and pointed her finger at him, the man grabbed at his throat and began gasping for air. No one was touching him. He fell to the ground dead in a matter of moments, and the other soldiers with him carried him out. She started to run up to her mother to ask what happened to him, but a servant named Leone stopped her. "But I just want to know what happened to him," she said to the servant girl.

"He disobeyed the empress," Leone replied, swiftly gathering up the dolls to take Mira out of the room.

"What do you—"

"Shush!" she had whispered quickly. "Come, let's go play in your room now." And Leone had escorted her out of there with haste. Mira had looked back at her mother, trying to process what she had just seen. The empress had looked at her daughter coldly, not saying a word.

Mira has seen her mother's dark powers at work and is reluctant to face her now. She can avoid her for the moment but will be expected at the dinner table. She is sure her mother will seek her out to question her privately after they eat. She must be sure to bring the vial of poison with her to show her mother. Vespes is going to continue to act weak and sickly, which isn't hard, considering his body is still recovering. Everyone knows to be careful what they say around the empress. They will play the part of a happy family excited for the wedding ceremony in the morning.

Knowing the empress is now inside the castle, Mira starts to turn away from the window, but in the corner of her eye she sees a hand waving. She looks out and realizes it is Arten, and her heart begins to race. She lifts a hand to wave back at him, and he makes a motion with his hand for her to come outside. She shakes her head no, thinking it will be too dangerous, and also because she is still upset with him for leaving her without a word.

He runs his hand through his hair in frustration and makes the motion again, a pleading look in his eyes.

"I can't!" she mouths the words back to him. He continues to look up at her and then nods in understanding. Then he walks back over to Vico, and they take their horses over to the stable area with the other soldiers. She follows him with her eyes, wishing she could run down to him, but she is afraid.

Has he come back for me? Can I trust him, or is he working with my mother now? She thinks on this for a few moments, then decides she doesn't care. *I still love him. I have to believe he is on the right side.*

There is good in him, I know it! She puts her hopes on him seeking her out later that evening so they can speak. He knows where her room is. She will leave it up to him.

An hour goes by, and there is a knock on her door. "Yes?" she calls out.

"Dinner is served, milady," says Ceyla. "Would you like to walk down with me?"

"Yes," says Mira, checking her face in the mirror one last time. "I'm coming." She braces herself and heads out the bedroom door. Ceyla is standing there with a grin on her face.

"Princess, your mother, the empress, has arrived! She will be so glad to see you," Ceyla remarks as they walk down the hall together.

"Yes," says Mira, not wanting to say anything more. They descend the steps together, and Mira takes a deep breath and exhales before entering the dining room. Everyone is already seated at the table, and all eyes turn to look at Mira. Vespes rises from his chair slowly, and a servant rushes to pull out a chair for each of them.

Feeling everyone's eyes upon her, she can feel her cheeks flush as she looks around the table. She is seated next to King Vespes and across from her mother. The empress looks at her and smiles in greeting, but there is a coldness in her eyes. "My daughter! How lovely you look. I think being in Silvenia agrees with you."

"Yes," she responds, "I've been very happy here." She clears her throat a bit and continues, "We are so glad you have come in time for our wedding tomorrow. Aren't we, Vespes?" Out of the corner of her eye, she sees Arten watching her. Purposely, she grabs Vespes's hand on the table and looks at the king with affection.

"I wouldn't have missed it!" says the empress. "Also, I was hoping you would show me your wedding dress this evening and that we could have some private mother-daughter time together." Mira knows from the look in her mother's eyes that this is a command, not a suggestion.

"Of course, I would love that. We can go to the dressing room after dinner," she responds, determined to remain calm. *The sooner we get this over with, the better,* she thinks to herself, trying to eat but not really tasting any of the food. Her stomach is tight, but she forces herself to look cheerful and composed.

She glances over at Arten and sees he is talking politely with Commander Vale. He looks back at her, and she quickly looks away. Determined to continue the charade, she goes on talking about the honeymoon plans with her mother and the king.

"We are planning a tour of the Southern Isles," says Vespes convincingly. "Of course, we might have to wait a few days after the ceremony, until I am fully recovered."

"Yes, I heard you have not been feeling well. I do hope you are on the mend now, especially with your big day tomorrow," says the empress.

"I am sure I will be perfectly fine by morning. I don't want anything to delay our marriage," he says, smiling at Mira. Mira looks back at him and notices a hint of sadness behind his eyes. She squeezes his hand gently, feeling regret at the pain she has caused him once again. He withdraws his hand from hers and picks up his fork to begin eating. Everyone follows suit, and they are served three courses before dessert. Cora and the other servants work rapidly and quietly around them, removing plates and filling their cups.

Kara and Dominic are seated purposely farther down the table, close to Delvana and King Greffen, to avoid being questioned by the empress. The empress makes an attempt at conversation with Delvana and King Greffen, asking about the kingdom of Volkenland. She listens attentively. Mira notices this, that she is probably marking it down on her list of territories to take over.

Kara and Dominic do their best to keep to themselves, avoiding eye contact with the empress. Finally, she calls them out. "And you, Lady Kara, is it? And Sir...?"

"Dominic," he responds with a quick bow of his head. "Lady Kara is a cousin of King Greffen, and I am her chaperone here. We are honored to meet you, Empress Celia."

"Yes," she responds, and deciding they do not interest her at the moment, she turns back to Mira and Vespes. Dessert has been served, and the king begins to excuse himself, saying he is tired and wants to be well rested for tomorrow. "I will see you in the morning, my darling," he says to Mira, kissing her on the hand.

"Yes, I will be up in a little while to say good night. I want to show my mother the beautiful wedding dress that was made for me." She looks at her mother, who is watching Vespes slowly get up from the table and head out of the room. Mira feels Arten watching her as well, and her cheeks flush pink. She tries not to look at him and gets up from the table also. "Shall we go to the dressing room now, Mother?"

"Yes, I can't wait to see it!" she responds. The empress looks up at Cora with a meaningful glance as the head cook takes her plate.

"I hope everything was to your liking?" she asks.

"Yes, thank you," she responds. As they walk out of the room, the empress hands Ceyla a small piece of paper. "Ceyla, would you please ask the head cook to write down that delicious souffle recipe for me? I would love to have our cook at home learn how to prepare that."

"Of course, Empress Celia," she says with a small curtsy and heads over to the kitchen.

Mira can't stop herself from glancing back at Arten as they leave the room. Their eyes meet for a brief moment, and she can see a look of love and determination in his eyes. Her heart beats rapidly, both from seeing him again and also because she is about to be alone with the empress. She can no longer hide behind any polite conversation.

They make their way down the hall to the dressing room and enter without a word. Hanging up in the center of the room is her wedding dress. It glitters with tiny jewels sewn onto the bodice, and white satin is spread out in layers of descending length around it. Her eyelet lace veil is draped over a chair and is also long and layered, with a glittering crown attached to the top.

"My, how lovely," remarks the empress in a chilling tone of voice. She waits for Mira to shut the door behind them before her interrogation begins. "Are you ready for tomorrow? Have you followed all my instructions?"

"Yes, Mother." She reaches into her skirt pocket and pulls out the vial to show her. "I have been diligent to obey you, and all is in place for tomorrow. You have seen how weak the king is already."

"Lower your voice!" commands the empress. "And put that away before someone sees it." She then puts her finger under Mira's chin and lifts her head to look her in the eyes. "We are so close, my daughter. So close to achieving our goals. But you do not look happy. What is the matter? You don't truly have feelings for this King Vespes, do you?"

"No, I don't," she whispers, turning away. "But he is decent and nice. He is a good king, and the people of Silvenia respect him."

"He is a young fool! You can do much better, my daughter. Let me position you in your own little kingdom, and then you can have whatever man you choose. But first, I must claim Silvenia as our territory. Our kingdom will continue to expand and grow in power, and no one will be able to come against us! You must harden your heart against these weak and foolish ones who are so easily deceived. Have no compassion for them. To be a strong and powerful queen, you must show no mercy—that is the only way!" She looks down at Mira, as if sizing her up for the task.

"Yes, Mother. I will do as you say," she says as convincingly as she can, returning her mother's gaze without looking away.

"Do you still have the scroll?" counters the empress.

"Yes," she replies quickly. "It's up in my room, hidden away."

"Very well." She nods, accepting this response. "You must give the king ten drops from the vial on your wedding night. My men are ready and waiting for me to give the signal to seize control of the kingdom. We will make this as quick and painless as possible, providing everyone cooperates as they should. Otherwise, it could be quite a bloody battle," she asserts, with emphasis on the word *bloody*. "But don't worry, Mira. I never lose!"

Mira shudders inwardly, faking an agreeable smile. "Yes, Mother. Is there anything else?" she says, wanting to flee the room.

"That is all for now. I will see you in the morning looking quite beautiful in this dress, I'm sure."

Mira opens the door and starts to head back out into the hall. Her mother grabs her by the arm and jerks her back around. "Mira," she says forcefully, "you must not fail me!" Nodding silently, Mira pulls her arm back and heads out the door. She doesn't breathe normally until she is safely back in her room, with the door shut behind her. She collapses onto her bed, shaken from her mother's dark words but refusing to let fear take her over. "This will all be over soon," she whispers to herself, sure she will not be able to sleep at all this night.

While Mira is busy with the empress, Arten seizes the moment and asks to speak with Commander Vale. He brings Vico along with him, and they meet in Vale's private room. While in there, he reveals his true intent to overthrow the empress and assures the commander that he and one-fourth of their army are ready to turn against the empress and help Silvenia defeat her. King Vespes, Marcus, Kara, and Dominic are brought into this secret meeting as well, and they begin to formulate a new plan together with Arten and Vico. The king is glad to know that now they have even more soldiers on their side.

Arten addresses the king. "The empress is full of hatred and murderous intent. She has no compassion and has confessed to me that she will kill even her own daughter if she gets in the way. In fact, she has instructed me to kill her if she is found to be a traitor. I tell you, she will stop at nothing to overthrow this kingdom, and must be killed—it is the only way to stop her."

"We must arrest her and give her a trial first," asserts the king. "Just as we would do with any other criminal."

"But if she resists, my king," interjects Commander Vale, "we must consider the threat to your life and defend as necessary." Vespes agrees to this with a nod.

"She will most certainly resist," says Arten. "And the first thing she will do is command me to kill you and her daughter, Mira, and the battle will begin. Both you and Mira are in great danger."

"But we are one step ahead of her and already know that you will not comply with that command."

"There is one complication," says Arten. "She has ahold on my younger sister, Gaelyn. She's been keeping her as a maidservant close to her side as a pawn to control me. If I don't follow her commands, she will kill her as well. I cannot allow that to happen."

Vico speaks up. "We can get Friedrich to help with Gaelyn. He is small, and we can hide him under a pew close to where the empress and Gaelyn will be. We will tell Gaelyn the plan and tell her to be prepared to run. When the arrest is announced, he can be there to block the empress and help Gaelyn escape quickly from the room. I will be there as well—you know how quick I am with my bow. I won't let her harm your sister."

Arten cringes slightly. "Are you sure we should bring the boy into this?"

"He volunteered for this!" Vico reminds him. "And I will do my best to protect them both."

Arten nods in agreement and then turns to the king. "King Vespes, I have been thinking about these plans to defeat the empress for some time now. I know you are planning to retreat to your safe room with Mira and the others. I have another idea I would like you to consider."

Vespes looks at him curiously. "Yes, what is it?"

"First, I want to confess to you that I care deeply for Princess Mira and I want to protect her. I know the empress will be enraged and try her best to kill her tomorrow. I have seen her kill before. She has dark powers that could be hard to overcome. I think the best thing to do is to have Mira escape before the wedding."

Vespes looks over at him, considering. "And how do you propose we do that? You can't have a wedding ceremony without a bride."

"You could have someone stand in for her. Doesn't her wedding attire have a veil? The stand-in would be veiled, and the empress won't know the difference until it is time to remove it, and we will have her arrested by then."

"That would never work," says the king. "She would recognize it's not Mira, even with the veil—"

"No, he's right!" I say. "I've seen the veil, and it completely covers her face. I could do it. I could take her place."

They all turn and look at me.

"We are about the same height and build. My hair isn't as dark as hers, but it will be covered with the veil. Even if the empress notices I'm missing from the ceremony, you can just say I got sick and stayed in my room. That way, Mira will have a head start and can get far away from her mother before everything unfolds."

"But where will she go?" asks the king.

"She can go stay with the windfolk," interjects Vale. "She has a connection to them by her grandmother Londine. I can send a messenger bird ahead of her, and they will come to meet her and protect her within their borders."

"Mira is a descendant of the windfolk?" asks Arten, clearly surprised at this new information.

"Not exactly," says Commander Vale. "Her grandmother Londine was adopted by them as a small child and raised as one of their own. The story is, she was found alone in the woods by the windfolk, far from any neighboring towns. There was no sign of her parents anywhere, so they took her in and raised her. She lived with them until the age of fifteen and then tragically was kidnapped by Danere, an evil agent of Mercurio. She was taken to the underground realm and forced to marry him there. She bore him a daughter, whom you know as the empress Celia."

Arten counters, "Even if this is so, I'm sure they know how wicked the empress is. Why would they want to take in the daughter of a known enemy? Why would they trust her when she could bring evil to their land?"

"I will explain to them what has occurred. That Mira has left the empress and her dark ways, not wishing to end up like her. I will request that they give her shelter and protection, in memory of Londine, her grandmother. Lady Vallora will remember and honor this. She is my personal friend and will trust my word."

"Who will go with her?" asks the king. "She won't know the way, and it is a long journey to Elmwood from here."

"I will take her," says Arten. "I will protect her and make sure she gets to their land safely."

So for the next hour, they discuss this new strategy and work out as many details as they possibly can. I agree to take Mira's place in the chapel while Mira escapes through the underground tunnel to the guesthouse. Arten will have horses waiting there for their quick escape while the queen is confronted during the ceremony. He will also instruct Gaelyn to run there with him as well, and the three of them will escape together into the woods.

Arten knows he needs to put as much distance as possible between Mira and the empress once her betrayal is revealed. He knows that she will seek revenge and show no mercy if she catches them. He tries to persuade King Vespes that once they have her detained and locked in a cell, a close watch needs to be kept on her at all times with numerous armed guards. He relays his own stories of seeing her kill with a word and a point of her finger.

The king listens closely, and they all agree to adhere to the plan they have set. Arten will go to Mira this evening and explain this new strategy to her as well. Vico will speak with Gaelyn and Friedrich, and King Vespes will inform his sisters and King Greffen.

Before they adjourn, King Vespes has me speak to them about what God has shown me and that He is on our side. I encourage them to be brave and not fear, and then I lead them all in a prayer for victory over the enemy. I also take Dominic's Bible and hold it up in front of them. I feel boldness and strength fill me as I remind them of the power of the Word of God and read to them from the book of Joshua: "Have I not commanded you? Be strong and of good courage; do not be afraid, nor be dismayed, for the Lord your God is with you wherever you go" (Josh. 1:9 NKJV).

The Battle Begins

The morning comes quickly, and servants rush around in the kitchen, preparing the wedding feast. There are white flowers and ribbons everywhere, adorning the chairs in the dining hall and the pews in the chapel. I go down early in the morning to hide in the dressing room and wait for Mira to show up. I leave Buddy safely in my room, curled up on my bed, sleeping peacefully. Creeping quietly down the hall, I pass the kitchen, where Cora is busy preparing the cake. I am quiet as a mouse, and no one notices me enter the dressing room. Mira arrives a few minutes later.

Mira helps me fasten the last of the buttons on the back of the wedding dress and then assists me with the veil. Under layers of the satin skirt, I have tied the green-and-gold scarf that I found in the tree to my thigh. I saw it on my dresser this morning before I came down and felt like I should take it with me. Not really knowing why, instinctively, I grabbed it and brought it with me to the dressing room.

Mira takes a metal clasp and attaches the veil securely to my hair. Thankfully, the veil provides good coverage of my hair and face, and Mira makes sure the crown is set well, holding the white lace fabric in place. Then, together we check my appearance from every angle, making sure my true identity will not be on display. Standing in front of the looking glass, Mira remarks to me, "Kara, you are truly a beautiful princess! Thank you again for everything." She says this sincerely, squeezing my hand.

I reach down to a side table and hand Mira a small package.

"What is this?" she asks, peeking inside.

"It's a Bible. I found some in the palace library. Vespes said I can give it to you. Take it with you on your journey and read it every day.

It will help you to know the God who saved you." I smile at Mira as she accepts it gratefully.

"Thank you. I will always keep it with me."

I asked Marta to wait outside our door, both to alert us if the empress comes around and also to lead Mira safely to the secret door to the underground tunnel once the ceremony begins. None of the other servants know of this door except for Marcus. Since Marcus will be busy helping Commander Vale and the king, I convinced them to also allow Marta to assist with Mira's escape. The door is behind a bookcase in the small red-and-white parlor down the hall from the chapel. There is a lever behind one of the books that slides the bookcase over to reveal the narrow door. When the door closes again, it automatically slides the bookcase back into place.

Marta waits outside the dressing room, pretending to dust and hang more decorations in the hallway. She is to knock three times to give the signal that the ceremony is about to begin, and four times to alert us if she sees the empress approaching. If the empress tries to enter the dressing room, Marta is to tell her that the king has told everyone to take their seats in the chapel now. She sincerely hopes she doesn't have to deal with her. Hopefully, the empress will just go directly to the chapel and take a seat.

Marta didn't have to worry about explaining where she was to Cora; apparently, she was in the chapel already to attend the ceremony. And the other servants were too busy and didn't bother to ask where she was going when she left the kitchen. Feeling nervous and excited, she is glad that the king and I have trusted her enough to include her in this secret plan.

The organ begins to make music, and Marta hears it echo in the hall. "It's time!" She sees the empress and her army commander walk past her quickly along with a few others and enter the chapel. She breathes a sigh of relief. Peeking into the chapel, she waits for a moment, making sure all the king's family is in there. The room is filled with guests, both with family, military, and a few servants. She sees Cora seated in the same row as the empress, on the other side, with a few servants. There are guards by all the doors, and she can feel the tension in the air. The king is standing at the front, flanked on the steps by King Greffen and Commander Vale.

Princess Trea is at the back of the chapel by the door, waiting for the bride. Delvana is seated on the first pew along with Dominic and close to her husband, King Greffen. Marta looks back at the organist and sees him point at her, giving the signal that all is ready. Nodding, she turns back to the dressing room door.

"Three knocks—it's time!" I say. I grasp Mira's hand and say quickly, "Remember, wait until I am all the way to the altar before you and Marta head to the secret door. That way, everyone's eyes will be at the front of the chapel."

"Yes! Goodbye, Kara. I hope I will see you again!" We hug one last time, and I head out the dressing room door, bouquet in hand. It feels like I am in a dream.

As I stand at the chapel door, the organ pipes up again and everyone stands and turns to watch me come down the aisle. I walk steadily to the front, feeling all eyes upon me. King Vespes is waiting for me at the front, dressed regally in his full military uniform and crown. He takes my hand to assist me up the steps. With my back now to the people, I breathe out a nervous sigh of relief. I have made it this far!

The minister gives a brief welcome and then begins the ceremony. I hear myself repeating the wedding vows, and then Vespes does the same. Through the lace of the veil, I can see his eyes. Once again, I have that strange feeling of being drawn to him. *It's probably just the romance of being dressed as a bride and saying these vows...vows!* I suddenly feel alarmed at this. *But we won't get through the whole ceremony. It's not a real wedding, after all,* I reason within myself.

Vespes looks at me as he repeats the words. *She looks so brave and beautiful! How come I never noticed before?*

He is surprised at his own thoughts. His heart beating rapidly, he realizes he must stay focused on the task at hand, which is to arrest the empress and protect the kingdom of Silvenia. He puts his attention back on what the minister is saying.

"Do you have the rings?"

There is silence for a moment. That is the signal.

Commander Vale raises his hand to alert the guards. Then, walking to the front of the altar, he stands in front of the king and pulls out a scroll. Opening it, he reads, "Empress Celia Tremonde, you are under arrest for attempted murder in a plot to kill King Vespes of Silvenia. You will be detained here until time for your trial…" He goes on reading the order while soldiers from Vespes's army begin to surround her, fully armed.

She begins to laugh out loud. "You have no power over me! Kurt, Arten, do as I have commanded you!" Kurt jumps up and grabs Princess Trea, holding a knife to her throat. Arten hesitates, looking over at Gaelyn. He can see she is also being held around the neck by Cora, the cook. She has a knife pressed to his younger sister's throat. And he thought she would be safe since she was not seated near the empress! Arten begins to walk slowly toward the veiled bride, sword in hand.

"You must kill Mira and the king. Do it now!" yells the empress.

"Ahhh!" Cora screams, feeling a stabbing pain in her calf from Friedrich's dagger. She drops the knife, and Gaelyn flees from her grasp. At the same moment, Vico shoots an arrow at Kurt, striking him in the shoulder, and he falls to the ground next to Princess Trea. But he catches on to her dress as she tries to break away, and she ends up falling down beside him. He grabs her around the neck and then begins to reach for his fallen sword.

Arten yells, "Now!" into the air, and a soldier pulls out a horn and blows. Soldiers run into the chapel from outside, and soon there is fighting all around, with swords clanging and people yelling and running in every direction. Filled with rage, the empress rushes the altar with a steel blade in her hand, knocking back everyone who comes toward her with some kind of power coming out of her hands. Arten raises his sword to strike the empress, and she holds up her hand in front of him. Her eyes are pools of darkness, and she is speaking out venomous words as she walks toward him. He is pushed back with a surge of power coming from her hands that causes him to stumble backward to the ground, banging his head against a wooden pew.

"The weakness of men!" she hisses at Arten. "I'll kill them myself!" she shouts, raising her knife in the air and rushing toward me. Suddenly, she halts. Reaching up to my face, she rips off the veil. After a moment of shock at seeing my face instead of her daughter's, she bellows, "Where is she?"

"You will never find her!" I say, backing away.

"You will die for this!" Celia hisses, lunging at me violently. She raises her knife again to strike me, and Vespes throws himself in front of me, taking the stab of her steel blade into his arm. Commander Vale rushes at the empress from behind and pulls her back by the arms, causing her to tumble down the steps with him.

Keeping ahold of her tightly, Vale calls for help from his soldiers as the fighting continues all around. One soldier comes with handcuffs and manages to get them around her wrists while Vale holds her from behind. She begins to speak out loudly in a menacing chant, her words forming a spell, and Vale quickly puts his hand over her mouth to silence her. "Quick, bring me a cloth to tie around her mouth!" he orders.

Once this is accomplished, he orders twenty of his men to surround and hold her there until they get the battle under control. Both armies are still fighting against each other inside the chapel and out on the grounds. While Vale was restraining the empress, Vico had rushed forward and pulled Arten to his feet. He urged him to quickly escape the palace grounds with Gaelyn and Mira.

With the empress being held, Marcus is now able to usher the king and his family out to the secret room below—all except for Trea, who is still in the clutches of Kurt. She is kicking and struggling to get away from him, and he is keeping a firm grip on her and still trying to grasp his sword. Even wounded, he is quite strong, refusing to let her go. Vico sees what is happening and runs forward, kicking the sword out of his reach and punching him in the face. Even with the arrow stuck in his shoulder, Kurt punches him back and they wrestle each other to the ground, close to Trea. "Run, Princess!" yells Vico as he tries to hold back Kurt's large frame from overcoming his smaller one.

"Hurry, Trea, come this way!" she hears Vespes calling to her as Marcus leads them toward the exit door. Trea looks back at Vico, and instead of running, she lunges for Kurt's sword, picks it up, and stabs him in the back with it. Kurt collapses on top of Vico, blood streaming from his jacket. Vico pushes out from under him and grabs Trea's outstretched hand. She hands over the bloody sword to him with a look of revulsion, and together they run over to where Marcus and the king are waiting by the exit door.

"Go with the king!" Vico instructs her, pushing her in front of Marcus.

"Come with us!" she pleads, reaching back for him.

"I must stay and help the others. Please go!" And leaving her, he runs back into the midst of the fighting. As Trea runs down the hall with Vespes and me, she sees Delvana up ahead of them with King Greffen and Dominic. They all climb through the narrow door and into the tunnel. It closes behind them, and Marcus runs to the front, leading the way with a torch. I am alongside Vespes, and I see he is trailing blood from his arm where the empress stabbed him. I remember my scarf and stop for a moment and pull it off my leg.

"Kara, hurry! We mustn't stop until we are safely in the room!" he says, trying to pull me along.

"Wait," I say. "Let me see your arm." I gently take ahold of his arm and tie the scarf around it to stop the bleeding. "There, until we can do better."

"Thank you," he says, grabbing my hand. "Now let's go!" And we run to catch up to the others. As we hurry to the secret room, Delvana suddenly falls to the ground with a cry.

"What is it, my darling? Are you all right?" King Greffen stiffens, realizing that Nancy, her midwife, is not with them, and he braces himself for her reply.

"It's the baby!" she gasps. "I think it's coming now!"

"Oh my god, Della!" yells Trea, running toward her sister. King Greffen reaches down and lifts her up, carrying his young wife the rest of the way to the room.

"It's just ahead," says Vespes. "Hurry, Marcus, unlock the door!"

They hurry inside, and Marcus quickly locks it behind them. Greffen gently lays Delvana down on the small bed as she moans from the pain. She grabs Greffen's hand and squeezes it tightly until she is able to speak again. "The pains are coming fast, Greffen," she whispers. "Please help me!" She closes her eyes tightly, and a tear slides down her face.

"Please, who can help her deliver the baby?" says Vespes frantically. "Kara, can you do it?"

My mind flashes back to a picture in my memory of seeing a baby being born in the hospital during my nursing school training. I have watched a doctor do this once but have no experience myself. I look at Trea questioningly, hoping she might have some skill in this area. Trea quickly shakes her head no, with a fearful look in her eyes. Gripping Delvana's other hand, she encourages her sister to breathe. "Please, Kara," she says pleadingly, "will you help my sister?"

I whisper a prayer under my breath as I step forward to become Delvana's midwife. As I position myself, I notice that there is an awful lot of blood. The bed beneath her is soaked with it. I can see the baby's head is crowning and urge Delvana to push with the next contraction. The pushing continues with each contraction for what seems like hours. Finally, the baby's head emerges, and I can see the infant's face—it is blue, with the cord wrapped tightly around the baby's neck.

"God help us!" whispers Trea, who is standing beside me now with a towel in her hand.

"Push, Della! You're almost there! One more time!"

As she pushes the baby out, I try to slip my finger under the cord and release the pressure. "Trea, help me grab the baby underneath," I say as I pull the slippery baby forward under its arms. Trea positions the cloth underneath the baby, and together, we grab ahold. Blood continues to pour out of Delvana as she pants for air now, her breathing rapid and shallow.

"It's a girl!" exclaims Trea excitedly. The baby is still blue and has not taken a breath. I quickly turn her over, using my finger to release the cord from her neck and then try to sweep fluid from the baby's mouth. I tell Trea to use shoelaces to help tie the cord, and then we use Vespes's knife to cut it. I pat the baby on the back and thump her tiny feet.

Nothing. The baby lies still on the bed, getting bluer by the minute. I look up at Vespes with desperation, not knowing what else to do.

"My baby, let me hold her," says Delvana softly, glad to have the baby out and unaware of the crisis. Greffen grips her hand tightly, looking at his dead baby girl, and he hangs his head in sorrow. He cannot speak.

"Why isn't she crying?" Delvana asks. "Greffen, what's wrong! Give me my baby!"

Trea begins to cry, and I pick up the lifeless infant and lay it gently on Delvana's chest into her outstretched arms. "God have mercy on me! God have mercy on me!" she screams inconsolably, clutching her lifeless baby to her heart in anguish.

My heart is undone. Feeling waves of compassion, I lay my hand on the back of the baby and pray with all my might. I feel a powerful warmth go out from my hands into the baby's cold skin. The warmth continues to grow until it feels like fire! I look down and sees pink flesh beneath my hands. The baby suddenly begins to move!

"She's alive!" shouts Trea. "Look! Look at her!"

Delvana gets quiet and feels the baby move on her chest. Then she hears the infant's cry. "Oh, God, I thank You, I thank You!" she says, hugging her baby as tears pour down her face. I quickly help Delvana adjust the baby in her arms with the towel wrapped around her, and Greffen reaches down and enfolds them both in his embrace. Trea and I hug each other excitedly, both still crying, and then my eyes meet Vespes's, and we break forth into sounds of laughter spilling out from relief and joy.

After this, I slump down into a chair and feel the tension leave me. "Thank You, God!" I whisper, closing my eyes for a moment. For the next hour, we remain in the safe room, tending to Delvana and the baby. The baby is fully pink now and seems perfectly well. Delvana, on the other hand, has lost a lot of blood. She is happy, but very weak. I instruct Trea to keep giving her fluids and watch to make sure the extreme bleeding has stopped. Finally, Delvana and the baby are both resting well, and Vespes and Marcus take turns listening at the ceiling vent by the door to see if they can make out what is going on upstairs.

While all this was taking place in the secret room, Marta and Mira have made it safely through the tunnels and are hiding out in the guesthouse, waiting for Arten and Gaelyn to join them. Vale has positioned armed guards outside the door to help protect them, and there are four horses tied to the nearby trees in the woods so they can make a quick escape.

As they wait, they suddenly hear three knocks on the trapdoor below. Marta quickly lifts the wooden opening on the floor, and Dominic climbs up to join them. "I'm here to see you off safely and then report back to the king," he says. "Arten and Gaelyn are not far behind me."

A moment later, they hear them approaching, and soon Gaelyn is climbing up the steps. Arten follows behind her, and they lock the trapdoor shut and cover it back over with a rug. Arten embraces Mira, and she smiles happily, holding him tight.

"Come now, there's no time to wait!" urges Dominic. He peeks his head out the cottage door and looks at the guards. "Is it safe to go now?" he whispers to them.

They nod, and one of them says, "Follow me."

They all crouch down low in the tall grass and hurry toward the waiting horses. Dominic and Marta watch from the doorway and wave goodbye to them once they are all safely mounted up and ready to go.

"Thank you!" Mira gestures with her hand. Arten gives a salute, and they turn and head into the forest, following a trail that leads to a hidden back gate out of the kingdom. One of the guards stays with them until they safely reach this woodland gate and exit to the outside. There are miles of thick forest ahead of them, for they must take a secluded route and stay off the main roads.

Inside the palace, the fighting has ceased. Once the empress's men realized she had been arrested, it was only about a matter of time until the rest of her army surrendered to King Vespes's soldiers as well. Her army is now detained in the courtyard, and the empress is being led up to the tower cell by Commander Vale himself and twenty of his men. Her arms are cuffed behind her, and she walks up the stone steps in silence.

She does not resist them now and quietly walks into her prison cell at the top of the tower. Vale removes the cloth from her mouth for a moment when she raises her hand in a questioning gesture.

"Can you just loosen this a bit? It's so tight that it feels like it's cutting into my mouth!" She gives him a pleading look with her eyes. Frowning, he ties it back on, a bit looser this time. He leaves the cuffs on her wrists, behind her back, after seeing the damage she can do with her hands.

Once she is locked inside, she turns her back on them, her face to the stone wall. Commander Vale leaves four guards with her just outside her cell. They are instructed to keep watch on her in shifts. If she makes any attempt to use witchcraft or escape her cell, they are to blow the trumpet and call for immediate aid.

As Commander Vale descends the stairway, the empress smiles to herself. "They should have known better!" Under her breath, through the loosened cloth, she begins to recite softly, "Danere, my father, take me from here. Away from their sight. Danere... Danere!"

With the four guards watching, she vanishes before their eyes in a cloud of gray fog that fills the cell. The first guard blasts the horn, and Vale comes running back up the stairs with the other men. He shakes his head in amazement. "What happened?" he questions them.

"She just whispered something and then disappeared in a puff of smoke! She's a witch, to be sure!"

Vale has them check everywhere along the tower and throughout the palace to be sure, but she is nowhere to be found. He has to inform the king.

Back on the main floor, there is still a lot of chaos, with dead soldiers being carried out and others being treated for wounds. Vale speaks with Daniel, his second-in-command, and he takes charge of locking up the empress's soldiers for the night in the south building; they have many holding cells there and will position them there until they figure out what to do with them.

Commander Vale heads down to the tunnels to report to the king. Marcus greets him at the door, and Vale is welcomed in, everyone wanting to know what has happened aboveground. Vale's eyebrows raise as he sees the sleeping princess and her baby off to the side.

"Delvana had her baby while we were in here," says Trea. "It's a girl!"

"Congratulations!" he says to King Greffen, who also comes forward to hear the news.

"What do you have to report, Commander Vale?" asks King Vespes.

"We arrested the empress, Your Majesty. I regret to report, however, that as soon as we locked her in the tower cell, she vanished from our sight."

Trea gasps out loud, covering her mouth.

"She has escaped," the king repeats, not wanting to believe it.

"Yes, my king. But her army has surrendered and the fighting has ceased. It is safe to come back up now, but with your permission, I would like to keep extra guards by all our rooms and throughout the palace at this time."

"You have my permission," agrees Vespes, shaking his head. "We should have listened to Commander Arten and killed her before she had a chance to escape."

"Where do you think she could have gone?" I ask.

"She will probably try to track down Mira and Arten," realizes Vespes. He looks at Commander Vale. "Can we send some of our men after them to help warn and protect them?"

"Yes, I will assemble a search party. We know the way they are headed. It is at least a two-week journey through the deep forest to Elmwood and the mountains of Shazir."

"Let us pray our men can get to them before the empress does," says Vespes. "May God protect them!"

So the king and his family go back through the tunnel, with Vale leading the way. Trea watches as Vale speaks with the men in the chapel. Vico is the first to respond and becomes the leader of the search party, along with Friedrich, Korin, and three other soldiers. Without delay, they head out to give aid to Arten, Gaelyn, and Mira.

Slowly and deliberately, order is restored in the Silver Palace. Cora, the head cook, is among those arrested and being led away to the south building. Trea looks sadly at the woman she thought she knew so well being escorted away as a traitor, limping from the stab wound in her leg.

The servants are bustling about, picking up overturned chairs and china that has been smashed on the floor. But at least they are safe. The empress is gone, and the king and his family remain. The kingdom of Silvenia will have peace again.

While birds flit about in the evening sky, Trea, King Vespes, and I watch from his balcony as the search party rides out into the forest. Vico, astride his gray horse, leads them on. The first moon is already visible, low on the horizon, and the kingdom of Silvenia rests from the tumult of the day.

The Tree in the Meadow

It's been five days since the battle at the palace, and Vespes is beginning to feel like his old self again. The wound in his arm is healing well, and his strength has returned. He has been going out to ride on his horse every day, and I have been joining him. He finds his broken heart has been quick to heal, and we are getting to know each other better every day.

I have begun to tell him bits and pieces about my home and the land I came from. He begins to understand that my Earth is in a different time dimension from his. I tell him how I came through some sort of doorway, a portal, into Paredonia. And I don't know how to get back. It is selfish, he knows, but he is glad that this is so. He does not want me to leave.

More and more, my feelings for Vespes have grown, and it is apparent to everyone at the palace as well. Dominic remarks to me one morning as we head down to breakfast, Buddy following close behind, "Kara, I've noticed how happy you've been these past few days. Could it be you are falling in love with the king?"

I blush. "What? I mean…I don't know. I do enjoy spending time with him. But this is not my home. I cannot form that kind of attachment here."

"Why not?" he says with a grin. "Perhaps you were meant to come here not only to fulfill your assignment but also to find a new and happy life? Maybe that's why you didn't bring your leaf key with you."

I ponder this for a moment. "But I didn't know I was supposed to bring it. And my family…" I pause, thinking how sad it would be to not see them anymore. "I've always thought I'd be able to find my way back to them."

"Have you asked God about it?" he asks me.

"Well, no. I guess I've been so preoccupied with everything going on here and my assignment to fulfill…"

Dominic looks at me thoughtfully and pulls on his beard. "I would talk to God about it, my friend. He brought you this far, and I believe He will show you your next step as well."

"Yes, I will do that. Thank you, Dominic. You are a good friend to me."

He smiles and pulls out a chair for me in the dining room, and we sit down at the table together. The king and Trea walk in a few minutes later and join us for breakfast. We enjoy good conversation together while eating a hot breakfast of bacon, eggs, and fried potatoes.

Vespes looks up at me. "Shall we go riding again this morning after breakfast? I want to show you Windmere Park today. There are many trails we could take through there on the horses that I think you would enjoy. In fact, Dominic, why don't you and Trea come along too? It's very scenic, and it's a good day for it."

"Not me," says Dominic. "I'm looking forward to reading and taking a nap this afternoon. That's enough excitement for me!"

"And I am going to enjoy as much time with the Della and the new baby as I can before they return to Volkenland," says Trea. "I love being an aunt!" She smiles.

"Well, I guess it will just be the two of us, then," I say. "I'll go change into my riding clothes."

Later, as our horses trot along the path, I am taking notice of all the exotic-looking birds in the trees.

"Those are red swans," he says, pointing at the long-necked graceful birds that are swimming in the pond. "When they are babies, they are covered in gray down, then they turn a deep red and white as they mature."

"They're beautiful!" I exclaim. "I've never seen such a lovely bird."

"Have you ever seen a sterrador?" he asks.

"Yes, actually. When Dominic and I were traveling through the swamp area, there was one that swooped down at us through the trees. I caught one of its feathers. I still have it in my sack back at the palace."

"Really? You will have to show it to me later."

"Yes, I will."

We go over a little hill and come to a small meadow with a large tree in the center of it. "Why don't we let the horses rest for a bit by that tree over there?" He points.

As the horses enjoy grazing, Vespes looks up at the tree. I notice it looks similar to the one I got stuck in on the way to Silvenia. It has a large trunk and many long winding branches, like an oak. "My sisters and I have climbed up in this tree many times," he remarks, smiling at me.

"I can see why. It looks like a good climbing tree."

"If you climb up high enough, you can see over Silvenia's gates into Fir Forest."

"I want to see!" I say, grabbing a low branch to hoist myself up.

"All right," he responds. "Let's see who can reach the highest branch first."

Together, we begin climbing up the sturdy tree. The branches are thick and fairly easy to reach, and soon we are high up above the horses. Looking through the branches, we peer out over the stone walls surrounding the city and see the dark-blue-green trees of Fir Forest.

"Is that the forest Mira and Arten are traveling through?" I ask him.

"Yes, but they should be well past that by now. I would think they should be close to Oakendale by now, which is in the valley just before they enter the mountains of Shazir. Once they cross over to Elmwood Forest, they will be protected within the borders by the windfolk."

"I pray that they are safe," I say sincerely.

"I pray that also," he agrees. "Kara, can I ask you something?"

"Sure, what is it?"

He looks over at me, hesitating for a moment.

"Wait, what is that?" I say, pointing out through the branches at the sky.

"Do you see something?" he asks, looking over to where I am pointing. "All I see are clouds."

Between the branches, I see large puffy clouds, but what has caught my attention is a bright circle that has opened up in the center of the clouds. It's not the sun, which is to our left. "There's a bright opening in the clouds there. Do you see it?" I ask.

"I think so," he says, peering in that direction.

As I watch, I see two bluish-black birds fly up into this sky portal and disappear. And then, as I gaze into this opening in the clouds, it becomes like a movie screen before my eyes. I see Julia! She is standing beside a hospital bed, and she and a young man I don't recognize are both leaning over a patient. They are holding hands and praying with intensity. The image starts to become clearer, and I try to make out who the patient is. "It's me! They're praying over me!" I say, both shocked and startled at the vision before me.

"Kara? What are you talking about? What do you see?" Vespes tries to get over to my branch to see what I am looking at.

"Vespes," I say excitedly, "it's my sister. I can see her!"

As the image becomes clearer, I see there is something in my sister's hand that she is holding as she prays. It is colorful and vibrant-orange, green, and purple. *The leaf!* Without thinking, I feel drawn in and reach for it. Suddenly, I feel light as a feather. I can't feel the tree anymore. It feels like I am flying, and the light around me gets brighter and brighter. It becomes so bright I close my eyes very tight.

"In Jesus's name. Amen." It's Julia's voice.

I blink and open my eyes.

"Oh my god, it worked!" screams Julia, jumping up and down. Will laughs, and they both look down at me. "Kara, you're awake! I knew you'd wake up! I just knew it! Thank You, God!" She hugs me repeatedly while I struggle to make sense of what is happening.

"What happened to me?" I manage to whisper, discovering my throat is extremely dry.

"You had an aneurysm. You've been in a coma," says Julia, hugging me again. "I'm so glad to see you awake. I've been praying and praying." A nurse rushes in the door now and is startled to see me with my eyes open. She stands there frozen for a minute and then calls the head nurse.

After a few minutes, the head nurse and a few others who have been attending to me all come rushing in to see. "It's a miracle!" says the nurse.

"Welcome back!" says another. "I'll go call the doctor!" says the head nurse, rushing back out.

I look up at my sister. "How long have I been like this?" I ask as confusing thoughts race through my head. *Was it all a dream?*

"It's been about two months," Julia responds. "This is Will. He's my friend. We've both been praying for you. But today we decided to come in here together and pray over you, agreeing together that it was time for God to wake you up. And He did!"

"But I was in another place. It couldn't have been just a dream. I don't understand." I feel myself tearing up and look at Julia. "Julia, can I talk to you alone for a moment? I'm feeling a bit overwhelmed."

"Of course," she replies, looking up at Will. He nods and quickly exits the room.

"Julia, please believe me. I was in another world. I went through this door, and it was a real place, with real people in it. It was a beautiful land called Paredonia, and it had strange birds and colorful trees with…" I pause for a moment and look down at Julia's hand. "With colorful leaves," I say, reaching for the leaf still in Julia's hand.

"I found this in your room," says Julia. "I started to carry it with me everywhere as a way to keep you close in my thoughts." She places it in my hand.

"This is a leaf from that place," says Kara. "I know it was real. Do you believe me, Julia?"

"Of course I do." She smiles. "And I want you to tell me all about it."

"But first, the doctor needs to have some time with her," says the nurse, pushing back through the door, with him following close behind her. "You can come back to see her tomorrow, Julia. We'll take good care of her until then."

Julia starts to protest, but the nurse insists. "Besides, you need to go tell your parents the good news as well!"

"Yes, I do!" she says excitedly and gives Kara a parting hug. "I'll be back with them first thing in the morning! I promise!"

Hope

Vespes sits on the ground beneath the large tree in the meadow, his head in his hands. "How could she have just disappeared? I don't understand this. God, what is happening?"

As tears form in his eyes, he allows himself to feel the pain in his heart. It's unbearable. He looks up into the sky again, and the portal he thought he saw before in the tree has now disappeared as well. "God, why did You take her from me? Weren't You the one that brought her here? I thought You did that for me!"

He shakes his head in confusion. "I thought she was the one! Was I wrong to think this?"

He sits there in silence, waiting. Suddenly, he hears a gentle voice on the inside. "No, my son. You were not wrong. She will be waiting for you to find her again."

"But how will I find her?" he says out loud, with desperation in his voice.

"I will help you."

Vespes lingers there under the tree, hoping to hear more, but nothing else comes. He notices Kara's horse has begun to wander off, and he gets up to go bring it back. He leads it home, next to his horse, and soon is back at the Silver Palace. He sighs as he goes inside, knowing he now has to explain to everyone that Kara is gone. Fortunately, no one is around as he enters except for Dominic, who is sitting in the library, reading a book and smoking his pipe.

Dominic looks up at him as he comes in and sees the sad expression on his face. "She's gone back, hasn't she?" he says quietly.

"Yes," says Vespes. "I have to find her," he says, his voice filled with emotion.

Dominic nods, puffing out a plume of smoke. "If there's anything I can do to help…"

Vespes looks at him. "Thank you, Dominic. I think I am going to take you up on that offer."

Later that evening, as Vespes climbs into bed, he spots the green-and-gold scarf lying on the floor next to his dresser. He reaches over and picks it up. It is stained dark red with his blood from the empress's knife wound. He remembers Kara tying it onto his arm to help him stop the bleeding. He presses it to his lips and then places it inside a small treasure chest that also holds his mother's crown.

Lying in his bed, he stares up at the ceiling as sleep evades him. He reaches over to the Bible Kara has put in his room and opens it. He begins to read from Proverbs. When he gets to a certain verse, it seems to jump off the page at him. He reads it out loud: "Hope deferred makes the heart sick, But when the desire comes, it is a tree of life" (Prov. 12:12 NKJV). He repeats it a couple of times to himself, feeling like it was meant just for him.

"I will find you, Kara," he says into the night air.

Outside his window, the second moon has risen and lights up the sky. Deep in the woods, flashes of light flicker and float in the air. The wind blows through the trees, and leaves begin to fall—orange, green, and purple.

About the Author

Susan A. Mills grew up reading and loving fantasy and adventure stories such as the Narnia Chronicles by C. S. Lewis and many others. A detailed and vivid dreamer and storyteller, she also enjoys traveling and worked for the airlines for a time before having children. She obtained many creative ideas and descriptions of scenery from the places she got to travel to. And she considers New Zealand to be one of the most beautiful places in the world.

Along with being a homemaker and author, she is also an ordained minister through Hunter Ministries. She gives God all the credit for the inspiration to write. She is happily married to Ian Mills, who works for NASA. They currently reside in Texas along with their four grown children—Shelby, Melanie, Joseph, and Peter—who are all the loves of her life.

Susan was born in the beautiful state of Pennsylvania but has also lived in Indiana and Texas. She is currently at work on the sequel to *The Leaf Key*. You can find her on Facebook as Susan A. Mills—Author, or visit her website at susanamills.com.

CPSIA information can be obtained
at www.ICGtesting.com
Printed in the USA
BVHW081708230321
603272BV00003B/218